THE GRAND OLD LADY OF VINE STREET

THE CINCINNATI ENQUIRER

1841 1991

150 YEARS

GRAYDON DeCAMP

COPYRIGHT ©1991
THE CINCINNATI ENQUIRER

ALL RIGHTS RESERVED.
NO PART OF THIS BOOK MAY
BE USED OR REPRODUCED IN ANY
MANNER WHATSOEVER WITHOUT
WRITTEN PERMISSION.

LIBRARY OF CONGRESS CATALOG
CARD NUMBER: 91-073718
ISBN 0-9630442-0-6

PRINTED IN CINCINNATI, OHIO
THE MERTEN CO.

CONTENTS

THE STAFF

GRAYDON DeCAMP
AUTHOR

MR. DeCAMP IS FORMER ASSISTANT CITY EDITOR
AND MAGAZINE EDITOR OF *THE CINCINNATI ENQUIRER.*
HE IS SENIOR EDITOR OF TRAVERSE MAGAZINE,
TRAVERSE CITY, MICHIGAN.

RON HUFF
DESIGNER

MR. HUFF IS DESIGN DIRECTOR OF
THE CINCINNATI ENQUIRER.

ROBERT CLERC
RESEARCH

MR. CLERC IS AN EDITORIAL WRITER AND COLUMNIST
FOR *THE CINCINNATI ENQUIRER.*

RAYMOND ZWICK
RESEARCH

MR. ZWICK IS THE LIBRARIAN OF
THE CINCINNATI ENQUIRER.

J. DENNIS DOHERTY
EDITOR

MR. DOHERTY IS DEPUTY MANAGING EDITOR OF
The Cincinnati Enquirer.

WELCOME TO THE ENQUIRER

And welcome to the inside story of this newspaper and its relationship with the citizens and city it has served for 150 years since April 10, 1841.

We marked our sesquicentennial with a special section on our anniversary date, but that edition provided only a thumbnail sketch of our history.

The Grand Old Lady Of Vine Street gives you a more in-depth look. This book introduces you to the great journalists of our past, reveals the personalities of the people who shaped the character of *The Enquirer* and, in so doing, helped shape the character of Greater Cincinnati.

Most of all, it reveals the love story of this newspaper and the city it serves. The relationship is like a good marriage: the newspaper and its city have supported each other, quarrelled, struggled together, grown together and prospered together..

As we celebrate our first 150 years, we invite you to enjoy this story of the newspaper and the city. We have already started work on the next 150.

William J. Keating

William J. Keating
Chairman and Publisher
The Cincinnati Enquirer

GETTING OUR STORY STRAIGHT

> *"We are confident of our assertions in this book, have tried to hedge candidly when uncertain, and to be careful not to pass along exaggeration as truth."*

This book should carry one of those warning labels: "Caution — Not everything in here was written by the authors."

After all, this is the history of a newspaper, an institution built on the written word. It would have been presumptuous (if not foolhardy) for us to produce a history of *The Enquirer* without leaning heavily on the journalistic and editorial skills of our contemporaries and predecessors at the paper.

This is not your ordinary business history, because newspapers are not ordinary businesses. In places, we confess, we descend into the recitations of boards sat upon by publishers, of circulation milestones, awards won, advertising goals surpassed, pages printed. But we have tried to make this history interesting, rather than definitive.

It is, after all, about some of the most interesting people on earth — newspaper people. In few other lines of work, except possibly sports and entertainment, are there so many interesting people — bright and competitive people, sometimes zany, sometimes eccentric.

But always interesting. The stereotype of the gruff-voiced editor with a heart of gold is a stereotype because it is true. So is the stereotype of the quiet, tenacious reporter who plugs away against all odds until he or she has the story, of the eager but untutored cub who succeeds beyond anyone's expectations.

As you will see by leafing through this book, much of it was written for us, over a period of 150 years, by people who toiled at *The Enquirer*. Fortunately, these *Enquirer* people felt constrained every so often to publish something of themselves, thus becoming unwitting historians of the very paper they produced.

Two pieces in particular stand out as authoritative sources of who was who and how things were at *The Enquirer* of yesteryear. One, published without byline on New Year's Day in 1878, was a long, and richly detailed account of how the paper was produced in that era of hand-type and gaslights. The other was a rich, warm, personal history, written in 1926 when the paper moved into new quarters in the present Enquirer Building.

The librarian in the 1920s, Harry Pence, was also a fine and sensitive writer, a sentimentalist who produced many brief pieces — and a few long ones — about earlier days at *The Enquirer*. His accounts have such a ring of truth about them, such a patina of careful research and forthrightness, that whenever we encountered an apparent conflict of fact, we chose Pence's version as true. His work is a remarkable resource.

However inadequate its space —then or now — *The Enquirer* library, or "morgue," is a marvel of an "attic." There's no telling what will turn up there. And there are no lengths to which librarian Ray Zwick won't go to look for something, even when he knows

Continued on next page

perfectly well it doesn't exist. When it comes to obscure facts, Zwick is a master sleuth.

And his staff of assistant librarians and clerks are trained as exhaustive fact checkers. *Enquirer* Editor George Blake borrowed this old news-bureau line for the newsroom's unofficial motto, and it guided our research: "If your mother tells you she loves you, check it out."

Very few things got Zwick's curiosity up as much as his discovery that the file of back issues of *The Enquire*r has some very mysterious gaps. For long periods in the 1860s, for instance, there are no Sunday papers in the file. In some weeks, the issue numbers for Saturday and Monday are consecutive, while in others, the issue number skips one — indicating that there was a Sunday paper but that it wasn't filed.

Worse, still, was the realization as he looked at the files for 1864 and 1865, that there were papers on Monday every week. What was bad was that almost every published history in our hands says that *The Enquirer* stopped publishing Monday papers when it began publishing on Sunday in April of 1848, and didn't resume Mondays until December, 1866. That was when it moved to Vine Street above Sixth after the Opera House fire and became a true, seven-day "daily" for the first time.

So, we found ourselves ask - ing, if those other histories are right, then why were there Monday papers in 1864 and 1865? The answer is, we don't know. We can only guess. One guess is that the editors decided to put out a paper seven days a week during the Civil War, then simply made it permanent in December, 1866.

The really big issue this forced us to confront was the possibility that *The Enquirer's* claim to having America's "oldest continually published Sunday paper" might be false. Maybe it's true, and maybe it is just a myth. Later in this book we look at this in depth.

What muddies all these waters are gaps in the record, and inconsistencies that make it hard to figure out what and whom to trust. Things must have gotten a bit out of hand in the library in the old days because for some time in the 1860s the paper carried volume numbers indicating it had been founded in the 1830s, not in 1841. To make the records even more suspect, we found one year in which the first issue number is 91, not 1. And in another year, the issue numbers ran as high as "371," which was a few more days than there were in the year, even back then.

Further complicating things is the fact that *The Enquirer* itself has not kept its own bound files for every year since 1841. The "files" we refer to with such easy familiarity in our book are actually on microfilm, put there in recent years by various commercial contractors. They used *The Enquirer's* own, bound, back copies where possible, but for many early years had to rely on other sources such as the Public Library, the Ohio and Cincinnati Historical Societies, and private collections. Some microfilmed copies have pages missing. Gaps exist, some for days in a row. The record is especially spotty before March 22, 1866, the day Pike's Opera House caught fire, destroying as well *The Enquirer's* building next door and everything in it — including bound copies of back issues.

Sorry to say, we never uncovered the origins of either the official seal of the paper — the naked printer of old, pressing out yet one more copy — or the sobriquet "Grand Old Lady of Vine Street."

We think the seal stems from the 1920s, when *The Enquirer* moved into today's building. It appears in gold foil on a leather album of photos of the new building.

We think "The Grand Old Lady of Vine Street"was originally a derisive term applied in print to *The Enquirer* in a less polite era by one of its competitors. After *The Enquirer* triumphed in a 19th century circulation fight, our theory goes, publisher John R. McLean turned the nickname to his own use.

We are confident of our ass-ertions in this book, have tried to hedge candidly when uncertain, and to be careful not to pass along exaggeration as truth.

Of one thing we are absolutely sure: This history is far from complete. We chose at the outset to make it interesting and accurate. However, we recognized not only that we could not possibly include everything, but that we would almost certainly omit many things deemed by others to be important.

So, if your great-grandfather was the first *Enquirer* compositor to use the Linotype and we omitted his name, forgive us. But by all means drop Ray Zwick a note, so he can put it in the files for whoever writes the 200th anniversary history of the Grand Old Lady of Vine Street.

MOSES DAWSON'S ADVERTISER

Although Moses Dawson did not edit, write, report or even work at *The Cincinnati Enquirer*, he was crucial to its birth. He was, so to speak, its grandfather—the editor and publisher of the newspaper that, in 1841, became *The Enquirer*.

This editorial patriarch was an immigrant from Belfast, Ireland. Born in 1768, he was growing up during the American Revolution, and boyhood heroes for whom he would later name two of his sons were Ben Franklin and George Washington. He became a teacher, but more notably, he also became a political activist opposing English oppression of Ireland. Arrested and jailed twice, he fled first to Scotland when he was 48 and then, when the crown put a price on his rebellious head, to Philadelphia a year later in 1817. Since the government had seized all his property in Ireland, his wife, Jane, and their seven children, ages five to 18, were without funds to join him.

Dawson found his way in 1819 to the fastest-growing, most exciting city in the American West, Cincinnati. His family followed in 1821 when the English — perhaps pleased to be rid of him — relented and released his property. After a failed effort to establish a Quaker school, he used his writing talents to find steady work as associate editor of one of Cincinnati's dozen-odd newspapers, the *Advertiser*.

Cincinnati was a boisterous, exciting town, only three decades removed from the community the settlers had established on the broad Ohio River bottomlands across from the mouth of the Licking River.

Secured by a fort and an army garrison, Cincinnati had grown by 1820 into a prosperous river port of 10,000 with a bright future as a center of manufacturing, meat-packing and river transportation. West of the Alleghenies, it was America's leading city.

Within two years, the stocky, red-headed Moses Dawson was the *Advertiser's* editor. And in 1823, at the age of 55, he bought the paper and became its proprietor and publisher as well. His interest was political, not journalistic. Most American newspapers in those days were partisan political organs, and the *Advertiser* was the all-but-official voice in Cincinnati of the populist, Democratic Party of Andrew Jackson.

Dawson, whose politics had brought him across the Atlantic, brought to Cincinnati an editorial style that was passionate and pugnacious. He signaled his politics in the very first issue under his ownership with a sharp editorial attack on John Quincy Adams. And when he criticized President James Monroe, the conservative opposition labeled him an alien and sought to prove he had not been legally naturalized.

The *Advertiser* was composed by hand, one character at a time, and printed on a hand-fed, flatbed press in a shop on the south side of Fifth Street between Main and Sycamore. It was published each afternoon but Sunday, and contained news aside from politics — merchants' notices of new ship-

Continued on next page

> *"The* **Advertiser** *was composed by hand, one character at a time, and printed on a hand-fed, flat-bed press in a shop on the south side of Fifth Street between Main and Sycamore."*

ments, news of arriving and departing river boats, and "exchange" notices reprinted from other cities' papers.

Dawson's editorial causes were those of the common man. He supported the Monroe Doctrine and wanted an America free of European influence. He favored secularized education, abolition of public debt, and broad access to opportunity, including ownership of land. He knew that trade and a strong economy meant jobs and opportunities for working people, and he used his newspaper to favor major civic undertakings—fire-fighting forces and police forces. He backed a citywide water system but opposed city ownership, fearing it would become a source of patronage and corruption. He strongly supported such keys to prosperous trade as boat-building, river-shipping, canals and roads. Above all, he supported Andrew Jackson and his policies.

And for most of his two decades

Andrew Jackson

at the *Advertiser*, his archenemy was Charles Hammond, publisher of the Whig paper, the *Gazette*. They were bitter editorial rivals, trading daily jabs, gibes, and arguments, and Hammond often wrote of Dawson as "the old gentleman of the *Advertiser*." Privately, however, according to some accounts, they were amiable enemies, often keeping each other's company in the saloons.

One *Enquirer* historian called Hammond "the more adroit debater" but portrayed Dawson as having a broader, more worldly, general knowledge, remarkable integrity and honesty, and an abiding democratic belief in civil liberty. By most accounts, he distrusted government, bitterly opposed privilege based on wealth, and abhorred political patronage

Moses Dawson

and favoritism. Dawson, said one historian, "was more democratic in conviction and sentiment than the leaders and most of the rank and file of the Democratic Party of that era."

Naturally, in 1824, the *Advertiser* supported Andrew Jackson against three opponents, including the conservatives, Henry Clay and John Quincy Adams. Jackson lost, but it was so close that the outcome was decided in the House of Representatives when Clay withdrew in favor of Adams and then was named secretary of state. Dawson smelled a deal and furiously redoubled his efforts on behalf of Jackson. Four years later, helped measurably by the growing influence of the *Advertiser*, Jackson turned the tables and defeated

Adams by a wide margin. In 1832, he was re-elected by an even wider margin over Clay.

Like most Cincinnatians in the 1830s, Dawson and Hammond took sides on the issue of President Jackson's withdrawing government deposits from the Bank of the United States in Philadelphia. The ensuing credit crunch hit Cincinnati and the fast-growing West especially hard and split the old Democratic Republican Party wide open. Hammond sided with the pro-bank conservatives and businessmen opposed to Jackson, while Dawson and his *Advertiser* supported him against the "moneyed aristocracy."

Dawson, an immigrant himself, was strongly sympathetic to the interests of the city's working class, composed largely of Irish and German immigrants. Independent of spirit, often preyed upon by bankers and speculators but constantly struggling to become landowners, they grew in political strength with the arrival of each new wave of immigration and they in turn became the backbone of the

John Q. Adams

Democratic Party. Dawson's *Advertiser* was their voice in an era when journalism and politics were all but synonymous.

In the 1830s, Cincinnati became a focus of national politics. The West's largest city, it was on the cutting edge of a fast-growing nation. Moreover, nearby North Bend was the home of the old military hero, William Henry Harrison, the elder statesman who would be the conservatives' presidential candidate in 1836. Dawson knew Harrison, and had written a warm, friendly biography of him soon after acquiring the *Advertiser*. But when the Democratic Republican Party divided in the mid-1830s, leaving Harrison and Jackson on opposite sides, Dawson decided Harrison had no "democratic edge" and rejected him as presidential material. He expressed his change of mind with an editorial rhyme:

When this old hat was new, the people used to say,

The best of all the Democrats were Harrison and Clay.

In fact, concluded Dawson, Harrison and Clay never were Democrats. The Whigs chose Harrison in 1836 to run against Jackson's vice president, Martin Van Buren, a New Yorker who was not popular in the West. The *Ad-*

CINCINNATI'S FIRST NEWSPAPER

The first newspaper in Cincinnati—indeed, in the entire Northwest Territories—was the *Centinel of the Northwest Territories.*

Its publisher was William Maxwell, a Revolutionary War veteran who crossed the mountains in 1793. Intent on starting a newspaper at Cincinnati, he led pack horses that carried his type and a simple press similar to Ben Franklin's.

The *Centinel* was born Nov.9, 1793, in a log cabin at Front and Sycamore Streets, near today's Riverfront Stadium. Maxwell distributed it to readers in Cincinnati, and he had agents in the nearby settlements of Newport, North Bend, Colerain and Columbia. The *Centinel* appeared each Saturday for three years. Its four 8-by-10-inch pages of three columns contained local news and reports from back East and abroad, along with occasional poems and witticisms. The first issue contained an account of Indian raids on white settlements to the

EXTRA! EXTRA!

north and west of town, along with news (60 days old) from New York and Philadelphia, and a dispatch from London dated July 15. Advertisers offered dry goods and land and rewards for return of stray livestock and runaway apprentices. One early issue carried a notice of a $168 bounty for 'every scalp having the right ear appendant, for the first ten Indians who shall be killed. . .'

Maxwell introduced himself in the first issue merely as "*The Printer*," and did not use his paper to further his own causes or politics. Its motto was stated atop page one:"Open to all parties—but influenced by none."

When Maxwell was appointed Postmaster at Cincinnati in 1796, he sold the *Centinel* to Edmund Freeman, who changed its name to *Freeman's Journal* and, in 1800, moved it under another name to the new territorial capital, Chillicothe.

vertiser provided crucial western support, and Van Buren won with a popular-vote margin larger even than Jackson's.

But it was a last hurrah for Dawson. Despite political successes, things were not going well for him. His eldest daughter had died in 1832, his wife in 1834. In the next four years, three of his sons died as well. He was

71 in 1839 when a fire burned out the *Advertiser's* shop on Fifth Street. He tried to rally, resuming publication as the *Advertiser and Phoenix* until party leaders persuaded him it was undignified. The years were beginning to tell and the fire only added to the burden. The next year, when Harrison and the conservatives ousted Van Buren and the Democrats,

Dawson may well have decided that politics and newspapering suddenly just weren't the fun they used to be.

As a result of the same election, two Ohio Democrats had lost their jobs as well—John Brough as state auditor and his brother, Charles, as a state representative. The ambitious Broughs had published a Democratic paper in Lancaster, Ohio, and were eager to move up. In those parts, "up" meant Cincinnati. The Broughs were hardly strangers to Dawson, and they surely had his and the party's blessings as suitable heirs to the *Advertiser's* Democratic spirit. When they arrived in town ready to buy, Moses Dawson was a ready seller.

Shortly before turning his paper over to the Brough brothers, Dawson published an editorial farewell. "For more than half a century," he wrote, "we have ever been the persevering advocate of civil and religious liberty, and with truth we can assert that we have never lent our aid to man or measure which we believed or even suspected to be opposed to, or inconsistent with, the rights and privileges of the great mass of the people" And Cincinnati was ready for a new paper.

THE BROUGHS GIVE CINCINNATI ITS ENQUIRER

When John and Charles Brough moved to Cincinnati from Lancaster, Ohio, in 1841 and bought *The Enquirer* from Moses Dawson, they had already made quite a name for themselves, both in politics and journalism. It may well be that they came at the invitation of leading Democrats in the West's leading city.

John Brough, born in 1811 in Marietta, Ohio, was the elder by two years. Orphaned at age 11, he had apprenticed to a printer in Marietta and, nine years later, founded his own paper, the *Western Republican*. In 1833, he sold the *Republican*. With his brother, Charles, he moved to Lancaster and purchased an old paper, the *Eagle*.

Because politics and journalism were so intertwined, editors and publishers often sought election or appointment to office. In 1835, John Brough went to Columbus, appointed as clerk of the Senate, and while he was there, doubled as correspondent for the *Eagle*. Two years later, at 26, he was elected to the state legislature and named to head the powerful, important committee on banks.

Banks were a hot issue in those days. Most issued paper money, and supposedly would redeem their bank notes on demand in government coins or in "specie." However, the market value of a bank note depended on the bank's health. Banks were not uniformly robust, and some that invested too speculatively stopped paying full value for their paper — or quit redeeming it altogether. Bankers called it "suspension," critics such as John Brough called it "repudiation," and it upset ordinary working folks a great deal.

State law required banks to pay a penalty on suspended payments, and in 1841, when the Broughs established *The Enquirer*, bank-friendly Whigs in the legislature were trying to repeal the penalties. Working folks who wanted value for their bank notes were demanding that the fat-cat bankers pay up, and such staunch Democratic publishers, editors and politicians like John and Charles Brough were their champions.

John Brough became a powerful voice for fiscal conservatism, both in the legislature and then as state auditor in 1839 and 1840. He battled repudiation, demanded more capital of the bankers, sought higher real-estate taxes to pay off state debts incurred in building canals and

John Brough

roads. Calling on big-city financiers in Cincinnati and the East, he secured loans for the state.

In 1840, however, political winds shifted. A Whig, William Henry Harrison, was elected president and carried Ohio in an election that put the Broughs out of office. They had made a good name for themselves among Democrats, however, and out of office hardly meant out of work. Democratic leaders in Cincinnati needed someone to succeed old Moses Dawson at the helm of the party newspaper, and the Broughs not only were loyal Democrats, they were accomplished journalists—John a publisher and Charles an editor. Moreover, they were ready to move up to the big city.

It was hardly a coincidence that on the very day William Henry Harrison was sworn in as president, the Broughs negotiated the deal that would give them the newspaper. Harrison died before Volume 1, Number 1, of *The Daily Enquirer* appeared.

As a pair, the Broughs were well-suited to their new enterprise. As one *Enquirer* historian, Harry

Pence, wrote in a 1926 history of the paper, "John was the leader and spokesman, Charles the studious master of routine and detail. Of the two, the younger is said to have been the more graceful and forceful writer and the deeper student of political problems, but the senior of the team was also an eloquent and powerful orator."

The Broughs' primary contribution to the history of *The Enquirer* is that they founded the name in the process of taking over the official voice of the Democratic Party. They made their *Enquirer* the party's leading paper in Ohio, but they didn't stay long. John sold his share after just two years and moved on, becoming a successful promoter of railroads in Indiana and Ohio. During the Civil War, he returned to politics and, in 1863, was elected governor.

Ironically, *The Enquirer* did not endorse its former publisher. He was elected largely because of his popular pro-Union, pro-war stance, and *The Enquirer's* new owners had stopped supporting the war after Lincoln's Emancipation Proclamation the previous January. John Brough declined renomination in 1865 and died later that year.

DISPATCH FROM THE MEXICAN FRONT

On Nov. 22, 1847, *The Enquirer* devoted four columns to a dispatch from the editor and co-owner, Col. Charles Brough, describing action in the Mexican War. Dated October 25th, 1847, it dealt in part with the relief of U.S. troops under a Col. Child, besieged by Santa Ana's men in a fort near the town of Ajacito:

"To the Readers of the Enquirer:

"It is a long time since I have conferred with you. At Vera Cruz, pressing duties, some illness, and a short stay, prevented, and the almost absence of facilities for sending a communication, have since kept me silent.

". . . Our information was that Gen. Rea with a large force of lancers and guerrillas and some regular infantry and artillery, occupied the city. Everyone looked upon a fight as a certainty. . .but contrary to all expectation, the enemy was vamoosing as we entered the city — a remainder corps of lancers and guerrillas being left to cover his retreat.

"The Ohio boys were first in the town, and were saluted by a rattling fire from the roof of a church by the wayside. Nobody down! But a shout and a volley in reply — ineffectual — the assassins were already jumping down into a back street. One half the regiment, under the Colonel, was then ordered to take and hold the main plaza, in conjunction with the Indianians, — the remaining half, under Lt. Col. Moore, to push the enemy in another part of the city. Not a few were the leaden pellets from roofs and windows, as we marched towards the plaza, and right well were they returned. Simultaneously with the Indiana boys we reached the plaza and a few volleys sent the enemy's stragglers scampering. Lt. Col. Moore's division, in conjunction with some few of the Pennsylvanians, fell in with a considerable number of them in the western part of the city, and peppered them from street to street, until he drove them utterly east, leaving some twenty or thirty dead behind them . . . .

"In half an hour, the city was completely in our possession. I really thought the released men of Col. Child's force would have gone mad with joy. For many days they had no meat and but a scant allowance of other food and were targets for Mexican sharpshooters whenever they ventured beyond their breastworks.

"That very morning a party from the fort had gone into the city prematurely and to the number of twelve were massacred and horribly mutilated by the rascals whom we drove out. Haply we lost not a man, and at evening the Ohios were quartered and quietly making their coffee in the spacious monastery connected with the church from whose roof they had been fired at, on their entrance."

Charles Brough had remained as editor of *The Enquirer*, in partnership with various co-owners. In 1846, he recruited a regiment and went off to the Mexican War as a colonel. His dispatches, sent back by mail and Pony Express, reported the war as viewed by troops at the front and set standards for vivid candor unrivaled until Ernie Pyle's coverage of World War II.

Charles sold his share of the paper on his return in 1848, served one year as a judge in Hamilton County, then died in a cholera epidemic in 1849. The man who bought him out, James J. Faran, was no stranger to *The Enquirer*. The veteran Democratic legislator's letter — on repeal of Ohio's bank penalties — had appeared in the very first issue in 1841. Faran's association with the paper would last for years.

HOW THE NEWS GOT ON THE FRONT

The first issue of *The Enquirer* in 1841 had some news in the first column on page one, but it was not the publishers' intent to devote page one to news. News, in those days, went on page two. The reason it was on page one in *The Enquirer* was probably that the paper didn't have enough advertisers in 1841.

By 1846, that had changed, and page one was all ads. In fact, most were long-term ads, which meant that page one seldom changed from day to day. Atop one column, day after day after day, for instance, was a woodcut illustration that must have been boringly familiar to Cincinnatians, showing the hand-operated flatbed press of "Case, Bagley & Co., Book & Job Printing. Publishers of *The Cincinnati Daily Enquirer*."

Then, on Aug. 11, 1846, something interesting happened. The U. S. had just gone to war with Mexico, and public interest was high, and the entire right-hand column of page one was given to a

dispatch from Monterey "as the army of emancipation has commenced its advance upon the interior."

It was not just a wartime aberration. The next day, the column contained a mix of poetry, commentary and fiction. One day soon after, a running comment on local

phenomena, weather, and customs appeared. War news frequented the space, but the column was obviously not just for major news. Nor was the editor limited to one column. On July 13, 1848, for instance, three front-page columns were devoted to President James Polk's announcement of the Mexican War's end.

In 1854, publisher Hiram Robinson moved the news from the right-hand columns to the left side of the front page, but the content still was not always hard news. One day's entry, "A Thrilling Story," was a reminiscence of a flood about ten years ealier.

Although the use they made of it varied — in content and column — it was plain from 1848 on that the editors had a toehold on page one and clearly intended to stay.

Today paid ads do not appear on page one of *The Enquirer*. News dominates. Examples of famous front pages through the years appear in this book.

ADS DOMINATE FIRST EDITION

In its first two decades, *The Enquirer* consisted of four pages, of which at least two, and often three, were filled with advertising.

In the beginning, page one was entirely advertising, although even the largest merchants' ads more closely resembled today's classifieds than anything else. The earliest ads were generally small and consisted almost entirely of type, and were stacked one above the other, never more than a column wide.

By today's standards, rates were incredibly cheap. One column inch cost less than a dollar a day; for $5, an advertiser could have one inch for a whole month, and for $20, it was his for a year. All of this, of course, if the advertiser agreed not to change it in any way. Setting new type was expensive and time-consuming, and the advertiser who agreed to let his ad stand unchanged got a huge break.

The editorial offices of the paper and advertising offices were the same at first, but from the mid-1850s onward, they were separate. The advertising office was called the "counting room," and it usually was in the very front office.

By the 1880s, *The Enquirer* regularly consisted of eight pages each day, one or two of which were devoted to what we'd now call "classified" ads. They were variously known as "personals" or "wanteds." The traffic in these ads had been heightened no end in the 1870s when John R. McLean took over the paper from his father, Washington McLean. Young John, in a spectacularly successful bid to boost circulation, took the revolutionary step of making personal want-ads free.

In the early 1880s, a gentleman from Sidney, Ohio, visited *The Enquirer* and then wrote this description for his local paper on his return upstate:

"In the counting-room where the business is done, here are two round stands with slips of paper, where all 'the personals, miscellaneous wants, help wanted.' &c., are written that will always be found on the third and seventh pages. We need not tell you how valuable the space in this paper is, yet column upon column is given free under the heads of situations wanted, &c. A few minutes in the room is a study. We see here the young ladies and gentlemen that use the personal column and the workingmen and women that want situations, the business men that use the columns as preferred space for advertising. At ten and eleven o'clock this room is crowded and all writing 'ads,'which are passed over to the clerks and sent upstairs."

"Upstairs," of course, was the composing room, where typesetters set the handwritten advertisements into type, one letter at a time. Setting "display" ads was considered premium work in the days of hand-type, because printers were paid according to the amount of space they filled, not the time worked. When you were setting big type for department store ads, you filled space much more easily and quickly than

Continued on next page

when you were setting baseball box scores or long columns of tedious political news.

Keeping track of the classified ads has always been an exacting task. Today, computers keep track of which ones run, when and how often, and where and in what sequence, page after page after page. A century ago, and until the end of the "hot type" era in the 1970s, it was much more complicated. For one thing, the ads were in hard metal, and after each day's paper

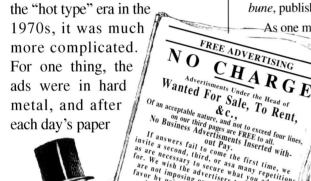

SOME PAPERS HAVE STAYING POWER

O n April 10, 1841, the day *The Cincinnati Enquirer* appeared, another newspaper made its debut: Horace Greeley's *New York Tribune*. The *Trib* later merged with the *Herald* to become the ill-fated *Herald Tribune*. Its name remains today only as the *International Herald Tribune*, published in Europe.

As one modern *Enquirer* editor said, on learning that Greeley's *New York Trib* and Cincinnati's *Enquirer* were born on the same day 150 years ago: "Some papers have staying power, some don't."

Greeley, of course, is famous in American history for (among many other things) having urged, "Go west, young man." What he didn't specify, was how far west. In 1850 in his *New York Tribune*, he wrote:

"It requires no keenness of observation to see that Cincinnati is destined to become the focus and market for the grandest circle of manufacturing thrift on the continent. Her delightful climate, her unequaled and ever increasing facilities for cheap and rapid commercial intercourse with all parts of the country and the world; her enterprising and energetic population; her own elastic and exulting youth; are all elements which predict and insure her electric progress to giant greatness. I doubt if there is another spot on earth where food, cotton, timber and iron can all be concentrated so cheaply. . .such fatness of soil, such a wealth of immense treasures. . . .How many Californias could equal in permanent worth the valley of the Ohio?"

was printed, were removed from the page forms and either melted down in the hellbox for reuse of the metal or carefully filed on metal galleys in the proper sequence — alphabetically and by classification

— for the next day's paper. It required close attention to detail.

For the first 30 years of this century that exacting task fell to a printer named John Ferrell, who headed a crew of three or four experienced men. Ferrell started at *The Enquirer* in 1884, a decade before the Linotype, and worked in the composing room setting type by hand and helping make up the want ads. When his boss on the classified pages, Don Davis, died in 1899, Farrell took over.

Near the end of his career, he recalled that when he began, it was the era of John R. McLean's free-ad policy, and "nearly all the ads were free, and most of them listed something for sale"— rooms for rent, or personal services offered.

"When ads were free," he recalled, "only one ad was supposed to come in from [any] one person, so several persons would send in extra ads by their friends and relatives to get as many ads in the paper as possible. Gradually," Ferrell remembered, "the free ads were done away with until all ads were paid for."

In the early years of this century, exactly two men sold all the local display advertising in *The Enquirer.* One of them was Bill Hunting, a young man who started in the department in 1904. He and his one colleague solicited everything from patent-medicine ads and "at-home" cards to big stores' accounts. Bill handled banks, financial houses and department stores, and when he celebrated 25 years' service, he reminisced about the early days and about how long the hours were.

Continued on page 18

A&P

YOUR GUARANTEE OF QUALITY

BALDWIN

YOU are cordially invited to come and see the Ellington, Howard and Valley Gem Pianos just arrived from our factory. Some in Mahogany and some in Oak cases. Natural wood finish if you prefer it.

It is often better to buy a used piano of well-known make than to pay the same money for a new piano. We have few pianos of very prominent makes, taken in trade during the holidays. Usually one of these pianos would cost you at least $350. Now it is $150.

The Pianola overcomes the prejudice most people have against mechanical musical instruments. The endorsement this instrument has received from such men as Messrs. Sieg and Rosenthal must impress even the most skeptical.

Here's A Man Will Tell You that

Coca-Cola

has the call

The standby of the thirsty— the delight of the hot and tired— the treat for the multitude

Delicious and Refreshing

Demand the genuine by full name— nicknames encourage substitution.

Whenever you see an Arrow, think of Coca-Cola.

THE COCA-COLA CO.
ATLANTA, GA.

Dust does it—makes the complexion look like a London fog, thick, dingy, dull. Wise men and women combat dust with

Woodbury's Facial Soap

Cleanses and purifies each minute pore. Revivifies the skin, leaves it as smooth, clear and rosy as a baby's cheek. For faces.

Your dealer has it. 25 cents a cake.

Special offer Our booklet, trial size package of Soap and Facial Cream sent for 6 cts to pay postage; or for 10 cts, the same and samples of Woodbury's Facial Powder and Dental Cream. Address Dept. I.

THE ANDREW JERGENS CO.,
Sole Owners,   Cincinnati, O.

GROCERIES

Of the finest quality, at prices that speak for themselves. The reason we can sell Groceries at these remarkably low prices is that we buy not only by the carload, but frequently by the whole trainload. The consumer gets the benefit of our large purchasing power for cash. We deliver to all suburbs, and our prices are for all day long. CUT THIS OUT and TAKE IT TO THE STORE NEAREST TO YOU. See that you get the goods just as they are advertised.

Canned Goods.

Pickles.

Sauerkraut.

Star Candles.

Soup.

Beef, Wine and Iron.

Candies.

Navy Beans.

Buckwheat.

Lenten Goods.

Matches.

Corn Meal.

Golden Syrup.

Catsup.

Chili Sauce.

Coffees.

Flour.

Toilet Soaps.

Smyrna Figs.

Evaporated Apples.

Evaporated California Pears.

Tobacco.

New Prunes.

Cigars.

Lard.

Dates.

Peanuts.

Webb's Cocoa.

B.H. Kroger's
18 Tea and Grocery Stores

408 East Pearl Street, East of Broadway.
810 East Pearl, bet. Sycamore and Broadway.
308 and 810 West Sixth Street, near Plum.
840 West Sixth St., near Central Avenue.
1151 Central Avenue, bet. David and Wade.
Northwest Corner Thirteenth and Main.
461 West Sixth St., South Side, near Mound.

532 West Court Street, near Mound.
Northwest Corner Hunt and Spring.
116 and 117 Elder, Corner Pleasant.
Northeast Corner Liberty and Freeman Ave.
87 East Court Street, near Walnut.
740 State Avenue, South of Eighth Street.
Southwest Corner Massachusetts and Hopple, Camp Washington.

2430 Gilbert Avenue, Southeast Corner Curtis, Walnut Hills.
Northwest Corner Corry and Vine Sts., Corryville.
N. E. Cor. Warsaw and Purcell Aves., Price Hill.
Corner Fifth and Columbia Streets, Newport, Kentucky.

GOODS DELIVERED TO ALL SUBURBS.

SEND FOR OUR PRICE LIST. MAIL ORDERS PROMPTLY ATTENDED TO.
Our NEWPORT STORE, Cor. Fifth and Columbia, IS NOW OPEN.

You tell 'em, Camels, you've got the mildness!

PUT Camels in comparison with any cigarette you ever smoked in so many hundreds for ways they'll prove a delight to your taste—and never stir it, no matter how liberally you smoke!

And, you'll want to tell from the house top that Camels leave no unpleasant cigarettey aftertaste nor unpleasant cigarettey odor!

Camel CIGARETTES

B. H. Kroger placed this, his first Enquirer ad on March 21, 1897. Competition from the Great Atlantic and Pacific Tea Co. (A&P) developed as well as product advertising. Coca-Cola appeared regularly by 1915 and the ad for Camel cigarettes was popular in 1920. Baldwin's ad of Jan. 4,1900, was crude but attention getting. Woodbury's soap, in this 1903 ad, was a product of Cincinnati's Andrew Jergens Co.

Miss St. Louis Says, **HATS OFF TO THE** B.&O.S.W.

THE NATURAL GATEWAY TO THE **WORLD'S GREATEST FAIR**

WATCH FOR OUR TRAIN SERVICE AND SCHEDULES

FOR **ST. LOUIS** Everything New.

WORLD'S FAIR BOOKLETS FREE ON APPLICATION.

TICKET OFFICE   420 WALNUT ST. (Traction Bldg.)

No. 111 Canopy Top Surrey

A Thing of Beauty and Service

JUST THE KIND OF FAMILY CARRIAGE YOU ARE LOOKING FOR

SECHLER & CO

"Have You seen the New *Buick*?"

The first ad for an automobile to appear in The Enquirer offered a Rambler for $750 on May 24, 1903. Transportation ads regularly appeared from the 1840s on. Steamboat ads (this from March 20, 1865) and buggy ads (March 21, 1897) were common. It cost $9 to take the train to the 1904 World's Fair in St. Louis. By 1923 auto ads, like this one for a Buick, had acquired a subtler style. This ad for the 1932 Chrysler exemplifies modern auto advertising.

Rambler

$750

Climbs GILBERT AVE with ease on its highest speed. A slight pressure of the thumb controls it. Has all of the latest improvements and is so simple a lady can operate it. A free demonstration given for the asking.

THE **Cincinnati Automobile Co.,**
807-809 RACE STREET,
CINCINNATI, O.

CHRYSLER with patented **FLOATING POWER**

AUTOMATIC CLUTCH • SILENT GEAR SELECTOR • FREE WHEELING • HYDRAULIC BRAKES • OILITE SQUEAK-PROOF SPRINGS • DOUBLE-DROP GIRDER-TRUSS FRAME

Chrysler Eight Sedan **$1475**
125-inch wheelbase—100 horsepower
4 other body styles $1435 to $1695

Theater advertising started in **The Enquirer's** *first edition with a one-column ad for* **The Lady of Lyons.** *By 1897, ganged ads for opera and Shakespeare rubbed shoulders with grand proclamations for the "Smallest Comedian on Earth" at a museum on Vine Street. Valentino headlined a silent movie in 1922 as the Midnight Rounders performed in vaudeville at the Shubert. Talkies and Garbo were big in 1932, and Cinerama arrived 30 years later. Competition to the movies began in Cincinnati on Sept. 19, 1939, with the first showing of television at Pogue's department store.*

THE CINCINNATI ENQUIRER **21**

Alms & Doepke's address in 1887 was the Erie Canal. Ten years later the Fair Store called itself "Cincinnati's Great Department Store" while McAlpin's cut its prices on Mme. Yale's remedies. On Wednesday, July 21, 1920, Shillito's offered men's Palm Beach suits for $12.50. Mabley & Carew put 2700 suits on sale for $7.50 each on July 5, 1883. And Swallen's announced a new line of Sunbeam products on June 1, 1962.

ROLLMAN & SONS.

SPRING OPENING --- 1897 --- SPRING OPENING

In 1897, The Big Store and Rollman's, where you could buy a silk cape for $5, were doing business on Fifth Street. Nathan Wolf, tailor, offered a discount for cash in the same year. By 1939, a handcrafted suit cost $45 at Burkhardt's on Fourth Street.

MAX RUDOLF

Conducts the

Cincinnati Symphony Orchestra

AT MUSIC HALL

Subscribe Now!

20 FRIDAY MATINEE CONCERTS—20 SATURDAY EVENING CONCERTS

Season Tickets from $16.50

1958-59
SUBSCRIPTION CONCERTS

Oct. 10-11 OPENING CONCERT	Jan. 23-24 ZINO FRANCESCATTI, Violinist
Oct. 17-18 ROBERTA PETERS, Soprano	Jan. 30-31 CARL SEEMANN, Pianist (U. S. Debut)
Oct. 24-25 GYORGY CZIFFRA, Pianist	Feb. 6-7 SIR JOHN BARBIROLLI, Guest Conductor
Oct. 31-Nov. 1 JOSEPH FUCHS, Violinist	Feb. 13-14 PETER MAAG, Guest Conductor (U. S. Debut)
Nov. 14-15 MARIA TIPO, Pianist	Feb. 20-21 ARTUR RUBINSTEIN, Pianist
Nov. 21-22 JOSE LIMON and DANCE COMPANY	Mar. 26-28 EASTER CONCERT
Nov. 28-29 ROBERT CASADESUS, Pianist	Apr. 3-4 MICHAEL RABIN, Violinist
Dec. 5-6 BEETHOVEN MEMORIAL CONCERT	Apr. 10-11 GOLD and FIZDALE, Duo-Pianists
Dec. 12-13 BACH'S "CHRISTMAS ORATORIO"	Apr. 17-18 HANDEL'S "JUDAS MACCABAEUS"
Jan. 2-3 NEW YEAR CONCERT	
Jan. 9-10 RUTH SLENCZYNSKA, Pianist	

SUBSCRIBE TO SYMPHONY NOW!

Write or Phone the Symphony Office

111 E. Fourth St., Telephone CHerry 1-6146 or CHerry 1-2538

The Zoo, Chester Park, Coney and the Reds wanted Cincinnatians' entertainment dollars on Sunday, May 31, 1903. Rudy Vallee, Jimmy Ames and Miss Holland (hmmmm?) wanted the discretionary buck in 1949 at Beverly Hills, the Latin Quarter and the Gayety, respectively. Lunch was 85 cents at Grammer's in 1958, when the phone number at the Maisonette was PArkway 1-2260. And a season ticket for the symphony that year was $16.50.

FLAMES LIGHT WAY TO 617 VINE

"They bought a building on the west side of Vine, north of Sixth, for $84,000, then set about erecting a new building next door for a printing plant."

The paper's original office was on the south side of Fifth Street, between Main and Sycamore, where Moses Dawson's *Advertiser* had been when John and Charles Brough bought it from him and renamed it *The Daily Enquirer.* A directory of the day listed it as on "Fifth at Dennison's." (A hotel by that name stood in that block for more than a century after that, until it was razed during recent decades of urban renewal.) Today, the site is occupied by the Central Trust Center.

Producing a newspaper has always required a unique combination of intellect, knowledge, editorial craft and industrial skill. The production requirements in 1841, however, were far simpler than today, and the "back shop" of a newspaper office was usually the production and printing plant. Most early editors were also printers. The trades went hand in hand.

The Enquirer stayed on Fifth through the Broughs' two years of ownership and the subsequent partnership between Charles Brough and Hiram H. Robinson. Then, in 1846, the paper moved. Directories from that year carried this reference: "Eliphalet Case Jr.,

Publisher, Enquirer, Northeast Corner Main and Third." The paper stayed there until about 1850, through a period when ownership was shared by a confusing array of various partners — committed Democrats who had been importuned to help support the party newspaper. In 1849 and 1850, according to old directories, the paper was published on a site at the intersection of Main and Third Streets.

In 1850, the new owners, James J. Faran and Hiram Robinson, moved the paper to 88 Main St., between Third and Pearl streets, where it remained for seven years as The Enquirer Co., publishing the paper and (like many newspapers) doing brisk commercial printing business. There it stayed most of the 1850s, in relative stability, producing a daily paper as well as business forms, illuminated show bills and circus posters.

In 1857, Faran and the industrialist, Washington McLean, acquired control of *The Enquirer* and moved it to the corner of Vine and Baker, just below Fourth Street. Today, this is at the rear of the Provident Tower, but in those days, it was 138 Vine St., which was next to Pike's Opera House.

On the night of Thursday, March 22,

1866, Mr. Pike's Opera House was the wrong thing to be next to. A tremendous explosion blew out the back of the building, causing the worst fire Cincinnatians had ever seen. Not only did it destroy the opera house, but half the businesses in the block — including the Enquirer's building.

The paper missed only one day of publication. It might not have missed that one, except that the fire began late at night, forcing printers to evacuate the building even as the paper was on the presses. It was simply too late to do anything about it. Next day, Calvin W. Starbuck, publisher of the

Continued on next page

competing *Times*, offered publishers McLean and Faran the use of his shop. From there, *The Enquirer* reappeared on Saturday, the 24th. Other publishers offered help as well, and in the days to follow, *The Enquirer* accepted the offers. In an editorial in its first post-fire issue, *The Enquirer* thanked its helpful competitors publicly:

"This . . . calamity which has fallen upon us has been modified in part by the generous and kindly spirit manifested by our brethren of the other daily papers, Messrs. Starbuck & Co. of the *Times*, Mr. Halstead of the *Commercial*, and Messrs. Smith & Co. of the *Gazette*. We owe to their establishments a debt of gratitude that far exceeds mere thanks and complimentary mention, which we hope we never shall be able to repay in kind. . . .

"To Messrs. Starbuck & Co. of the *Times* and Mr. Halstead of the *Commercial*, we are especially under obligation. Before the flames had consumed our building, and while the conflagration was in progress, these generous proprietors made the tender of their extensive offices to us, which we accepted and by means of which and the

ENQUIRER SURVIVES FIRST FIRE

From *The Enquirer* of Tuesday. Feb. 28, 1865, comes this report of what was to be the first of two devastating fires at the paper within 13 months. This one, luckily, came on a Sunday morning. The Saturday-night crew had finished printing Sunday's paper. There was no Monday paper in those days, so employees would have had Sunday off. By Monday afternoon, enough salvage work had been done to let work proceed on an abbreviated Tuesday paper, and *The Enquirer* did not miss a day's publication. That Tuesday's paper began its description of that fire this way:

"About half past seven o'clock on Sunday morning the quiet of the Sabbath in our city was disturbed by the cry of fire, the incessant ringing of the alarm bells, and the rumbling of the fire engines and hose carriages along our streets. It was soon discovered from the dense volumes of smoke issuing from the Enquirer

assistance rendered by them, we are able to issue today."

Such lofty sentiments of gratitude cooled as quickly as the embers of the conflagration. Soon *The Enquirer* would turn on Murat Halstead with a vengeance rarely seen in Cincinnati newspaper rivalry.

buildings that our establishmment was seriously threatened with total destruction. . . .

"The fire broke out in the upper story, which is used as our news room and storage department for pictorial bills, cuts, etc. How the fire originated we are at a loss to know, although there are various theories expressed — one of which being that the drippings of oil from the cog wheels and machinery of the hoisting apparatus into some rubbish produced spontaneous combustion. . . .

"The engines Citizens' Gift, Fourth, Fourteenth, Tenth, Fifth, and First, were speedily on the ground and almost instantly were at work throwing their great streams of water on to the burning element. The black immediately gave way to a white smoke, but such was the tenacity with which the fire clung to the building, that three hours of incessant labor was performed before the element was subdued and conquered . . . ."

Within the year, McLean and Faran moved into new quarters. They bought a building on the west side of Vine, north of Sixth, for $84,000, then set about erecting a new building next door for a printing plant. When production began at the new plant after the opera house fire,

The Enquirer added a Monday paper. Now producing a paper seven days a week, it became Cincinnati's first true "daily."

Those buildings on Vine Street lasted six decades, through a golden era starting in 1872, when Washington McLean's son, John R. McLean, made *The Enquirer* into one of America's premier newspapers. In 1924, eight years after John R. Mclean died and left the paper in a trust, the managers and trustees decided it was time to replace those old buildings and their antiquated presses with a new plant and the most modern of equipment.

The old "building" was really a collection of four buildings, three facing Vine Street and one in back. The former Wesleyan Female College residence hall at 617 Vine was "the Enquirer Office." Parts of the paper were next door above the Atlantic Gardens saloon, some in the building erected by Washington McLean in 1868 at 619, which was the paper's address for many years.

It was an awkward agglomeration, but old-timers in the 1920s wrote with keen sentiment of its passing. In the hand-type

Continued on page 28

OPERA HOUSE CONFLAGRATION CANCELS EDITION

Cincinnati's great Pike's Opera House fire of 1866 broke out as *The Enquirer* was preparing to print the paper of March 23. No one ever learned what caused the fire, but the most likely explanation was that something ignited gas from a leaking main in the Opera House. The fire went undetected until an explosion blew out the rear of the opera house.

The flames roared into the rear of the adjacent Enquirer Building so suddenly that they chased the printers from the building before the presses got rolling. The paper didn't reappear until Tuesday, when *The Enquirer* printed its account of the fire and of how the paper resumed publication. In an accompanying editorial, the publishers, James J. Faran and Washington McLean, explained *The Enquirer's* one-day absence and thanked competing publishers for offering their shops, equipment and presses to let *The Enquirer* resume publication:

"Our city subscribers yesterday needed no apology, for the non appearance of our paper. The blackened walls and smoldering ruins of what was once the Enquirer office too

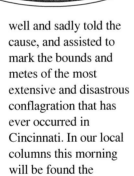

Ruins of Pike's Opera House (wall with arches) and the two-story Enquirer *to its far right smoulder on Vine just south of Fourth Street. Inset shows opera house before fire.*

well and sadly told the cause, and assisted to mark the bounds and metes of the most extensive and disastrous conflagration that has ever occurred in Cincinnati. In our local columns this morning will be found the particulars of this disastrous and exciting catastrophe, which for years to come will be a memorable and talked-of event. We, of the Enquirer, have been of late peculiarly unfortunate. Twice within little more than a twelve-month span the Enquirer office has been in ruins from the same devouring element, which it seems has marked us for its own. We had hardly repaired and made good the damages incurred by the fire of Feb., 1865, when we are involved in a far severer and more complete loss in March, 1866, which has swept our printing house clean from top to bottom. The first fire originated within, the second from without, and so sudden and overwhelming was it that our printers and other employees had barely time to escape with their lives from the building then threatened with the most terrible destruction. . . .

"Topmost upon the ruins of this establishment lies. . .the huge iron safe, strange to say, in a perfect state of preservation, and its contents unscathed. It is feared, however, that the four-cylinder Hoe press, if unwarped by the flames, lies beneath the burning mass of flooring and crushing weight of brick is in so broken condition as to render it utterly useless hereafter.

"*The Enquirer* office is insured at $38,000, and had on hand $50,000 worth of printed matter and printing materials of which $18,000 worth belonged to Jno. Robinson's Circus. Four boxes of show-bills were only yesterday delivered to Lipman's Circus Company.

"The Enquirer building was owned by the publisher. . . Many of the printers and attaches of the office only saved themselves by a precipitous exit from the house — some of them leaving their shoes and other wearing apparel behind."

era, before unions and automatic typesetters stabilized back-shop employment in the 1890s, printers were a rowdy, unpredictable lot. As one veteran reminisced: "Printers came and went. Drinking was customary, heavy drinking by no means rare, and the general morale such that College Street (the alley behind the buildings] was colloquially refered to as 'Battle Alley.'" The news departments and advertising "counting room" were in one building, the composing room in another, and the two were joined by a footbridge. Long after *The Enquirer* moved into its new building in 1926, editors spoke of going "over the bridge" to the composing room.

Fond of the old buildings or not, by the time the Roaring '20s arrived, *The Enquirer* had out-grown them, and it was plainly time to build a new Enquirer Building. The project, however, would pose a formidable problem because newspapering is not like making widgets: You can't

ENQUIRER HAS MISSED NINE PUBLISHING DATES

Newspapering is like show business: Come hell or high water, the show must go on, and the paper must get out. Only nine times in its 150 years has *The Enquirer* failed to appear when scheduled, and one of those times, the show didn't go on, either. That was the day after a great fire that, on March 22, 1866, destroyed Pike's Opera House on Fourth near Vine, and took with it *The Enquirer's* premises next door at the corner of Vine and Baker streets. Within 24 hours, the paper had recovered its balance and, in an abbreviated edition printed on borrowed presses, reported its own temporary failure along with the news of the Great Conflagration.

It was following that fire that *The Enquirer* moved to new quarters on the very same site as today's Enquirer Building at 617 Vine St.

The day after the opera-house fire was only the third time *The Enquirer* had missed publication. The first two had been less than a year before: An announcement atop the editorial column on page two on Saturday, April 14, 1865, said there would be no paper on Sunday so that employees "may participate in the general celebration today" of the impending end of the Civil

From left, the late George Palmer, reporter, and Charles Hubbs, former managing editor, broadcast the news during the 1967 strike. At left, a note found in the files to explain the absence of the paper on March 23, 1866.

War. Had there been a paper on April 15, of course, it would have reported the shooting the night before of President Lincoln at Ford's Theater in Washington. Because of the "general celebration," that news was not reported in *The Enquirer* until April 16. (And it was such a big story, that the exact same type was repeated the next day, April 17.) Again on July 5, 1865, there was no paper because employees were given the day

off to attend Fourth of July celebrations.

Labor disputes lay behind *The Enquirer's* remaining failures to appear. In 1943, a pressmen's walkout halted publication for a day. The paper was down for three days in 1967, when other trades honored a photoengravers' picket line. In 1973, a Teamsters strike produced paperless days on Nov. 24 and 26 (on Sunday, Nov. 25, the "newspaper" consisted of comics and other sections that had been printed before the strike).

On Oct. 28, 1977, a computer failure put *The Enquirer* within an eyelash of not appearing, but 11th-hour electronic improvisations permitted a single, tardy edition.

During that 1967 strike, the electronic media discovered how hard it is to fill a newspaper's shoes. Both *The Enquirer* and the *Post and Times-Star* were absent, and TV tried to fill the gap by tripling newscast time. WKRC radio turned *The Enquirer's* newsroom into a makeshift studio and produced an oral version of the paper, complete with reporters and columnists reading copy on-microphone. The late George Palmer, then an *Enquirer* reporter but formerly a radio and TV newsman, anchored the broadcast. Expanded coverage or not, it was not the same; readers found that TV just can't deliver what a newspaper does. TV doesn't do classified ads, or crosswords, editorial cartoons or box scores. Or TV listings.

just stop making the product for a few days while you move to a new home. Moreover, the new building was to be built on the exact same site as the old.

The trade publication, *Editor & Publisher*, featured *The Enquirer*'s new building in its issue of April 14, 1928, not long after *The Enquirer* had moved.

"Construction of the new plant proceeded in three stages over and around the old plant without an hour's interruption of publication. . . . First an adjacent lot was bought and cleared, and a four-story building with basement was erected to a stage permitting its use. This was Building No. 1, and in it was erected a new, 16-unit Goss press and two Wood junior autoplate machines in their permanent positions in the basement. On the floors above were located temporarily the offices from the building on Vine Street. The latter was then torn down, and the whole front [of the new building] erected complete to 14 stories, after which the offices were moved from Building No. 1 to more or less permanent rooms in the new structure, their places in the first building being occupied by the

Above, the 1882 news staff: seated, from left, Harry M. Weldon, Ed H. Anthony, George S. "Dirty Shirt" Brown, Frank E. Tunison, Elliott Marfield, Thomas McConn and George M. Roe. Standing, from left, are Theodore Horstman, Claude Meeker, Alex C. Sands Jr., Charles Scanlon, Charles L. Doran, Ren Mulford Jr. and Henry Walter. Left, In April, 1894, these four reporters posed: James M. Cox, W.A. Draper, Harry Shaffer, and James Allison. Cox went on to lead other newspapers and ran for president in 1920. Draper later became president of Cincinnati Street Railway Co.

composing room, mail room and associated activities. In the meantime, the new presses had been put into operation. The old structure was then wrecked and the new building completed."

Cincinnatians marveled at the erection of the new Enquirer Building, literally around the old, especially during the deep excavation for the basement pressroom when workers put extensive shoring under the adjacent Public Library and the Palace (now Cincinnatian) Hotel buildings to avoid undermining their foundations.

The new Enquirer Building's cornerstone was laid Dec.4, 1926, some months after the first paper to come off the new presses in the adjacent "Building No.1" early in the morning of June 6, 1926.

The Enquirer was printed there, deep below Vine Street, for more than half a century, until a new era of electronic publishing. The new electronics allowed production apart from the editorial and advertising offices, nearer the transportation needed for urban distribution, and on a site better suited to the complex, industrial process that newspaper production had become. In 1978 *The Enquirer* began building just such a plant on Western Avenue in Cincinnati's West End, near the site of the Reds' old ballpark, Crosley Field.

The readers' first preview of the new plant's product was a special section inserted in the Christmas Day editions in 1978. After those early test runs, more and more of the paper was printed at the new plant, although type continued to be set in the old composing room at 617 Vine St. Finally, on the weekend of April 21-22, 1979, the rest of the mechanical departments moved. The editions of Monday, April 23, were entirely produced at the new plant, from typesetting, composing and photoengraving, to platemaking, printing and distribution.

Above, **The Enquirer** *at 619 Vine St. and , right, the "new" building built around it. Opposite page, top, construction of the 617 press room two stories below Vine Street. Bottom, Mrs. W. F. Wiley, center, at cornerstone laying. Box in fore-ground is a time capsule.*

This poem first appeared in *"Pi Lines,"* a composing room publication during World War II. The author, unknown, writes about traveling printers.

SIX-ONE-SEVEN VINE.

There are times I like to travel,
And roam from town to town,
Where'er I get a chance to hold
A situation down;
But away from Cincinnati
The thought is always mine
That I must hurry back again
To Six-One-Seven Vine.

No matter is it East or West,
And North and South's the same,
For life is but a checker-board
And I just play the game;
But when I get a-going good
And everything is fine,
'Tis then I get to thinking
Of Six-One-Seven Vine.

I've worked in New York City,
In Chicago looped the loop,
In the Southland I have wandered,
But still my spirits droop,
Until my heart persuadeth me
To drop my folks a line
And tell them I am coming back
To Six-One-Seven Vine.

When I'm far across the country,
And sad as I can be,
Just homesick for a happy land,
Then this thought comes to me —
O'er the hills of Cincinnati
The golden sun may shine,
And so I hurry back to home
And Six-One-Seven Vine.

THE CINCINNATI ENQUIRER.

VOL. XXXIV: NO. 179. FRIDAY MORNING, JULY 7, 1876. PRICE FIVE CENTS.

WASHINGTON.

The Impeachment Trial Begun in the Senate.

A Tilden and Hendricks Ratification Meeting.

The Feeling Over the Indian Atrocity.

An Exciting Debate on Finances in the House.

A Fond Farewell to the Hopes of Ohio.

Samuel Cox Sits Down a Mr. Garfield.

FORTY-FOURTH CONGRESS.

SENATE.

CUSTER'S COMMAND.

The Terrible Tale of Its Butchery Confirmed.

Further Details of the Fight—Particulars of Reno's Command.

The Wounded Arrive in Minnesota by Steamer.

The War Department Officially Notified of the Butchery.

The Feeling of Horror Throughout the Country.

The Frontiersmen Preparing to Avenge the Death of the Martyrs.

A Full List of the Butchered Officers.

The Broadbrim Peace Policy Denounced by the Country.

THE GREAT STORM.

Over Sixty Persons Killed and One Hundred and Fifty Buildings Blown Down.

Great Damage to Property Throughout Iowa and Missouri.

FOREIGN.

THE WAR IN THE EAST.

THE FIRST McLEAN TAKES OVER

A partnership forged in 1857 between two East End Cincinnati neighbors and friends named James J. Faran and Washington McLean marked the beginnings of *The Enquirer* as a newspaper with interests beyond Democratic politics and a horizon beyond Ohio.

Only a few years before, a marvelous invention called the telegraph had ushered in an era of instant long-distance communications. Along with the railroad, it was bringing the world closer to Cincinnati, and vice versa. It was an exciting time in the news business. Newspapers, for the first time ever, could tell readers in detail of events that happened only hours before, half a world away. And their papers could be distributed by train for hundreds of miles around within hours of publication. The modern newspaper was being born.

Washington McLean, not yet 20, had come to Cincinnati from Pennsylvania in the early 1830s and entered the iron and steel business. He eventually expanded into boiler-making and steamboat building and grew prosperous as a manufacturer as well. He lived in the East End—where the city's boatbuilding industry was centered. His neighbor and close personal friend was James J. Faran, a lawyer who was also a partner in, and editor of, *The Enquirer.* For nearly a decade, while McLean operated his boatbuilding business, Faran had been running the paper in partnership with various other men, including Hiram Robinson. Through the early 1850s, with Faran and Hiram Robinson as partners, *The Enquirer* enjoyed stable prosperity in both the newspaper and the job-printing business.

Both were active politicians — Faran as mayor of Cincinnati from 1855 to 1857 after his years as a legislator, and Robinson as U. S. marshal. When Robinson resigned as marshal amid controversy and moved from the city, he sought a buyer for his share of *The Enquirer*, and Faran turned to his friend and neighbor, Washington McLean. The boatbuilder became a publisher. What neither man knew was that the name McLean would continue to be associated with *The Enquirer* for 94 years.

Naturally, with McLean as a pro-prietor, the paper solidly supported causes that benefited river commerce, especially commerce with the downriver South. McLean maintained close ties with Southern businessmen, ties which influenced his editorial views on abolition, the Civil War and Reconstruction.

But he was also a keen student of politics and had been a staunch Democrat since his early 20s. He quickly grasped the potential advantages of becoming co-owner of his party's leading editorial voice in the West. It would provide him a wider stage in a shrinking world.

Yet, for all the journalistic and

Continued on next page

financial success *The Enquirer* enjoyed under Faran and McLean, most of the years when they ran the paper together weren't particularly happy ones for the Democrats. McLean and *The Enquirer* opposed abolition before the war, and while he opposed secession as well, he was only lukewarm in support of Lincoln early in the war after the South did secede.

Then, after Lincoln's Emancipation Proclamation in January, 1863, *The Enquirer* turned sharply against him and towards the anti-war, or "Copperhead" position.

By war's end, McLean was not only on the losing side politically, his party was itself divided and out of power. Yet he had stuck tenaciously to his position and won a certain admiration, even from opponents. Washington McLean had great strength of character and resolve. *The Enquirer* bitterly opposed the government's harsh Reconstruction policies well into the 1870s.

repayment of Civil War debts. Rich conservatives back East favored slow repayment in gold, a policy that plagued Cincinnati and the fast-growing West with

extremists, he waited for a contender he could safely back as a presidential candidate in 1868, and finally settled on George Pendleton of Cincinnati. Leader of Ohio Democratic moderates, Pendleton had won the state party's blessing with a compromise plan to pay some debt with gold, some with greenbacks, some with spending cuts, some with tax increases. It wasn't what *The Enquirer* had been demanding, but it was a potential winner (and besides, Pendleton was a home-town man).

Washington McLean, left, was a successful steamboat builder before he purchased part of **The Enquirer.** *Steamboat building was the city's major industry for much of the 19th century.*

Washington McLean remained a powerful voice in national Democratic Party deliberatons virtually until his death in 1892, especially after both he and his son moved to Washington, D.C., in 1882. But the elder McLean's postwar maneuvers to regain prominence, now as a presidential kingmaker, were in vain.

One issue he tried to ride was chronic shortages of credit and cash. Expansion-minded westerners and western Democrats played to long-standing regional distrust of Eastern bankers by demanding the government simply print greenbacks to repay the war bonds. McLean's *Enquirer* favored this inflationary plan. Playing Democratic moderates against green-back

The Enquirer swung behind Pendleton wholeheartedly but the newspaper didn't immediately grasp the importance of also supporting its candidate's moderate views. It kept trumpeting its old extremist position loudly enough to help ruin Pendleton's chances at the 1868 Democratic convention. The party picked an Easterner, Horatio Seymour, who lost to Ohio's Ulysses S. Grant.

EDITOR FARAN CHAMPIONS NEWS' INDEPENDENCE

The name James J. Faran appeared on the masthead of *The Enquirer* for nearly 40 years, through associations with Hiram Robinson, Washington McLean and his son, John R. McLean. He was a widely respected lawyer, legislator and civic-minded thinker who lent editorial stability, dignity, integrity and style.

He was born in 1808, attended Miami College in Oxford and studied and practiced law under a distinguished judge, O.M. Spencer. Well before his name first appeared in *The Enquirer*, he served nearly 10 years in the Ohio Senate. In 1855 he became mayor of Cincinnati.

His link to *The Enquirer* dates to the very first issue, on April 10, 1841, which carried a letter he had written as a state representative defending his position on a controversial banking bill. He frequently contributed to the paper before becoming an owner himself.

Faran's first formal connection to the paper was when he bought a small share in 1844.

But he was serving in Congress at the time and left the newspaper business to others, mainly Hiram Robinson.

In 1848, Faran had left office and bought an even larger share from one of the several part owners, and, in partnership with Robinson, moved the paper to 88 Main St.

Together they ran it there until 1857, when Faran was simultaneously serving as mayor of Cincinnati. He was finishing his term as Robinson decided to sell his share of the paper. Faran persuaded his neighbor and friend, Washington McLean, to buy in.

When he bought his interest in the paper, Faran was 38, a knowledgeable public figure and an educated man, dignified and courteous, fair in reporting events and experienced as both a writer and as an editor.

Faran brought stability to the editorial helm of *The Enquirer*, a quality sorely lacking during the days of changing ownership. Most of the time he remained a co-proprietor of *The Enquirer* he wrote the editorials and most of those concerned politics.

He and Washington McLean were determined to make their newspaper useful beyond politics. They knew that to be free and independent, a newspaper also had to be self-supporting. That meant the paper had to deliver the news.

Faran and McLean brought *The Enquirer* to true prosperity not only as a paper, but also by building the commercial printing business into a huge enterprise. The owners also recognized that however important Cincinnati was in the "West," it was part of a wider world, and they tried to distance themselves from the sectionalism that surrounded and followed the Civil War.

Faran remained active as an editor until he was 75 in 1883. In that year, John R. McLean, Washington's son, bought him out. Faran died in 1892.

James Faran

RIVER FLOWS THROUGH ENQUIRER'S NEWS COLUMNS

The Ohio River has never been far from the mind of anyone who ever lived in Cincinnati., although in the mid-19th century the comings and goings of riverboats were far more a part of everyday life than now. Before the Civil War, and for some time after it, most of the city's commerce with the rest of the world was by river and was as regular a subject of news coverage as politics and government.

The Enquirer's proprietor and publisher from 1857 to 1873, Washington Mclean, had made a fortune in building riverboats and was always keenly interested in the river. Until the railroad prevailed over the steamboat late in the 19th century, the city's commercial soul was on the riverfront, and the Public Landing was more important than the airport has ever been.

The Enquirer had a full-time river editor until the 1920s. River news consisted largely of reports of the movement of vessels and cargoes. After the telegraph made long distance communications almost instant, the Associated Press provided regular reports on river traffic. During the Civil War, they often dealt with movement of troops, munitions and prisoners, and were of extra interest. These reports

As 19th-century passengers board the steamer **Sherlock**, *a sign advertises departures for New Richmond, Moscow, Foster and Chilo aboard the steamer* **Tacoma**.

generally came from Cairo, Ill., strategically placed where the Ohio meets the Mississippi. Like this one in 1863, they were terse dispatches, but spoke volumes to the merchant awaiting a shipment.

"LATEST TO ASSOCIATED PRESS NEWS FROM BELOW ON THE RIVER

CAIRO, February 27 — The steamer *Silver Spray*, from New Orleans for Cincinnati with 300 bales of cotton.

75 Confederate prisoners now confined in the Irving Block are to be sent to Johnson's Island shortly.

The steamer *City of Cairo*, arrived from Memphis with 240 bales of cotton for St. Louis.

Thirty bales of cotton belonging to a merchant in Memphis was burned by guerrillas a short distance above Memphis on the 23d."

The river editor required special knowledge of geography and commerce, of boats and their masters. For much of the late 19th century, the river editor was a man named Curly Lallance. When he died, his widow took over, and she was followed in the 1920s by her brother, Capt. George W. Budd, a former steamboat man himself. He was the last of the true rivermen to hold the job.

When modern towboats and barges took over river shipping, routine river news vanished from the paper. Most modern cargoes are commodities—grain, salt, oil, and coal, and the progress of them is seldom newsworthy. In recent decades, river news has dealt mainly with unusual shipments, new towboats named for prominent businessmen, the rise of pleasure boating, and the occasional river tragedy.

ENQUIRER OPPOSES ABOLITION, LINCOLN, CIVIL WAR

Cincinnati was a bastion of the Democratic Party in 1860, a fact to which *The Enquirer* — the Democrat's voice — owed its popularity and strength. The mainstays of the party were the the the Irish, the predominantly Catholic Germans, and mountain Southerners who had migrated north to jobs on the river and in the city.

These groups had a keen economic interest in the health of river commerce, since many of them earned their wages as warehousemen, boatmen, and wharf-hands, or in shops and factories dependent on river trade. One thing they were against was abolition. They feared that freed slaves would migrate northwards and take their jobs. Their view was not without foundation; well before the Civil War, blacks had supplanted many whites on the riverboats and landings.

As the '50s moved to a close, and secession — perhaps even conflict — loomed, the Democratic rank and file stood opposed to any war that might hasten abolition. *The Enquirer* was right behind them, although its interest in the issue was not necessarily woven from the same yarn. *The Enquirer* of Washington McLean and James J. Faran favored appeasement of belligerent secessionists because they knew war would disrupt Cincinnati's prosperous trade with the downriver South. Whatever the reasons, their position reinforced the paper's popularity among the Democratic rank and file. It also put the paper directly at odds with the local Catholic Church and Archbishop John Purcell, a staunch supporter of abolition, of the union, and if necessary, of war.

Despite **The Enquirer's** *opposition to the war, citizens would gather at the public landing to support the troops. Here the First Ohio Zouave Regiment leaves for Western Virginia.*

Once Fort Sumter had been fired upon, however, and war had begun. *The Enquirer* supported it, even if its support was only lukewarm. Support for the Northern cause was certainly not lacking in September, 1862, when rebel forces marched northward through Kentucky, menacing Cincinnati, and creating quite a stir. The entire city closed up shop and answered the call for its defense. A force of 15,000 volunteers, utterly untrained but ready to fight, streamed across the river and dug in on the Northern Kentucky hilltops to await the rebel assult. It never came, and the rebs turned back, leaving the city unharmed.

But on Jan. 1, 1863, when President Lincoln issued the Emancipation Proclamation, the paper turned against him and the war. Faran and McLean were among the anti-war Democrats derisively dubbed "Copperheads" by Lincoln Republicans, a term that referred to serpent-like treachery on the part of Northerners who seemed sympathetic to the South. Just as the isolationists discovered in 1941, people are not inclined to distinguish between being against a war and being for the enemy.

The Enquirer was a target of government efforts to silence anti-war dissent, an effort that took form in a military proclamation forbidding criticism of the government by editors or orators. It was a serious matter; when a prominent Democrat, Congressman Clement Vallandigham from Dayton, Ohio, harshly criticized the proclamation as a politically motivated violation of free speech, he was arrested by soldiers, convicted by a tribunal, and exiled to the South. Vallandigham found his way to Canada and campaigned from there for governor in 1863 after Ohio Democrats nominated him despite his exile. Ironically, his opponent was John Brough, one-time Democratic stalwart and founder of *The Enquirer.* Brough had bolted the party in 1848, objecting to its pro-slavery tendencies. His old paper endorsed Vallandigham, but

Confederate forces marched north in 1862 and 15,000 Union troops crossed a pontoon bridge from Cincinnati to Kentucky to meet the rebels. The Confederates didn't show up.

Brough won by a huge margin.

Vallandigham created a sensation the next year when, though still officially in exile, he appeared in Chicago to make a speech at the Democratic convention. The Lincoln administration, apparently realizing the error of having prosecuted him, took no action.

The Enquirer's anti-Lincoln stance was plainly visible in its coverage of his visit to Gettysburg in November, 1863, for a speech at the soldiers' cemetery there to commemorate the awful battle earlier that year. After arriving, but prior to his immortal Gettysburg address, Lincoln stepped to the balcony of his hotel and exchanged a few words with passersby. *The Enquirer*, in its anti-Lincoln zeal, mistook these words for the main event and was harshly critical of the "speech." Next day, while it reported the real speech, it denounced Lincoln for having a military escort on his journey from Washington. "Why a bodyguard of soldiers?" the editorial asked. "No other president has ever traveled so escorted." The writer went on to complain that Lincoln was "assuming the state and manner of a king," and concluded: "Conscience doth make cowards of us all."

During much of the Civil War, *The Enquirer* was banned in Kentucky. Many Northern Kentuckians continued not only to read it, but to receive it at home. One ferry operator smuggled newspapers across the river daily through the war, and faithful readers got their *Enquirers* wrapped inside copies of the *Commercial*.

An essay reproduced in 1929 in *The Little Enquirer*, a publication for *Enquirer* employees, spoke of the Civil War as "an awful time, an intolerant age when reason fled and rage and rancor dominated."

When the war broke out, the essay concluded, "all the political opposition against which this newspaper has arrayed itself in the past united in a violent determination to pillory it in public contumely as a disloyal advocate of secession. Misunderstood, misrepresented, and constantly and deliberately maligned, *The Enquirer* maintained its position. It declared against disunion, but asserted and exercised its right to judge and criticize the policies and performance of the government."

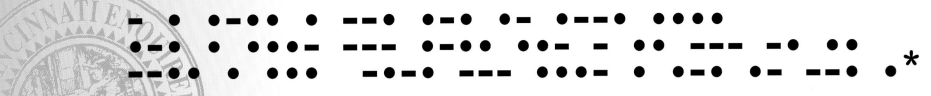

The newspaper editor's job changed radically in the late 1840s,when a new device called the telegraph brought virtually instant transmission of news.

Most papers in those days consisted of four pages, and one was the editor's to fill. It was usually page two of the paper, since page one was mostly advertising. The back two pages contained more advertising, and if the ads fell short, the editor might print the text of political speeches, legislation and other public notices.

Before the telegraph (and for years after it came, for that matter) the editor relied on other newspapers for news from distant places, always reprinting it with credit and sometimes adding his own comments or additional information he had gathered on his own. Newspapers regularly exchanged copies for this purpose and these sorts of items were called "exchanges." The term led logically enough to the title of "exchange editor" as papers and their staffs grew, and editorial tasks became more specialized.

Newspapers, conservative when it comes to the use of the language, are often slow to change old terminology. The "exchange editor" remained a fixture at *The Enquirer* into the 1920s, long after the paper's own network of correspondents and the wire services had all but rendered the position obsolete.

Early editors sometimes visited the state capital or other cities, "sending back by mail such news as he gathered," in one historian's words. Some persuaded a trusted acquaintance in the capital to provide news and comment by mail — that is, by "correspondence."

Until about 1850, these correspondents were not paid, and their names often did not appear in the paper.

The telegraph was invented by Samuel F. B. Morse in 1837. It carried its first intercity message in 1844 when Morse, in Washington, wired his famous question to Baltimore: "What hath God wrought?"

Within a year, wires were being strung between major cities. The first message to reach Cincinnati by telegraph was on Aug. 21, 1847, and within weeks, *The Enquirer* was printing news received by the "Magnetic Telegraph." The telegraph

had been carrying news for three years by the time most papers began the practice of paying their correspondents in 1850.

The Enquirer's proprietors apparently distrusted the machine at first, once referring to it in print as the "tell-lie-graph," perhaps because their firm views led them to distrust news from anyone except their own politically reliable correspondents.

The telegraph, like all new technologies, was expensive at first, and it was used initially for fast dissemination only of news of major interest and immediacy — disasters, war, assassination and the like. Routine news continued to flow via

Continued on next page

*TELEGRAPH REVOLUTIONIZES COVERAGE

the correspondents' mail for some time as the new medium spread.

In 1858, the telegraph had spanned the oceans, on Cyrus Field's underwater cable between North America and Europe, and most of the news of the Civil War reached readers by way of telegraph dispatches. By the 1870s, newspapers were sending and receiving telegraphic news dispatches of the most routine sort. New methods of gathering news meant new editorial tasks, and *The Enquirer* had a telegraph editor by the time of the Civil War. (War has a way of whetting the public's appetite for information; as one veteran Scripps-Howard editor once told a man who accused him of sensationalizing the news to sell more papers: "The only things that ever sold more papers were war, peace, and the Lindbergh kidnapping.")

Around 1880, *The Enquirer* established its own private circuit, on wires leased from Western Union, to keep the

An **Enquirer** *telegraph editor pulls a dispatch from a teletype machine. The newspaper established it's own telegraph line.*

editor in Cincinnati in close touch with the publisher, John R. McLean, in Washington. George Gilliland was the first telegraph operator in Washington, and the signature, "GI," with which he signed on and off

became the name of the private circuit. The GI wire soon expanded far beyond its original purpose and became a private newswire linking *The Enquirer* with its own correspondents in major East Coast centers and other Midwestern cities. When the paper's telegraph staff peaked during World War I, 10 regular operators were "pound-

ing brass" for the paper on Vine Street.

The GI wire was not *The Enquirer's* only source of telegraphic news. Associated Press dispatches have been appearing in the paper almost since the AP was founded in 1848 by six rival New York papers to take advantage of the telegraph. Like all new technologies, it was expensive; the founders reduced their cost by sharing the expenses of gathering and transmitting news from the rest of the country. They soon found it worked both ways and that papers outside New York were happy to join in the co-operative "wire" service. In 1875, the AP leased telegraph lines of its own between Washington and New York, only a few years before *The Enquirer* established its own leased GI wire between

Washington and Cincinnati.

A resident of Sidney, Ohio, in 1884, visited *The Enquirer* one evening and then wrote an account of the visit for his hometown paper. He was especially taken by the excitement in the telegraph editors' room:

"Four instruments are clicking away constantly," he wrote. "It's half-past ten and Gath's letter is coming over the wire. ("Gath" was the pen name of political correspondent George Alfred Townshend). It is a long one, taking up three columns of space.

"The four operators are kept busy now taking messages from New York, Washington and, in fact, from all quarters of the globe. . . . There have been thirty-five games of baseball played this afternoon; tomorrow morning we have them before us and can tell every individual play that was made. Besides this there are horse races, boat races and the like that takes up a page and a fourth of space, all sent over the wire. . . . Besides the four wires in the office, a telegraph messenger is constantly going back and fourth. A *special* comes in of half a column, and $50 worth of advertising is thrown out to make room for it. This is the very height of newspaper enterprise, and the secret of this great paper. News is first and advertising a secondary consideration."

The GI wire died in the 1920s, but the AP, of course, carries on. *The Enquirer* had begun replacing Morse-code transmitters with the brand new teletype machine soon after the AP introduced it in 1913. The AP began sending photos to its members by mail in 1926, and began transmitting photos almost instantly in 1935 on "wirephoto" machines (and you thought the fax machine was new). In 1947, at age 99, the Associated Press admitted radio (and, by extension, TV) stations to membership.

From the very beginning, telegraph editors — being responsible for choosing what to print from among a world of daily dispatches — required broad and worldly knowledge and were often among the most erudite and educated newspaper people. They wrote headlines for telegraphic news as well, and one early telegraph editor at *The Enquirer,* Charles L. Doran, wrote all his headlines in rhyme. Another, H. R. Smith, was so adept at finding the right words that he was known as "Alphabet" Smith.

The title "telegraph editor" no longer exists at *The Enquirer.*

This telegraph report of President Lincoln's death ran twice after the April 14, 1865, shooting because the paper took a holiday on April 15.

In 1979 the paper appointed a "Wire Manager" to edit all of the wire services at the paper. Old-timers persisted in calling him the telegraph editor despite the fact that no one had actually sent news dispatches by means of the telegraph key in nearly half a century. The teletype began to replace Morse code in 1913, and the clackety-clacking teletype, in turn, has all but been replaced by devices that pump news via fiber-optic cable and satellite, in silent streams of disembodied data, from computer to computer, unseen until the editor summons them onto a glowing video screen.

Efficient, yes. But it somehow lacks the color of the days when Alex Schaap was telegraph editor in the 1890s. He often did the work of an exchange editor as well, clipping foreign-language papers and rewriting their stories into sparkling English as a column called "Old World Chitchat." He could do that easily, for Schaap spoke 12 languages — and was clever enough to play poker in all 12 of them.

Eighteen Hundred Lives Are Lost in Atlantic Ocean When Leviathan Titanic Plunges Into the Depths; World-Famous Personages Are Among the Dead.

Iceberg Rips Open Hull.

Scores of Terror-Stricken Victims Plunge Wildly Into the Sea.

Lifeboats Are Sucked Into the Vortex When the Great Vessel Sinks.

"Save, Oh, Save!" Flashed Madly By the Little Band of Wireless Operators.

Women and Children Struggle With Men To Reach Lowering Emergency Shells—Engulfing of Steamship Is Believed To Have Been Witnessed From the Bridge of the Carpathia.

John Jacob Astor Drowns.

Bride of Noted Financier Rescued and Now Is on Way To New York.

Major Archibald Butt, Aid To President Taft, Reported Among Missing.

Charles M. Hays, Head of Grand Trunk Railway System, May

Others Unaccounted For Straus, F. D. Miller, J. Stead, Benj. Guggen Mr. and Mrs. H and Colonel

Ocean Disasters of Modern History Appalling; Thousands of Victims Are Asleep in the Deep

PRAYERS ARE RAISED.

LAST WORDS FROM SHIP.

Captain Edward John Smith.

MCLEAN SIRES SENSATIONALISM

The Broughs founded *The Enquirer,* and Washington McLean and James J. Faran made a successful, big-city morning daily out of it in the 1850s and '60s. It was Washington's son, John Roll McLean, however, who finally went the last mile and built the paper to prominence in the late 19th century — an era of fierce competition, when great newspaper empires were being built by the likes of Pulitzer, Hearst and Scripps.

Interestingly enough, newspapering is not what John R. McLean's father had hoped for him. The industrialist-publisher Washington McLean, as they say, tried to give his son, John, all the advantages and sent him to the very best schools — Harvard, Heidelberg, and the like. He could have read law (as his father wanted), or even studied medicine.

But what young John R. McLean seemed to want was to live in Cincinnati, play baseball, and be a newspaperman. His stay at Harvard was brief, and the reason for his departure unclear — some accounts say he was expelled for fighting,

others that he left voluntarily. Whatever the case, John R. McLean was one of those headstrong, determined men who get what they want. He returned to Cincinnati, played baseball, and became a newspaperman.

He was not afraid to start at the bottom and learn. He began at *The Enquirer* as cub reporter and worked in every department, learning newspapering from the ground up. He worked as a typesetter and a pressman and maintained a mutual loyalty and fondness with printers all his life.

He was headstrong as well as thoroughly modern, and it wasn't long before he even began finding fault with some of the paper's policies. At first the elder McLean treated his criticisms as youthful impudence and tried to ignore him.

Years later, in retirement, Washington McLean told how John demonstrated that he meant business as a newspaperman:

Young John, the story goes, took to kibitzing at stockholders' meetings, listening and watching, and more than once, his father brusquely sent him out of the room. This irked the

young man, who was determined to be taken seriously, and when he heard that a minority stockholder from out of town wanted to sell his shares, he bought them. At the next stockholders' meeting, he was primed and ready when his father told him to leave. Young McLean put his stock certificate down on the table and said that he fully intended to stay.

It was only a year or two more before Washington McLean understood fully how serious his son was about running the newspaper — and how good he would be at it — and

Continued on next page

decided to transfer his interest in *The Enquirer* to his son. Washington did not give him the paper; he sold it to him (although, as one *Enquirer* historian pointed out many years later, "the amount and terms were such as would not have been accorded to an outsider").

Exactly when control of the paper passed from father to son is not recorded. Accounts vary. Most histories put it in 1873. It

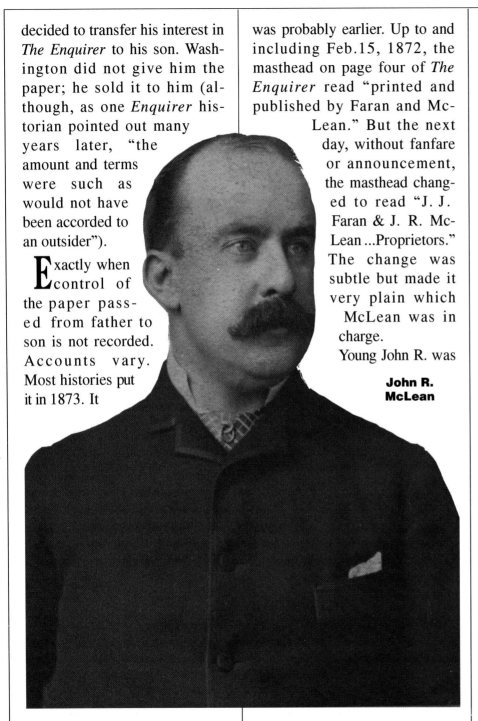

John R. McLean

was probably earlier. Up to and including Feb.15, 1872, the masthead on page four of *The Enquirer* read "printed and published by Faran and McLean." But the next day, without fanfare or announcement, the masthead changed to read "J. J. Faran & J. R. Mc-Lean ...Proprietors." The change was subtle but made it very plain which McLean was in charge.

Young John R. was

24 years old, handsome, debonair and popular. He was also ambitious and energetic, and he had big things in mind for *The Enquirer*. When he first assumed command, he put the editorial side of the paper in the hands of John R. Cockerill, a reporter who had learned leadership as a colonel in the Civil War and whose ideas about vigorous, aggressive, no-nonsense news coverage were right in line with young McLean's. One of McLean's first acts was to elevate Cockerill to managing editor.

For his part, McLean confined himself to advertising and circulation. It was there, he decided, that he would have to whip the competition, which was tough, indeed. The morning *Gazette*, a Republican paper, was larger, and larger still was the morning *Commercial*. Murat Halstead, publisher of the *Commercial*, was a nationally respected giant of American journalism, an editor more than a businessman, and conservative but independent. He was consulted by presidents, governors, and senators, and feared none of them. Once, unhappy with prosecution of the Civil

War, he had written of Lincoln as a "blockhead" and Grant a "drunkard."

When John R. McLean took over *The Enquirer*, Halstead had been publisher of the *Commercial* nearly 20 years, and he treated his brash, new, young competitor with contempt. "The boy manager," he called him, or "that presumptuous boy on Vine Street."

It was a big mistake.

McLean went after *Commercial* and *Gazette* subscribers with a vengeance that left the older men in shock. Halstead and the *Gazette's* Richard Smith attacked McLean in print, and he redoubled his efforts. Smith even took to vilifying *Gazette* subscribers who also took *The Enquirer*. A tough wordsmith himself, McLean boasted that the enemies alone of "Mother Halstead" and "Deacon Smith" were a wonderful source of new circulation.

The very day John R. McLean assumed command at *The Enquirer* he took dead aim on one of the *Commercial's* strongest assets and richest profit centers, its classified advertising.

The Enquirer announced it

would give away its want-ads free. It was as bold a move as it was simple, and it certainly worked. The office on Vine Street was soon jammed with so many people wanting to place ads that the paper had to impose limits, and it hit Halstead's *Commercial* right where it hurt, in the pocketbook. It cost McLean some revenue, but it all but wiped out the *Commercial's* key source of profits, and did grave harm to the *Gazette* as well.

Moreover, circulation of *The Enquirer* soared, thanks largely to the aggressive style of Cockerill and the bright young staff he began assembling. Colonel Cockerill had a sense of what modern readers wanted, and the leadership as an editor to give it to them. No one knew it then, but he went on to become widely recognized as one of the fathers of what we now call "yellow" journalism.

It wasn't long before merchants realized that if they wanted a big audience, *The Enquirer* had it. As circulation rose, so did advertising.

One of the things John R. Mclean did was to scrap the tireless political par-

J.R. McLean's Hottest Tip Was A Foul Tip

Baseball was relatively new in 1867, not far removed from being a sideline at Cincinnati's Union Cricket Club. The Red Stockings baseball team largely consisted of young men of some wealth and position, almost all playing as amateurs. Many of that 1867 team, for instance, were young lawyers, and most had attended such fine, eastern colleges as Harvard and Yale. Among these young baseball players was a 19-year-old catcher named Johnny McLean, whose career as a great newspaper publisher may have resulted from a foul tip.

It happened this way:

McLean was the son of the publisher of *The Enquirer,* Washington McLean. Among his teammates were men with such luminous names as Storer, Kemper, Ellard, Hoge, Wulsin, and Hickenlooper. Among the best of the baseball players was the club's treasurer and property man, Harry Wright, who had been paid to come to Cincinnati as a bowler for the cricket club and who had discovered baseball much to his liking. He was the club's first paid baseball player, and, in 1869, led the Red Stockings when, as the world's first professional team, they went unbeaten.

In 1867, baseball had become so popular that the Union Cricket Club spent $2,400 on a new clubhouse at its

grounds along Mill Creek, and $1,350 for a fence around the field so they could charge admission — 10¢ for games against local teams, 25¢ for games against out-of-town clubs.

The Red Stockings of 1867 played games at the Union Grounds behind Lincoln Park.

Catcher McLean was among the finest players, and the team's sole loss in 1867 was in a game McLean missed because of that foul tip.

McLean was as tough, aggressive and innovative as a catcher as he was later as a publisher. In his history of *Baseball in Cincinnati,* Harry Ellard, a descendant of one of McLean's teammates, tells of one game against an Indianapolis club in which an argument erupted between the teams over whether McLean had caught a ball. "Mr. Sharkey, catcher for the Indianapolis nine," wrote Ellard, "had the temerity to shake his finger in the face of Mr. McLean, who was then in prime athletic conition. Seeing the kind of material he had run against, Mr. Sharkey thought discretion the better part of valor and

allowed Mr. McLean's opinion to stand without further argument."

Ellard credits McLean with inventing the modern catcher's stance, crouched close behind the plate, where he could catch pitches directly rather than on the bounce.

Mr. McLean ,"he wrote, "was the first man to catch close behind the bat, with bare hands. In those days masks, gloves and protectors were unknown, and the catching of a ball in this manner was exceedingly dangerous."

The only game Cincinnati lost in 1867, out of 18 played, was on July 15 to the Nationals of Washington, 53 to 10. Four days before, the Red Stockings had played a local team called the "Live Oak Club" to prepare for the big game with the Nationals. Against the Live Oaks, Ellard wrote, "a foul tip from the bat of one of the players struck Mr. McLean squarely in the eye, closing it for some time. When he returned home, his fond mother was so grieved by the changed appearance of her boy that she forbade him taking part in another game of baseball."

Young John R. McLean obeyed his mother, took up newspapering, and built his father's *Enquirer* to national prominence in a career that lasted until 1916.

tisanship of his father's day. He not only objected to the old *Enquirer's* staid and longwinded coverage of the minutiae of partisan politics, he objected to the partisanship as well. It limited the potential audience, he reasoned. His paper would be so lively that everyone, regardless of their politics, would want to read it just to stay abreast. He made *The Enquirer* the first major daily to summarize even major political speeches. Then he used the space he saved to print news for readers interested in things other than politics.

Within two years, he had transformed *The Enquirer* into an almost non-partisan, wide-awake daily that covered everything from high society to low life, politics to crime, business to pleasure — and did it all with a vividness that sometimes made readers gasp. They didn't know it, but the age of sensationalism was being born, and McLean and Cockerill were the midwives. One of the able young reporters Cockerill hired (in 1874) was Lafcadio Hearn, now widely regarded as the first of the modern American journalists.

In 1880, Colonel Cockerill

Before moving to Washington, D.C., John R. McLean worked in this office in the Enquirer's *Vine Street building.*

went off to cover the Russo-Turkish war as *The Enquirer*'s correspondent. (Later, as managing editor of Joseph Pulitzer's *New York World*, he achieved his greatest fame). John R. McLean took over as editor-in-chief of *The Enquirer*. Not all the old hands could keep up with the new pace, and many left or retired. McLean replaced them with vigorous, aggressive, able young men.

It was all too much for old James Faran, the political intellectual and editorial elder. He didn't care for the brash, bold new style, the demotion of partisan politics, the sensational reporting, the aggressive pursuit of circulation. He and his young, new partner often found themselves at odds, and finally, in 1881, Faran agreed to sell out and retire. John R. McLean, at 33, became the sole proprietor of *The Enquirer*.

He turned out to be one of the

newspaper geniuses of the era. Some of the most colorful and famous of American journalists joined the paper during his tenure. Lafcadio Hearn was but one. James M. Cox, who later became governor of Ohio and the 1920 Democratic presidential nominee, as well as publisher of several Ohio newspapers, was an *Enquirer* reporter. James. W. Faulkner was among the best known political writers of the day. James S. Hastings delighted *Enquirer* readers as the columnist "Luke McLuke." And a reporter named Randolph Chester was widely acclaimed as a novelist and short-story writer in later years.

In 1882, after buying out Faran, McLean moved to Washington, D.C., in search of a broader stage, and put a succession of managing editors in charge in Cincinnati. But he kept them on a short leash, staying in constant touch via a private telegraph line. It was in Washington that he tried to become a press lord in the manner of the Scrippses and Hearsts, but didn't quite succeed.

McLean, however, took *The Enquirer* beyond Cincinnati and

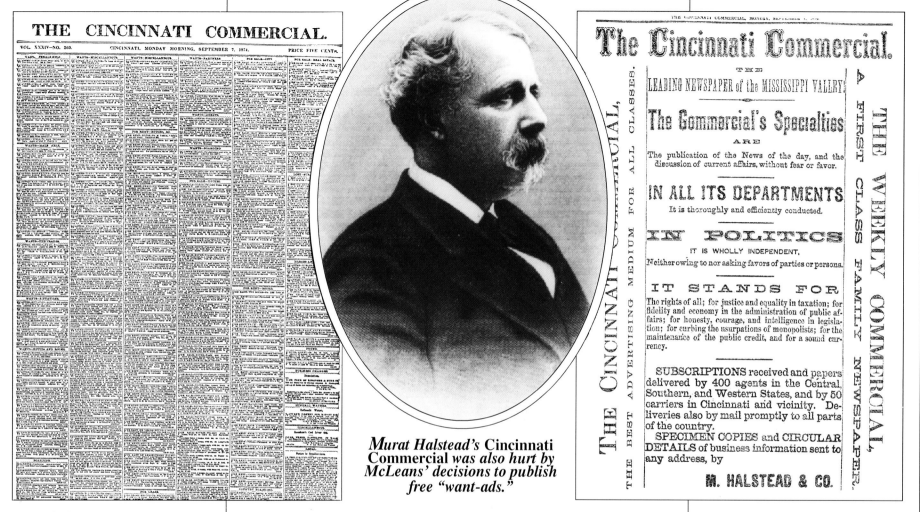

THE CINCINNATI COMMERCIAL.

The Cincinnati Commercial.

Murat Halstead's Cincinnati Commercial *was also hurt by McLeans' decisions to publish free "want-ads."*

made it into the newspaper for much of the Midwest. He maintained correspondents and telegraph bureaus in major cities from New York and Washington to St. Louis and Chicago. Indianapolis and Columbus were virtually local territory. For 15 years before and after the turn of the century, *The Enquirer*

delivered papers throughout Ohio, Indiana and Kentucky on its own, special, early-morning trains. By 1890, the paper was widely read in New York and Chicago.

Eventually, Halstead's *Commercial* was running on borrowed money, and Halstead was forced into foreclosure and

wound up as a hired editor on a paper in Brooklyn, N.Y. It was a sad end, considering that Halstead had helped *The Enquirer* survive in 1866 by unselfishly lending Washington McLean his shop and presses when *The Enquirer* was burned out by the opera house fire. The *Commercial* merged with the *Gazette*

and later became the *Commercial Tribune,* but it never threatened John R. McLean or *The Enquirer* again. *The Enquirer* finally bought it out in 1930, 14 years after McLean died, and almost immediately closed it down for good.

FINAL
Twenty-two Pages

VOL. XCI. NO. 328—DAILY

THE CINCINNATI ENQUIRER

*** WEDNESDAY MORNING, MARCH 2, 1932

THREE CENTS

WEATHER — Rain Wednesday; Thursday. Maximum, 62; minimum, 41. Campbell and Kenton counties, 60, 41.

LINDBERGH BABY IS KIDNAPED

Child Is Taken From Crib; Manhunt On In Two States For Driver Of Green Sedan

Chinese Army Withdraws On All Shanghai Fronts; Japanese Push Forward

China And Japan Accept Plan For Shanghai Peace Meeting In Future, But Reject Truce

RAIL LINE

Bombed By Fliers

To Hinder Troop Trains 35 Miles From City.

Nipponese Pilots Also Harass Defenders

Of Lithe, Near Landing Place Of Expedition.

Casualties In Day's Fighting Are Heavy On Both Sides

—Stores Reopen.

Official Information Sought By Stockholders Of Kroger On Company's Past Affairs

Roosevelt Holds Fate Of Bill To Continue Seabury Quiz

JUSTICE!

Life Term Meted To Former Felon Few Hours After Attack

Capture Is Made Shortly After Latest Incident

In Series That Boosts Rumor Of Violence.

Malone Is To Aid Barrow In Defense Of Four.

Accused In Slaying—To Sail This Month—Sister Of Mrs. Fortescue Reaches Pacific City.

ANSWER IS NO.

Divorce Plea Denied At Blanchester; Loss $100,000 Building Burns

Upon Japanese Woman On Honolulu Estate.

"GOLD RUSH"

Still Is On In England.

So, you're taking up with a two-timer . . . .

BASEBALL STARTS SPORTS PAGE

" From the earliest days of the fabled Red Stockings, baseball runs like a common thread through The Enquirer's sports reports."

In all likelihood, Cincinnatians fond of their sports pages can thank Harry Wright and the sport of cricket for them. Wright, a professional cricket player hired from the east coast by Cincinnati's Union Cricket Club in the 1860s, had taken up the popular new game of baseball and was so good, he switched. As one of the earliest paid professionals, he was the core around which the famous Cincinnati Red Stockings — the first all-professional team—were built.

The early *Enquirer* was a political paper and not given much to sport news. Politics was sport enough, and the occasional horse race or dog fight was reported like any other interesting news. But, following the Civil War, cricket clubs flourished, and the game credited to Abner Doubleday caught on. The team spawned by Cincinnati's Union Cricket Club was more than just adept at the game; it was nigh invincible.

That *The Enquirer* paid more than casual attention to the new game of baseball may also have been because one of the fine young gentlemen who played the new sport of baseball rather well for the Red Stockings just happened to be John R. McLean, the son of Washington McLean, publisher of *The Enquirer*. He was the team's catcher in 1867. When John R. McLean took over the paper's reins from his father in 1872 — three years after the fabulous 1869 Red Stockings went undefeated — his interest went along, and *The Enquirer* began devoting more space to sports. Of course, there wasn't the proliferation of sports we see today. There wasn't a sports editor, as such, until 1885, and even in 1895, sports editor Harry Weldon basically believed that only three sports warranted serious coverage—baseball, horse racing and boxing. The well-to-do had yachting, of course, but it was hardly popular in the streets of turn-of-the-century America.

But sports writers had, even then, begun achieving celebrity. In 1890 a brawny young writer for *The Enquirer* named Charley "Bull" Hammond was in great demand as a live model for students at the Cincinnati Art Academy. He was as ambitious as he was well proportioned, and with one of his colleagues, a part-timer named Thomas J. Slattery, who taught Latin at Covington High School in Kentucky, collaborated on a daily horse-racing chart that was widely circulated and quite lucrative.

Late in the 19th century, boxing enjoyed broad popularity, especially after the Marquis of Queensberry's rules brought stability to the sport in the '90s. Basketball had arrived by then, and college football had become as American as apple pie by

Continued on page 52

The undefeated 1869 Cincinnati Red Stockings: (top row, from left), Richard Hurley, George Wright, Doug Allison, Cal McVey and Andy Leonard; bottom row, from left, Charles Sweasy, Fred Waterman, Harry Wright, Asa Brainard and Charlie Gould.

RED STOCKINGS THRASHED LOCAL 'PICKED NINE'

In 1869, local news was on page eight — the back page — of *The Enquirer*, mostly in the form of paragraphs about events in the city. On July 1, that year, for instance, the customs collector at Cincinnati announced he'd paid $75,000 in interest on government debt from the war. A new hotel was being built in Yellow Springs, Ohio. Bond was set at $1,500 for a man who signed a false affidavit to get a Civil War pension, and a family named Kinney had recently returned from a railroad trip all the way to San Francisco. There was also this item:

"The Olympic baseball Club of Washington City, one of the clubs recently defeated by the Red Stockings, will arrive here this afternoon, at 5 o'clock [to] play a return game with our champions. The club is a good one and should be well received."

It was the tip of an iceberg. What lay hidden just around the bend of time was a whole new journalistic industry: covering baseball. The next day, *The Enquirer* devoted almost all its local columns to the triumphant return of the Red Stockings from a tour of Eastern cities on which they'd won every contest. The game against Washington that Fourth of July weekend began what we'd now call a long home-stand. Baseball was in the air, and the Red Stockings of 1869 had struck the spark of an enduring love affair between the city and the game. The next-day story began thus:

"Our victorious Red Stockings, the first nine of which met and conquered all the first-class baseball clubs of the country, after a tour of one month, arrived at home at ten o'clock yesterday morning via the Little Miami Railroad. . . . At an early hour our citizens commenced to congregate at the depot, and at ten o'clock, when the train arrived, there must have been fully 4,000 persons present. . . .When the boys, amid the enthusiastic cheers of the spectators, were escorted to carriages provided for the occasion, and taken. . . to the Gibson House preceded by the Zouave Band in an open transfer wagon, gaily decorated with flags and banners. Before starting, this band discoursed most eloquent music, playing "Hail to the Chief," "Home, Sweet Home," and other airs, which, together with the cheering of the crowd, the welcoming shouts of friends &c., formed a scene of excitement such as Cincinnati has seldom witnessed."

In an era without radio or TV to bring the play-by-play to eager fans, *The Enquirer* did. After lunch on the day of their triumphant return — and the day before their return match with Washington's Olympics — the Red Stockings' played an exhibition match against a local "picked nine," roundly defeating them, 53-11, as 3,000 paying spectators watched. Exhibition game or not, *The Enquirer* reported it in detail. Even though some of the rules were different, modern readers should have no trouble following what the Red Stockings did to the opposition in the bottom of the third:

"Cincinnati—Waterman was first up, and went out on a foul bound taken by Lowe. Allison, who came next, went to his first on three called balls. Harry Wright sent a high one to Grant in right field, who muffled it, and Harry got his first, sending Allison to third. Harry stole his second and Allison came home on a wild throw. Leonard came next and got his first on three balls. Harry came home on a wild throw and Leonard got his third. Brainard sent one to center field, making his first, stealing his second and bringing Leonard home. Sweasy sent a low one past second base, made his third and then stole home. McVey went out at first on a ball fielded by Brockenaw. Geo. Wright sent one way over center fielder's head, and got home, although the ball had been pitched past the home base before he reached it. Gould sent a pretty one to center, and made his second. Waterman sent a grounder in the same direction, and brought Gould home. He then stole his second. Allison sent one past second, brought Waterman home, and made his second; he then stole third; he came home on a short one to right field by Harry Wright who made his first. Harry then went to third on a wild throw of Lowe to first. Leonard sent a high one to Grant who muffled it, and he went to his second, bringing Harry home. Brainard went out on a low one fielded to first, and Leonard was left on third. "

The team was also honored at a banquet, duly reported in detail by *The Enquirer:* "It was pleasant to behold, as it were, the scalps of such honored and formidable organizations as the Mutuals, Nationals, Athletics, Atlantics, Harvards, Eckfords and Olympics. At the extreme end of the hall was a scroll, surrounded with cedar wreaths bearing the names of the conquering Nine and the inscription, 'Welcome, Red Stockings."'Cincinnati has taken its baseball seriously — and looked to *The Enquirer* for its baseball news — ever since.

the time Michigan beat Stanford 49-0 in the first Rose Bowl in 1902. Soon, the gentlemanly games of golf and tennis had moved from the society page to the sports page, and even bowling was fair game for the voracious appetite of the sports department early in the 1900s.

Soon after the turn of the century, *The Enquirer* had a sports writer named Benjamin Mayer, a licensed physician who preferred playing pinochle and writing about bowling. He later became a theatrical press agent and theater manager.

Sports editor Harry Weldon plainly never envisioned anything like Riverfront Stadium, teams named the Royals, Mohawks, Swords, Muskies and Bearcats, or the significance of baby tigers named Benzoo. He certainly wouldn't have recognized what was going on in 1988 when the Bengals went to the Super Bowl in Miami and *The Enquirer* dispatched a managing editor and 18 writers for a solid week to cover it. Only on the day after the Beverly Hills fire in 1979 has the paper marshaled so much talent to cover one story.

But Weldon and his contem-

Sports editor Joe Nolan with "The Visitors' Register," a book documenting the famous and not-so-famous who visited The Enquirer *for over 30 years.*

poraries might have understood the eight-page sections the paper produced after every game as the Reds swept the 1990 World Series. After all, in 1901, the paper was host to the nation's sporting press for a heavyweight title fight at Saengerfest Hall and produced a special section hailing its status as the "sporting headquarters of the middle and western states. . . the leading authority on all athletic and turf matters."

And Weldon would certainly

have recognized the name Reds and the city's unending enthusiasm for the team. From the earliest days of the fabled Red Stockings, baseball runs like a common thread through *The Enquirer's* sports reports. To Cincinnatians who love the game, the succession of *Enquirer* baseball writers is not unlike the succession of popes, kings, or third basemen. The first who wrote baseball may have been O. P. Caylor, whose name appeared on baseball

stories in the early 1870s. He was followed in 1879 by a reporter named Ren Mulford Jr., who covered baseball until 1904. Jack Ryder wrote baseball for the next 32 years, until he was succeeded by Lou Smith in 1936. Smith handled the job for 32 years.

All of Smith's successors together haven't covered the Reds as long as any of their predecessors did. Since Lou Smith, the paper's baseball beat has been in the hands of Bob Hertzel, Ray Buck, Tim Sullivan, Mike Paolercio, Jack Brennan and Rob Parker.

The earliest sports reporters were often ballplayers themselves, as John R. McLean had been. Weldon had played ball as a youth in Circleville, Ohio, although few of his colleagues in later years realized it because he grew a prodigious waistline to accompany his growling voice.

Weldon joined *The Enquirer* in 1881 as a reporter. His first big story was the Courthouse riot of 1884. The next year he was put in charge of the then-new sporting page. He spent 1886 as secretary of the St. Louis baseball club, then

VISITORS' REGISTER.

Enquirer Sporting Department.

Feb 27th 1923 Mr. and Mrs. Eddie Foy

une 5 1926 Don Miller   Defiance, Ohio   One of Notre Dame Four Horsemen

" " " " Edward P. Krumnyer   Chillicothe Ohio   Another One.

---

returned to *The Enquirer* for good. When his career began, reporters still wrote stories by hand and editors sent the hand written copy to printers who set it into type by hand. Weldon's handwriting was known at *The Enquirer* as "the compositor's despair." The head proofreader learned to decode his script, a colleague once wrote, only after discovering by long study that Weldon "used a limited vocabulary, and certain scrawls always meant certain words."

Weldon attempted the typewriter when it came into use about 1880 but never quite got the hang of it. "When he types," one colleague wrote, "the rattle can be heard all over the third floor with the connecting doors shut, and sounds on the floor below for all the world like a piece of heavy machinery sadly out of gear." Weldon, it seems, just couldn't master the shift key, and his typed copy was even worse than his handwriting. All his career, galley proofs of his copy were pulled on extra wide paper so the proofreaders would have extra space for corrections.

Like many editors, Harry Weldon was a gruff man, but gentle. One day, in 1900, he sent an assistant, a cub named Joe Nolan, out to fetch change for a panhandler, and the young man returned to find Weldon paralyzed by a stroke. He died after another stroke in 1902. He was 46.

Weldon was followed by Charles Murphy, but when Murphy went to work for the New York Giants in 1905, Nolan got the job. Nolan remained the "sporting editor," as he called himself, until he died in 1931. He specialized in boxing, which he regarded as the supreme sport, and is

Continued on page 56

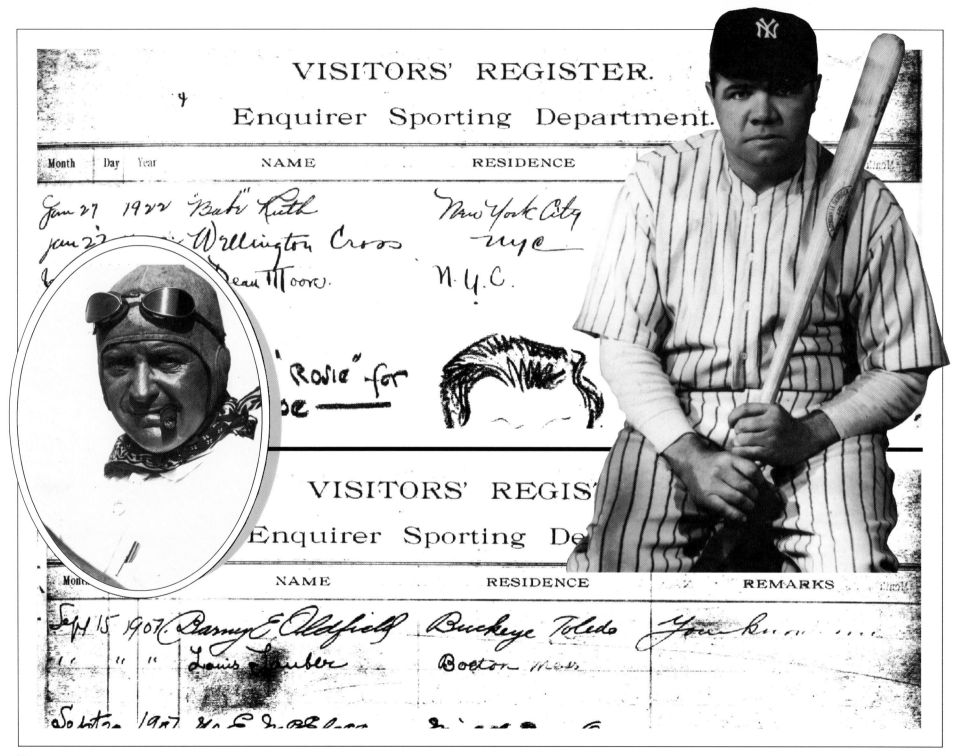

VISITORS' REGISTER.

Enquirer Sporting Department.

Month	Day	Year	NAME	RESIDENCE	
Jan 27		1922	"Babe" Ruth	New York City	
Jan 2?			Wellington Cross	NYC	
			Dean Moore	N.Y.C.	

"Rosie" for

VISITORS' REGIST

Enquirer Sporting De

Mon		NAME	RESIDENCE	REMARKS	
Sept 15	1907	Barney E. Oldfield	Buckeye Toledo	You know	
" " "		Louis Strober	Boston Mass		
So Lot?	1907				

VISITORS' REGISTER.
Enquirer Sporting Department.

Month	Day	Year	NAME	RESIDENCE	RE
March 11		1930	National Boxing Association		
			Championships March 11.		
			Jack Dempsey is my guest		
			Jack Dempsey	Los Angeles Calif.	the only thing I wish you...

VISITORS' REGISTER.
Enquirer Sporting Department.

		NAME	RESIDENCE	RE
EC 12	194	John L. Sullivan	A Boston Mass	Be good. will be
29.	1914	Lura Santa Cruz	Kansas City, Mo.	2 prospe
" "		Crystal E. Bennett.	Kansas City, Mo.	"The Kanso
" "		Alla Bennett	Kansas City. Mo.	

BASEBALL ALL SORTS BOXING
TURF

Today's emphasis on sports wasn't always so, and unless there was something extraordinary to report, such as a heavyweight title bout in town, sports seldom rated more than a column or two before 1900.

In the century's first decade, *The Enquirer* promoted sports more heavily, often devoting an entire page to major events in baseball, boxing, and racing. Outside of baseball, the coverage was mostly of sports on which people bet—notably boxing and racing. In season, however, the paper also reported on "lesser" sports such as football and basketball, golf, tennis, and bowling. Still, even in the sports-minded 1920s, sports often occupied but part of an inside page. Much depended on time of year, with greatest space given to sports in baseball seasons. But there was still no fixed, daily sports section until 1930.

On Feb. 28, 1930 — the first day of baseball spring training — a new top appeared on the front of an inside section, proclaiming "World Wide Sporting News." Sports shared the section with business news, classified ads and the comics. As baseball season approached, the header was dramatically changed, and a "SPORTS" logo appeared, complete with little action sketches of horse racing, baseball, boxing and golf, which would change in other seasons.

The promotional term, "World Wide Sporting Events" was relegated to a small box alongside the logo.

Afterward, a regular weekly page appeared on Sundays, titled "All Sorts," in which sports writers provided roundups and commentary, mostly on the usual major sports, but occasionally on the less-well-covered minor ones, from auto racing to swimming. The "All Sorts" page often appeared far from the regular sports section, often deep inside a section of business news of classified ads. It had a logo all its own, with more action drawings indicating "Turf, by Bob Saxton," "Baseball by Jack Ryder," "Boxing by Joe Nolan," and "Golf by Lou Smith." Nolan was sports editor. When he died, Saxton became editor.

The centerpiece of each front sports page, and of every Sunday's "All Sorts" page was a cartoon by Harold Russell, for years *The Enquirer* sports cartoonist, whose "typical fan" character, Danny Dumm, became so famous that many people called Russell "Danny."

immortal at *The Enquirer* because of an institution he began called "The Visitors' Register." It was a large ledger-style book, kept in the sports department, which all visitors (and staffers) signed. It was regarded as a breach of etiquette for any sports or theater figure to visit *The Enquirer* without calling on Joe and signing the book, and many famous non-sport figures signed in as well. It remains a treasured relic at *The Enquirer,* with such names as Miller Huggins, George M. Cohan, Jack Dempsey, Kid McCoy, Barney Oldfield, John L. Sullivan, Babe Ruth, Eddie Rickenbacker, Walter Johnson, and James J. Corbett. Even Carrie Nation signed in once, perhaps after deciding there were too many saloons on Vine Street for her ax.

Bob Saxton succeeded Nolan, then quit in 1948 to become a horse-racing official and was replaced by Lou Lawhead, who was known for hanging out in Kentucky's gambling dens with the Kentucky editor in the days when Newport was Sin City, U.S.A. Lawhead — a boxing writer whose own favorite sport was fishing — was a firm believer in amateur sports and brought new emphasis to them at *The Enquirer.*

Baseball writer Smith became sports editor in 1952 after Lawhead died; when he traveled with the Reds, the sports pages were produced by his two assistants, Saul Straus and Bob Husted. Like Weldon, Smith recognized some sports more than others, especially the one he covered. His regular column, "Sparks off Lou Smith's Forge," was always livelier and more interesting in baseball season.

Smith was very fond, too, of golf, and was forever frustrated because the golf and baseball seasons coincided. He'd begun newspapering in 1926 as a golf writer for the afternoon *Times-Star*. A low-handicap golfer himself, he always enjoyed spring training because of the time and weather it allowed for golf.

Smith, who retired in 1968, was living proof that a writer can cover only so many baseball games before he starts repeating himself, and by the end of his career, his game accounts were as predictable as dawn and dusk. Long home runs were "towering blows," especially the ones that cleared the fences of the "Western Avenue Orchard" instead of landing in the "right-field sun pews." Night games were always played "under the Mazdas," and the Reds never merely split a doubleheader, but spent "a long afternoon in baseball's revolving door" through all those awful postwar years when they had one ineffective pitcher after another who "served 'em up and ducked."

But the faithful readers loved it, which may only show that much of baseball's appeal lies in the comfortable ritual and familiar motions of the contest.

From 1869 until well into Smith's era, sports writers followed the teams by train. Today's reporters have laptop word processors, modems,

Hundreds of baseball fans jammed Vine Street and Gano Alley on Oct. 5, 1928, to watch **The Enquirer's** *World Series scoreboard. The Yankees were beating the Cardinals, 8-3 in the third inning.*

satellite transmission, and jet travel to cities far too distant to ever have been a part of the Big Leagues in the days of Pullman cars and poker games.

"They go in more for features now," said Smith when he retired. "We always had to be sure to get the score in the first paragraph." Two of those *Enquirer* sports writers who went in more for features were Barry McDermott and Tom Callahan. McDermott joined *Sports*

Illustrated before going into the real estate business. Callahan continued as a journalist and has written for the *Washington Star, Washington Post, Newsweek* and *Time.*

Electronic coverage dominates today, but within living memory, each year at World Series time *The Enquirer* erected a huge diamond on a billboard overlooking Vine Street, and recreated the games, play-by-play, with magnetic markers

as news of events came in on the wire. It was such a popular venue that traffic-blocking crowds would gather.

Sports writers and editors come and go more quickly, too. The careers of Weldon, Nolan, and Smith alone spanned half the history of *The Enquirer.* In the 23 years since Lou Smith, the paper has had six sports editors. Al Heim succeeded Smith but carried the title "executive sports editor." Jim Schottelkotte, followed Heim as executive sports editor and later was named sports editor.

Schottelkotte, a multitalented journalist, was promoted to news editor and managing editor after running the sports department for nine years. Succeeding him as sports editor were Jim Montgomery, Frank Hinchey, Mark Purdy, John Gibson, and Greg Noble.

Enquirer readers have always had favorite sports writers— Bill Ford and Dick Forbes, for familiarity and longevity of coverage of several sports; Dave Roberts for elegant prose as an outdoors writer; Denny Dressman (who went on to become editor of the *Oakland Tribune*) for elevating prep coverage to a new level; Barry McDermott,

The World Series Enquirer *front page of Oct. 10, 1919.*

Tom Callahan, Mark Purdy and Tim Sullivan for spice and strong opinion; and Bob Herzel for the sheer enjoyment of reading a baseball writer who knew his sport thoroughly, worked hard at it and wrote well. Many have labored in the sports department as copy editors, largely unsung. One such is Dick Macke, now but a few years short of retirement. His career encompasses more than 25% of *The Enquirer's* history.

Macke has specially fond memories of a young writer named Whitney Tower, who worked as a youth doing high school sports for *The Enquirer.* He was a wealthy young man related to the horse-racing Whitneys and the oil company Towers. And he was a fine writer.

In 1952, after covering the Olympics in Helsinki, Tower returned on the new ocean liner, *S.S. United States,* and wrote a piece about the crossing for *The Enquirer's* travel section that won a major prize.

Even as a young man, Tower made a name for himself at *The Enquirer* as a character. Each May 1, he would enter the office and recite a bawdy little ditty about sex and springtime that began, "Hooray, Hooray. The first of May. . . ." Macke remembers that even as a cub reporter he played his golf at Indian Hill's posh Camargo Club, yet he was sufficiently confident of his place in life that he sometimes was a bit careless in his dress.

"One day back when Everett Boyd was the editor," Macke remembers, "Whitney came in from a golf tournament wearing wrinkled, old khaki trousers with mud on the cuffs, a blue button-down shirt with a badly frayed collar, and a tweed sports jacket with a hole in the elbow. Ev Boyd didn't know him from any other young reporter, and when he saw him, he came over to me and wrinkled his nose in distaste and said, 'See if you can't get that young fellow to clean himself up a bit, will you?'"

Tower knew horse racing from the inside and went on to cover it as an associate editor at *Sports Illustrated* for years. And every May 1, for years after he had moved on, *Enquirer* sports writer Dick Forbes would send Tower a telegram saying: "Hooray. Hooray. The first of May."

MODERN JOURNALISM BEGINS

" Cincinnati lapped it up and The Enquirer's circulation soared with every Hearn story. Cockerill had found the key to what Americans wanted in a newspaper."

James B. McCullagh of the *Cincinnati Commercial* is credited as having been the first reporter ever to do a presidential interview. It was in 1868, and his subject was Andrew Johnson, then facing impeachment. The interview had a more far-reaching effect than anyone imagined at the time, because it set off a sequence of events that are now regarded as the beginning of modern, American journalism.

McCullagh's story — the idea and its execution — so impressed Washington McLean, owner of the rival *Enquirer*, that he offered McCullagh a job as his managing editor. McLean wanted him to boost circulation, and McCullagh had his work cut out for him. *The Enquirer* was not a flourishing success in those post-Civil War days, and its news columns lacked sparkle. Moreover, it was a highly political paper famous for partisan Democratic bias, and McCullagh was a Republican.

McCullagh realized, however, that partisanship limited the potential audience, and based his strategy on confining the bias to editorial columns and banning it elsewhere. And, except at election time, he told writers to cover little of politics and to summarize long-winded speeches. Then he ordered editors to condense the copy even further.

He also sought out aggressive, energetic young reporters. John Cockerill, publisher of a Hamilton, Ohio, paper, who had been a colonel in the war, typified the breed.

From this start at *The Enquirer,* and continuing throughout long careers in Cincinnati, Washington, St. Louis and New York, McCullagh and Cockerill literally invented the hard-hitting, tell-it-like-it-is style that came to be called "yellow journalism" in the 1890s. Their sensational manner has acquired more sedate maturity in today's mainstream press, but it remains most plainly visible still in the convenience-store tabloids.

McCullagh went on to Chicago and then St. Louis in 1872, about the time Washington McLean turned his interest in *The Enquirer* over to his brash, ebullient son, John Roll McLean, and one of young John's first acts was to make the equally young Cockerill his managing editor.

Cincinnati in the 1870s was self-consciously building a cultural life and inventing such civic institutions as the Zoo, The Fountain, and Music Hall. It did its best to ignore the stink of the sordid slums in places like Bucktown and Rat Row, where crime and vice ruled, and respectable people didn't go after dark. The good burghers — and especially their civic leaders — preferred to think about Saengerfests, the annual Industrial Expositions, the *gemuetlichkeit* of the Highland House and other beer-halls, and the new horse-drawn streetcars and inclines that were opening the

Continued on next page

hilltop suburbs.

Cincinnati was already a fertile place for aggressive young newspapermen in 1872, and when the Republican convention came to town that May and nominated Horace Greeley, publisher of the New York *Tribune*, it became even more so. Imagine how busy managing editor Cockerill was that year when he looked up one day to find a timid, misshapen, swarthy little man standing at his desk asking if the editor would read his manuscript.

Cockerill's characteristic brusqueness gave way to sympathy, so he read the stranger's work, noting (he later wrote) that he seemed "sensitive as a flower."

The young man's name was Lafcadio Hearn, and in the next few years, with Cockerill's blessings, he set the city on edge with graphically real accounts of Cincinnati's ugly underside that left astonished readers gasping for breath and demanding more.

"In a soft shrinking voice," Cockerill wrote, Hearn asked whether *The Enquirer* ever paid for manuscripts. Seldom, Cockerill replied, but when he read

'HICKS HANGS HIGH'

A danger of sensationalism is that eventually the real stories run out and a paper must begin creating them. One December night in 1880, a young railroad worker was slain in Ludlow, Ky., and on mere circumstantial evidence, police arrested a black youth of 18 named John Hicks. After a long, arduous trial and endless appeals, Hicks was convicted and sentenced to hang. All through the year-long appeals process, reporters visited him in jail to probe and prod him like a caged animal in hopes of provoking a sensational outburst with which to titillate readers.

Hicks bested them, maintaining his composure throughout the ordeal. He converted to Catholicism, steadfastly declared himself ready to meet his Maker, and defeated all their attempts.

One *Enquirer* reporter who visited him three days before the hanging went right for the jugular: "Do you think about how it will feel to have the rope around your neck?" he asked. "Do you imagine your own dismembered spirit hovering over the executioner?"

"No, suh," the reporter quoted Hicks' reply, with close attention to accent, vernacular and inflection, "I never think o' that. When I gits to thinkin' 'bout gittin' hung I gets my mind on somefin' else. What's de use o' makin' a fuss? Ef I'se got to go that's all they is to it and then this boil on my neck won't hurt no mo'. I knows when my time is, an' I'se ready, an' maybe dat's where I'se better off than you is, whose time may come befo' mine."

He proved an accurate prophet: The day before his hanging a workman building the scaffold fell, struck his head on a timber and died.

The Enquirer story of the hanging filled nearly four columns of space under the headline: "Hicks Hangs High."

Hearn's work, he made an exception, and asked for more. He gave Hearn a desk and sent him to interview local artists, such as Frank Duveneck and Henry Farny — good feature material in a city newly attuned to culture. Cockerill quickly realized that the young man's stories were a tonic for circulation. The editor turned him loose on the waterfront, the slums, the ugly back alleys of Bucktown and Rat Row.

The Enquirer, which had once led a campaign to rid the city streets of the pigs that roamed loose, now built circulation with lurid accounts of life in the impoverished, crime-ridden slums. Hearn went where respectable people didn't dare and told the city all he saw and heard, felt and smelled. Cockerill had him interview a grave-digger and write about the Bucktown Negroes who labored on the waterfront. He pricked the city's conscience with a piece about underpaid, overworked seamstresses. He wrote of prostitutes, grave robbers, murderers and drug addicts.

When a tanyard workman was viciously slain by a father who'd caught him in bed with his daughter, Hearn told in grisly detail how the victim had been beaten, choked, skewered with a pitchfork, and cremated in the tanyard furnace. Cincinnati lapped it up, and *The Enquirer*'s circulation soared with every Hearn story. Cockerill had found the key to what Americans wanted in a newspaper.

In early 1878, a new paper in Washington, the *Post*, hired Cockerill away to be its managing editor. In 1880, Joseph Pulitzer hired him to run the St. Louis *Post-Dispatch*, which he'd bought at bankruptcy auction for a mere $2,500 in 1878. In St. Louis,

HEADLINES DRIVE CALAMITOUS RIOT OF 1884

During the early 1880s, Cincinnati was a big city, genteel for the most part, but rowdy and unsavory in others, and with a dark underside that polite people tried not to notice. Most areas along the riverfront, and Bucktown along what is now Eggleston Avenue, were lawless neighborhoods where ordinary citizens did not stray after dark. Violence was everyday. Homicide was a common occurrence, and in recent years had increased and spread into other parts of the city.

By 1884, things had gotten so bad that *The Enquirer* undertook a campaign to clean things up. On March 9, in the wake of a fresh spate of homicides, the paper published a massive expose, calling the city streets a "College

The riot left 45 citizens dead, 125 wounded or injured and the courthouse and its invaluable records in ashes.

of Murder." It was complete with a rogues' gallery of drawings of recent killers and detailed, graphic recitations of their individual and collective lawlessness. The muckraking clean-up campaign proved altogether too successful.

Two weeks after the "College of Murder" expose, a trial began at the Courthouse of a man named William Berner. He was charged with murder, accused of killing his employer, William Kirk, and robbing him of $285. Largely because *The Enquirer* had fanned the fires of public concern, interest in the trial ran high, and the Courthouse was crowded to capacity. *The Enquirer* led the way in reporting the case, including details of Berner's confession to the jury and testimony about his supposed premeditation of the crime.

When the jury returned a verdict of mere manslaughter, a fresh cry went

Continued on page 62

---

ironically, Cockerill's competitor was his old boss, Mc-Cullagh, editor of the St. Louis *Globe-Democrat*. One day, after the *Post-Dispatch* called a prominent politician a coward, a friend of his entered Cockerill's office to complain and, during an argument, Cockerill fatally shot him. McCullagh, bitter rival or not, urged in print that

Cockerill not be judged until after a full investigation, and saw his stance vindicated when a grand jury learned that the visitor had also had a gun and cleared Cockerill. In 1883, Pulitzer bought the New York *World,* and Cockerill was the genius behind the *World*'s scandal-mongering sensationalism — stories of the super-

natural, features about freaks, stunts, promotions, and lurid crime stories.

Cockerill eventually had a falling out with Pulitzer and was not around in 1895 when color presses arrived and Richard Outcalt's "Yellow Kid" comic strip gave the sensational style its lasting name.

By then, Cockerill was in

Japan, as a correspondent for the New York *Herald*. One of the last stories he wrote before dying of a stroke in Egypt on his way back to New York was about an American who had become a Japanese citizen and a professor of English literature in Tokyo. The American expatriate was Lafcadio Hearn.

up. The paper called it an "outrageous assault upon society" and railed at defense lawyers' tactics of seeking acquittal "against all principle of law of justice."

Public reaction was swift. Some prominent citizens called a mass meeting at the city's new Music Hall on the evening of Friday, March 28. Outraged speakers told the crowd that defense lawyers had won an unjust verdict by such base means as bribing jurors and presenting perjured testimony. Speaker after speaker demanded action.

After the meeting, as the crowd poured out onto Elm Street, someone shouted for others to follow him to the jail. Thousands more joined in as the crowd marched east along the canal, and soon an angry mob of 10,000 surrounded the Courthouse on Sycamore Street. Some men found a heavy timber and battered at a basement door. Others hurled bricks and stones at windows and set to work on the massive front doors with tools and planks passed forward from the fringes. The doors soon gave way and the crowd poured inside.

Morton L. Hawkins, the sheriff, faced the mob with few deputies but good intelligence, some of it from sources developed when he had been city editor of *The Enquirer* before becoming sheriff. He knew what was happening at Music Hall and was ready. When the mob reached the Courthouse, he was wary of making a bad situation worse, so he ordered his men not to use their weapons. The mob roved through the jail in search of the killer they wanted to hang.

The killer, William Berner, and the headline that applauded the rioters.

What they didn't know was that immediately after the verdict, and with just such an eventuality in mind, Hawkins had ordered a deputy to take Berner out of the Courthouse and accompany him on a train to Columbus. What not even Hawkins knew was that Berner had managed to escape from the deputy and flee the train in Loveland, 20 odd miles east of Cincinnati. The crowd at the jail simply didn't believe Hawkins when he said Berner was not there.

The first city police to reach the jail were overrun by the mob, but fire bells soon summoned the entire police force from duty throughout the city, and at midnight the local militia had turned out. Together, after a night of hand to hand combat and volleys of blank rounds fired into the mob by the militia, the mob was driven back outside.

The Enquirer exulted at the stand the citizens had taken.

"AT LAST"

read the next day's headline,

"THE PEOPLE ARE AROUSED AND TAKE THE LAW IN THEIR OWN HANDS."

An uneasy calm prevailed on Saturday, as militia and police remained at the jail. But after dark a new mob formed — greater than the night before and now egged on by *The Enquirer*. Many had firearms, and they easily breached the outer defenses. Once inside the Courthouse, the mob began demolishing it. One historian's account says "the whole magnificent stone building seemed to become ignited at once." Gunfire erupted again, inside and outside the building, only now it was live ammunition. The Courthouse burned to the ground, taking with it 75 years of valuable documents and land records, and by the time federal troops had arrived and quelled the riot, 45 militiamen, police and rioters lay dead, and 125 more were wounded.

The Enquirer, finally realizing that the people had become a little too aroused, headlined Sunday's story:

"FIRE AND FURY. THE REIGN OF TERROR. AWFUL SCENES IN CINCINNATI."

And William Berner, the cause of it all, was recaptured late on Saturday afternoon, hiding in an old house in the woods near Loveland.

The law-and-order sentiment that spawned the riot did not fade. Judges began handing down death sentences right and left, and Hawkins spent much of the rest of his term as sheriff presiding at hangings. In subsequent elections, riot leaders took control of local government. Hawkins, one of the first victims, returned to *The Enquirer* as managing editor. The shift to the hard-line right eventually produced the notorious administration of "Boss Cox," (George B. Cox) whose defeat by Charter Committee reformers in the 1920s led to today's city-manager form of government.

VAGABOND LAFCADIO HEARN ARRIVES

In the 1870s, when young John R. McLean took over his father's stodgy, political paper, he was less interested in being politically correct than in being first in circulation, especially over the rival *Commercial*. While McLean had the last laugh, one of the most effective weapons both papers wielded was a strange young writer by the name of Lafcadio Hearn.

Lafcadio Hearn was 19 when he arrived in Cincinnati, a slightly built misfit, but determined, proud, and very, very bright. He spent but eight years in what he called "Beastly Cincinnati," only two of them at *The Enquirer*, and went on to far bigger things, but in those few years he pioneered the tell-it-like-it-is style that flourished anew in the 1960s and '70s. The best portrait of him ever to appear in *The Enquirer* was written in 1974 by an *Enquirer Magazine* writer named Bill Speers, from which the balance of this piece is taken:

Lafcadio Hearn

"Pop culturist Tom Wolfe has called Hearn a progenitor of the so-called 'new journalism,' and the *New Republic* declared him a bellwether of the American literary tradition, continued by Norman Mailer.

"Lafcadio Hearn may have been the finest writer—the greatest man of letters—ever to take up residence in Cincinnati. He had the courage to examine his own sorry life and tell honestly of it, without losing sight of the underlying beauty and excitement in the most meager of existences".

Speers continued his story. "The copy he filed was exceptional for his or any time. He gave his readers more than an account of events that happened while they slept or worked. He gave them insights into their lives, an awareness of the good and evil forces in their worlds.

"**P**atrick Lafcadio Hearn began life on June 27, 1850, on the Greek isle of Leucadia (hence his name). He was the product of a shotgun marriage between a handsome British Army surgeon and a young, black-haired, dark-eyed island beauty. At age 7, they abandoned him to an aunt in England, a religious fanatic. He rebelled at her efforts to Catholicize him and was expelled from Jesuit schools in England and France. His aunt sent him to America when he was 19, and he found his way to Cincinnati.

"**C**incinnati's 220,000 people made it the largest inland city in the U.S, and the convergence of rivers, canals and railroads made it the transport hub of the West. It was a publishing center, as well, a cultural oasis of what had been frontier in living memory. But pork-packing, soap-making and tanning made it a dirty, stinking place, too, and the busy river trade attracted newly freed slaves to lawless ghettos where all manner of vice and violence bloomed.

FACT

The number of pages in each day's newspaper was shown on page one until Nov. 21, 1956.

" Into this mad milieu, the 19-year-old waif was dumped, without money or means. His prospects were further dimmed by his physical appearance. He was short — 5 feet 3 — and slightly built, dark complexioned, and had a most unattractive face, with a beak of a nose and an opaque eye blinded in childhood. The strain on the other eye made it squint, as well.

"He lived as a vagabond and slept in crates until befriended by a printer named Henry Watkin, who took him in. He worked as a trinket peddler, waiter, salesman, showcard writer, messenger boy and bookkeeper. He haunted the Public Library on Vine Street to keep warm. Watkin helped Hearn get a more respectable job as a proof reader, but it taxed Hearn's eyesight, and he found the work tedious and boring.

"So, in October, 1872, he swallowed hard on his shyness, walked into *The Enquirer* on Vine Street, and entered the office of the newly appointed managing editor, Col. John Cockerill, a man nearly as young as Hearn, but large, confident, imposing and brusque. Cockerill later wrote his recollection of that meeting:

"'He drew from his coat a manuscript, and tremblingly laid it upon my table. Then he stole away like a distorted brownie, leaving behind an impression that was uncanny and indescribable. Later in the day I looked over the contribution which he left, a review of Tennyson's latest published portion of *The Idylls of the King*. I was astonished to find it charmingly written and full of ideas that were bright and forceful.'

"**S**oon Hearn was writing regularly for *The Enquirer*. For $25 a week, he wrote of the movements and vogues of his day. His reportage was damning to apostles of free love, spiritualism, abortionists, temperance advocates, phony astrologers and a myriad of self-styled saints. In an article titled 'Some Pictures of Poverty' he depicted the eroding influences of city life on the poor. In 'Slow Starvation' he told of the victimization of poor seamstresses. His 'Hebrews of Cincinnati'was a pioneer attempt at showing how a cohesive cultural group lived its life within the larger American experience.

"**S**trongly influenced by Poe and the 19th-century French writers — Gauthier, Baudelaire, deMaupassant and Zola — Hearn was fascinated by death, but reveled in its romantic aspects, rather than its gloom.

"He could write delicately and humorously as well as chillingly. He once described a spring day in Cincinnati:

"'The view from the summit of Price's Hill Elevator Building, yesterday afternoon, was little short of enchanting. The air was unusually clear but sufficiently tinged with summer haze to slightly empurple spires, woods and hills in the distance. The sunlight touched the faint blue of far spires with auriferous penciling; glistened in the glowing green of spring foliage, and shone in reflected flame from a hundred thousand windows.'

"Once, Hearn disguised himself as a woman to hear a 'ladies only' lecture by a woman who billed herself as an Escaped Nun.

"His feelings for women were deep and complex. He found himself comfortable only in company of women he considered outcast like himself. Hearn's first adventure into love led to his greatest unhappiness in Cincinnati, including the loss of the *Enquirer* job. Her name was Mattie Foley. She was a beautiful mullato, a freed slave, four years older than Hearn. It was a mismatch from the beginning. But they both were young and alone in a strange city, and they shared a tenderness and warmth. Ohio law forbade marriage between whites and Negroes, but Hearn managed to find a Negro clergyman willing to marry them.

"**T**hey moved to 114 Longworth St., and the union deteriorated almost immediately. Mattie, a lively, fun-loving woman couldn't cope with the silent, reflective moods of Hearn, who was spending more and more time away from home on his journalistic exploits. She took up with the levee Negroes. And the marriage became more tenuous.

"One day in 1874, Hearn arrived at *The Enquirer* to be told he was dismissed for 'deplorable moral habits.' Politicians and civic leaders unsettled by Hearn's articles had threatened the newspaper with a scandal over his alliance with Mattie, and under pressure from John R. McLean, Cockerill gave in and fired his star reporter.

"**H**earn was crushed. He had worked incredibly hard for *The Enquirer*, from 1 p.m. to 3 a.m., seven days a week. And those were days without autos and telephones, so he put many miles on his feet. And there weren't typewriters, so he often found himself scrawling out 12 columns of copy each day, his one good eye squinting within inches of the paper.

"The rival *Commercial* was apparently less concerned about Hearn's moral habits, and quickly hired him — for $5 less a week. And it was at the *Commercial* that he did his best work in Cincinnati — indeed, a gem of his entire life's work — in sketches of Negro life on the Cincinnati levee. The sketches stand today as the best single

'Ye Giglampz' Fling Flops

In the summer of 1874, reporter Lafcadio Hearn took a brief fling at moonlighting as editor of a weekly satirical magazine called *Ye Giglampz*, in partnership with a young commercial artist named Henry Farny.

Hearn had met Farny earlier, in 1872, while doing a newspaper article on Cincinnati artists. Jon Hughes, a University of Cincinnati historian and student of Hearn's career, wrote that Farny produced political cartoons and Hearn wrote satirical articles.

One of the articles was about the "Western Associated Press," a short-lived organization founded by

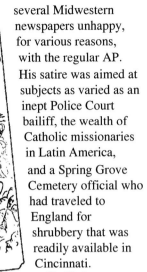

several Midwestern newspapers unhappy, for various reasons, with the regular AP. His satire was aimed at subjects as varied as an inept Police Court bailiff, the wealth of Catholic missionaries in Latin America, and a Spring Grove Cemetery official who had traveled to England for shrubbery that was readily available in Cincinnati.

Ye Giglampz was no smash hit. Hearn and Farny sold 35 copies of the first issue for five cents each. While they built circulation to about 500, they argued constantly over what to print, vacillated between satire and sophistry, and finally quit after nine issues, still losing money.

chronicle of post-Civil War Negro riverfront life.

"The levee was a wildly exotic and lawless world where few whites, including policemen, dared venture — an uncared-for slum peopled by criminals, addicts, vicious roustabouts and untamed women. Hearn saw beyond the poverty and brutality

and wrote of the levee's songs, dances, color, games, riddles, charms, cures, voodoo, proverbs and its people's love-hate view of their devil-mother, the river.

"'The dancers,' he wrote, describing a scene in a Rat Row hangout, 'danced a double quadrille, at first, silently and rapidly; but warming with the

wild spirit of the music, leaped and shouted, swinging each other off the floor, and keeping time with a precision which shook the building in time to the music. The women we noticed, almost invariably embraced the men about the neck in swinging, the men clasping them about the waist. Sometimes the men advanced leaping and crossed legs with a double shuffle, and with almost sightless rapidity the dancing became wild; men patted juba and shouted, and Negro women danced with the most fantastic grace, their bodies describing almost incredible curves forward and backward; limbs intertwined rapidly in a wrestle with each other and with the music; the room presented a tide of swaying bodies and tossing arms and flying hair.'

"**H**earn wrote of houses like the Blazing Stump, the Silver Moon and a place on Broadway called Butler's:

"'On opening the door you are saluted with a whiff of hot air, redolent of multifarious foulness —the stench of saliva squirted upon a red-hot stove, the odor of villainous tobacco, the familiar smell of salt fish, the sickening aroma of bad breaths qualified

ARCHBISHOP SCALDS ENQUIRER

One October Sunday in 1888, the Catholic Archbishop of Cincinnati, John Purcell, railed from the cathedral pulpit at *The Enquirer* as a newspaper "unfit to be read." The reason for this ecclesiastical scorn was the sensational, muckraking, vivid, plain-language reporting and writing that had been born on Vine Street and was still growing up in the young newspaper empires of Pulitzer and Hearst.

The style's godfather was John R. McLean, 24, who, early in his stewardship of the paper, discovered how avidly the reading public would snap up newspapers that gave them graphic, high-voltage copy that bristled with realism and detail.

"Stand up!" read a tract widely circulated in Cincinnati after the archbishop's sermon. "Scorched and Damned! Ecclesiastical Electricity! The Archbishop of Cincinnati. . . gives his verdict on the *Cincinnati Daily Enquirer* and its Proprietor. . . . We have right here in this city a daily newspaper owned by a young man who, I am told, is very rich. How did he make those riches? By publishing a paper that is unfit to be read by any human being, much less a Christian.

Every day it is filled with reading matter that is filthy, nasty, obscene and abominable. The amount of injury that paper is doing right in our midst is incalculable. I beg of you, fathers and mothers, who have the welfare of your children at heart, do not let their young minds be polluted by allowing them to read the vile sheet. And you yourselves should not allow it in your house. By reading that paper or allowing those whom Almighty God has placed you in charge of in this world to read it, you commit a grievous sin against your Divine Lord."

Archbishop John Purcell

with 40-rod whiskey, and one or two other stinks which it would not be decorous to name.'

"Cincinnati wore heavily on Hearn, however. He detested the unpredictable weather and was discouraged that despite his work, nothing seemed to change. His salary remained stagnant, and he was growing poor trying to cover Mattie's debts. Their marriage shrank into an unhappy, ugly relationship.

"One October day in 1877, Hearn abruptly announced to his managing editor that he was leaving Cincinnati and going South. It was a departure not only from the city but from the kind of sensational "new" journalism he had helped Colonel Cockerill design on *The Enquirer.*

"In New Orleans, he worked for the daily *Item* for 10 years, but as a more serious writer and literary critic. Then he accepted a commission from Harper's magazine to travel in and write about the West Indies. He stayed two years, then undertook a similar assignment in Japan.

"There, at 41, he met and married a 23-year-old native woman and decided to stay. He changed his name to Koizumi Yakumo, became a Buddhist, fathered four children and lived out his life writing and teaching in Japanese universities.

"Besides his newspaper work (which Hearn never considered literature) this 'civilized nomad' left behind a treasury — translations of 19th-century French romanticists, translations of French Creole and Japanese folklore and tales, travel guides to the U.S. South, Japan and the West Indies (he might even be called the first modern travel writer). He also produced volumes of interpretive works on Japan and the Eastern mind, critiques of art, literature and philosophy, poetry, scores of letters, two novels, and a Creole cookbook.

"On September 19, 1904, while looking forward to a trip to England as a guest lecturer at a university, he had a fatal heart attack. He is buried in a cemetery in northern Tokyo, more honored as a man of letters in Japan than the United States."

'IT'S ABOUT TIME WE HAD A GOOD MURDER'

Crime, from petty to atrocious, has long been standard newspaper fare. The glamor of the police beat— the "cop shop"— has a long history, and the police reporter occupies a special and romantic place in the history of American journalism. Indeed, an entire chapter of American history — the Watergate saga — began in the hands of a Washington police reporter covering a simple break-in.

Crime news covers a wide range. At the low end are such stories as the one in the *Daily Enquirer* in mid-1865, among reports of Civil War aftershocks, headlined "Interesting Gambling Case." It tells of a young man from back East named Ogden Meade, sent by his father with a sizable sum of money to be invested in a grocery in Tennessee. En route, however, the paper reported, young Meade "fell in with a gang of gamblers. . . and was induced to hazard $13,200" in a card game in which the gamblers used a sanded deck. "Meade," wrote the reporter, "lost, of course."

Atop the scale of heinousness is murder, and to the dedicated crime reporter, the more spectacular the better. Some crime-reporting connoisseurs in Cincinnati argue that the genre peaked with the ongoing drama of the Cincinnati Strangler's career in the 1960s, although some might argue for the after-the-fact revelations of

Anna Marie Hahn says goodbye to her son, Oscar, for the last time.

William Wigger-ingloh, baliff, escorts Edythe Klumpp to the court-room.

George Remus, right, killed his wife Imogene, in Eden Park. James Ruppert, above, shot and killed 11 members of his family on Easter Sunday in Hamilton,Ohio. Posteal Laskey, left, and Donald Harvey, are two of Cincinnati's most notorious killers.

the more prolific killer, Donald Harvey, in 1987. There's even a case to be made for the more mysterious killings of Audrey Evers Pugh in 1956 or the Dumler family in 1969. Or the fiery case of Edythe Klumpp in 1959. Easter, 1975, brought the horror of mass murder to the family of James Ruppert. And Anna Marie Hahn became one of the most famous killers in the nation when she was electrocuted for poisoning her husband. She was the first woman executed in Ohio, and her dramatic collapse on the way to the electric chair made headlines.

Whatever your choice, it's a fact that homicide has long had high priority in

the city room. As one old hand once said to the city editor across the desk, when a multiple killing ended a longdrought: "It's about time we had a good murder."

No crime reporting from any era surpasses the *Daily Enquirer's* coverage of the "Tanyard Murder" case for sheer grisliness of reporting. It broke on Monday, Nov. 9, 1874. A father had caught a young man in bed with his teen-age daughter and later, with two accomplices, waylaid him in the tannery where he worked. They beat and choked

him and, with a pitchfork, stuffed him in the hellish tanyard furnace.

The reporter on the story was named Lafcadio Hearn. Writing without byline, he referred to himself in the time-honored way only as "an *Enquirer* reporter" and reconstructed the horrible crime in sensationally graphic detail. After viewing the victim's remains in a coroner's coffin, he wrote of ". . .shapeless lumps. . . masses of crumbling human bones, strung together by half-burst sinews. . . The skull had burst like a

shell in the fierce furnace-heat; and the whole upper portion looked as thought it had been blown out by the steam from the boiling and bubbling brains. . . the brain had boiled away, save a small wasted lump at the base of the skull about the size of a lemon. . . still warm to the touch. . . .The eyes were cooked to bubbled crisps in the blackened sockets. . . .There is a horrible probability that the wretched victim was forced into the furnace alive, and suffered all the agonies of the bitterest death which man can die. . . ."

So lurid was Hearn's account that many citizens demanded he be fired.

CINCINNATI MATURES AS 19TH CENTURY WANES

The last three decades of the 19th century were a time of civic maturity in Cincinnati, a period when the city began to rise above its brutish, brawling, pork-packing past, embrace culture, and build many of today's venerable civic institutions.

It was the period when Cincinnatians built the Zoo, and a magnificent Music Hall for the Saengerfests that began in 1870, the year of the first of the annual "Great Cincinnati Expositions."

By then, the city was forgetting the rancor of the Civil War and looking to the future. The brilliantly engineered Suspension Bridge and the new Southern Railway promised prosperous commerce from the South. Civic pride ran high on the heels of the wonderful Red Stockings' baseball team that had gone undefeated in 1869. Who knew what splendid things lay ahead?

The cornerstone of the "new" Cincinnati, in a way, was laid on Oct. 6, 1871. The next day's *Enquirer* carried the story, next to telegraphed reports about industrial strikes in England, and about 35 crewmen who jumped ship when their cable-laying vessel reached England, complaining of "the wretched quality and insufficiency of the provisions."

The big headline that day in *The Enquirer* — on page one, which was rare in an era when the local news was usually inside — read:

UNVEILED TO THE PEOPLE OF CINCINNATI
The inauguration of the Tyler Davidson Fountain.
Fifty Thousand People in Probasco Place.

The reporter tossed civic modesty out the window onto Vine Street, writing that the day "will ever be remembered in the art history of the land." He effusively praised "the gift with which Henry Probasco, the retired merchant, the self-made man, the connoisseur, was to enrich his native city and perpetuate the memory of his employer, his partner, and his brother."

He wrote of "tens of thousands of visitors" streaming into town for the event, of "a fervor of anxiety on the parts of residents," and of 150 police stationed in the vicinity of the fountain to discourage disorder. (Even then, it seems, Cincinnati's finest believed that when people gathered 'round the Fountain on happy occasions, rioting would break out.)

In 1872, a steam rail line up the river to Columbia, adjacent to Lunken Airport, was extended up to Mount Lookout, where a new observatory was being built for a mammoth new telescope.

The street railways — horsecars, at first — had been operating in the old basin since before the war, but in 1872 pushed up the hillsides. Service to Walnut Hills began in 1872, the same year the first incline was built, up Main Street to Mount Auburn (ironically, that was also the year a machinist named George Brayton tested his remarkable invention, the gasoline engine, although it would be two decades before anyone tested a workable automobile).

Even through the five-year depression that began with bank failures in 1873, Cincinnati continued to blossom. By decade's end, it was in the full flower of cultural maturity, no longer a frontier town, where hogs ran the streets and crime ruled the riverfront.

More inclines followed the first, and in 1880 electricity came along. The hissing, flickering gas lamps that illuminated *The Enquirer's* offices and composing room through the long, winter nights, gave way to bright, incandescent electric lamps. The newsman's information-gathering arsenal, which had rested on the telegraph for four decades, was augmented by a marvelous new device, the telephone. First put in commercial service in 1878 in New Haven, Conn., Professor Bell's device reached Cincinnati but a few years later.

In those late years of the 19th century, Cincinnati, too, had begun to decline, even at a moment of greatness. The city grew much more, of course. In 1889, electric streetcars began replacing horsecars, and led to the city's rapid expansion beyond its own boundaries. Once-rural towns such as Silverton, Mount Healthy, Addyston, and Madeira became suburbs, and by the time Cincinnati realized what had happened, the suburbs had the city hemmed in with no place to grow.

Cincinnati's population grew but much more slowly than in the heady days when German and Irish immigrants made it the West's largest city and burgeoning river trade made it a world class port town. The Queen City simply sat back, fat, dumb and happy, enjoying riches amassed in its energetic, brawling youth, and confident that upstart towns like Chicago, Cleveland, and Detroit would never be serious rivals.

FACT

The first color page in **The Enquirer** *ran April 1, 1899— the day before Easter.*

ANNA HAHN FALLS AND IS CARRIED TO CHAIR; DIES AFTER SHE CRIES APPEAL TO SPECTATORS

Anna Marie Hahn

PAYS PENALTY

Current Hushes Prayer Of Cincinnati Blond Poison Murderer.

WRIT APPLICATION DENIED

Federal Judge Rejects Plea Just Before Electrocution Of First Ohio Woman.

BY JOSEPH GARRETSON, JR.

DEATH CELLS

Of 11 Men Passed To Electric Chair.

"Goodby Boys," She Replies When Doomed Group Voices Farewell

BY SARAH L. DUNE

DEMAND

Of Nazis Rejected In Italian Agitation For French Colonies.

London Shelves Colony Claims Of Reich.

Chamberlain Says Eden Will Give British Viewpoint In American Speech.

German Youths Join
In Italian Agitation
For French Colonies.

By Anna Hahn On Walk

To Call For Impeachment
Of Perkins, Thomas Says;
If Case Is Delayed Further

One-Judge Court Advocated
By Council For Traffic Cases
Proves Speed Afoot

PATROLMAN

FRENCH PLANES
To Serve Double Aim

POLITE THUGS
Rob Loan Association

Three Die, Several Are Hurt
When Fire Traps 11 Persons
In Rest Home At Columbus

McLean Empire Glitters In D.C.

The *Enquirer* and John R. McLean grew in each other's company to national prominence, and the paper became the foundation of McLean's personal wealth and fame. After moving to Washington in 1882, McLean aspired to — but never quite attained — a dynasty like Hearst's, but he erected quite an empire nonetheless.

It was an empire of political, economic and social power, as much as one of wealth. He counted presidents and princes among his personal friends, led what we would today call the lifestyle of the rich and famous, and attained wealth and celebrity enough to confer it on two generations of descendants.

His 44 years as owner-publisher were golden years on Vine Street. He raised the paper above partisan Democratic politics — while remaining as partisan as ever himself — and turned lively, aggressive news coverage and constant promotion into circulation triumph over his morning rivals.

But John R. McLean's empire-building had limits, and he never made it into the same league with the giant press barons. It was not that he didn't try.

John R. McLean and his father had moved to Washington seeking the greater wealth, power and prestige of a national stage. Leaving *The Enquirer* in the hands of hired managing editors (whom he closely supervised over a private telegraph line), McLean began carving out a serious financial presence in the capital. He bought into, and became president of, the Washington Gas Light Co., and was co-founder of a railroad into Virginia that strongly resembled Cincinnati's Southern Railway.

In a passage from her autobiography, written in 1935 but published years later, Evalyn Walsh McLean, his daughter-in-law, said he "knew the power of money" and was "always a businessman." But, she said, he exercised power over political figures the way J. Edgar Hoover did, by seeking out compromising information, letting them know he knew, then not publishing it.

He bought an old house on I Street and added a huge wing for entertaining, and maintained his offices in another house he bought a few blocks away. He also had a 75-acre estate called "Friendship," in what was then the country, although part of it is now an urban park, McLean Gardens.

The one market any serious newspaper magnate had to crack, even then, was New York, and McLean tried more than once, but never succeeded. The closest he came was in January, 1895, when he paid $1 million to Albert Pulitzer (Joseph's younger brother) for New York's successful penny paper, the morning *Journal*.

Continued on next page

" He (John R. McLean) also made use of his papers to do favors for friends, once influencing President William Howard Taft to commute the sentence of a banker serving a long sentence for misappropriation."

Washington McLean, right, and his son John R. moved to Washington, D.C. in 1882. They lived in this mansion within walking distance of the White House.

John R. McLean tried to make it into a serious, respectable paper, doubling the price and changing the tone, but he underestimated the power of established "respectable" morning dailies, and within nine months, awash in red ink and losing circulation, McLean offered the *Journal* to its principal competitor, William Randolph Hearst's *American*,

for $500,000. Hearst laughed, and McLean eventually sold for less than a third of what he'd paid. Hearst, who was a friend of McLean's but knew better than to put sentiment (or respectability) ahead of profit, turned the *Journal* back into a penny paper.

The New York embarrassment may have bruised John R. Mc-Lean's ego, but it didn't gravely

harm either his bank account or his notoriety, and he soon was back in the limelight. This time it was politics, and he was no more successful there —perhaps because both times he ran as an Ohioan even though he no longer lived there. He did, however, support the state's Democratic party handsomely and in 1896 was Ohio's fav-orite-son candidate for the

Democratic nomination for vice president. He led after four ballots but fell out in a compromise. In 1899, he ran for governor of Ohio but lost, engendering harsh criticism within the party that he was allied with big money more than ordinary folks. It was his last hurrah.

He had his eye on Washington newspapers, too, and in 1896 had supported the struggling *Post* with loans, in hopes of gaining control, which he finally did in 1905. He applied the same formula that he served so well in Cincinnati, making want-ads free, providing lively — even sensational — coverage of politics and government, crime and scandal, sports, entertainment and high society. He copied Hearst in making heavy use of circulation-building contests and promotional gimmicks (in 1895, winners of an *Enquirer* contest got free ponies, winners in Washington later got a free house).

Promotion of the papers' names extended even to such details as "The Enquirer Cocktail," a drink invented for the first edition of *The Bartenders' Guide* in 1899. In the 1870s, a

William Howard Taft

race horse named "Enquirer" had competed very successfully at tracks around the country, and when it died in 1897, McLean made news by putting a marker on its grave.

However aggressively he promoted his papers, McLean was not a self promoter, and his own name seldom appeared in print outside of the masthead, in either of his papers. When the McLeans hosted lavish parties for charity, their names did not appear in the extensive coverage he accorded the events. Their son Edward's wedding to a silver heiress ran less than half a column. McLean made an

George Dewey

exception only for his sister, Mildred, and her husband, Admiral George Dewey, the Spanish-American War hero who defeated the enemy fleet at Manila Bay in 1898; Dewey's every move was reported at great length. McLean also made use of his papers to do favors for friends, once influencing President William Howard Taft to commute the sentence of a banker serving a long sentence for misappropriation. One of McLean's reporters wrote that the man was dying, Taft commuted his sentence and the man lived 15 more years.

When McLean died, in 1916, at age 68, the *Washington Post*,

like *The Enquirer*, became part of his estate, controlled by the American Security and Trust Co. as trustees, for the benefit of Edward, an only child whom McLean and his wife, Mary Beale, had pampered and protected from birth.

After the turn of the century, John R. McLean's involvement in the news operations of his papers had diminished. What energies he devoted to the papers went mostly into the hard business of advertising and (his favorite territory) circulation. He set the general tone for editorials, paying closer attention only to such editorial positions that might affect circulation. In his final years, for instance, with an eye on the loyalty of German-born readers, he saw to it that his papers opposed American involvement in the European war. Where news coverage was concerned, he issued only vague, general orders to his managing editor in Cincinnati. But they were instructions that certainly didn't fit with *The Enquirer's* sensational past. "Be progressive," he urged in one letter in 1913, but "print always the good about the city. . .people don't want to read unpleasant news."

FROM PRESIDENTIAL POKER PARTIES TO LUNACY

After John R. McLean died in 1916, his son, Edward Beale McLean, became "publisher" of *The Enquirer* and the *Washington Post*, but he was hardly the man in charge. He had expected to inherit his father's wealth—*The Enquirer* and the *Washington Post* included— and was shocked to discover it had all been put in trust. Ned (as Edward was called), then just 30, would be a mere remittance man, collecting income but barred from beyond the grave by his father's will from doing anything on his own.

The assets would be managed by trustees — in this case, the bankers at Washington's American Security and Trust Co., in which John R. McLean had been a principal stockholder. Even in death, John R. McLean exercised power.

Ned and his silver-heiress wife, Evalyn Walsh McLean, contested the will, and the trustees agreed to name Ned "editor in chief" of both papers and to accept him as co-trustee.

Technically, he thus controlled both newspapers, and after a suitable mourning period, his name replaced his father's on the mastheads. For a while he even kept hours at the *Post;* he'd attended the 1908 Republican convention as a "reporter" (but apparently wrote nothing) and later had been "business manager" of the *Post* as well.

As to *The Enquirer*, he showed little interest except insofar as it provided income. The extent of his involvement is abundantly clear from an item in the *Little Enquirer*, the in-house employee publication, in 1929. Under a studio portrait of the dapper, mustachioed "Ned" Mc-

Edward B. McLean

Lean, it asked:

"How many *Enquirer* employees would recognize Mr. McLean if they were to encounter him in the building? For the benefit of those who have not had an opportunity to meet the publisher of *The Enquirer*, above is an excellent likeness. . . ."

This, mind you, appeared after Ned Mclean had been "publisher" of *The Enquirer* for 13 years.

The brief biography was a case study in good reporting under difficult circumstances. It properly credited McLean's father for the paper's "national power and prestige," and where Ned was concerned,

dwelt mainly on his hobbies, notably "a passion for horses and dogs, many of which are to be found at his country estate in Virginia. . . ."

It could be that John R. McLean, always a good judge of character, knew exactly what he was doing when he chose not to leave his wealth to his son.

Ned had been coddled and spoiled as a child by a mother who bribed playmates to let him win games. Ned developed a serious drinking problem. It got so bad that Evalyn had agreed to marry him, in 1908, only because he agreed to stop drinking and go to work. The "work" was that "reporter's" job at the *Post*, which lasted about as long as the pledge to go dry. At 21 he'd taken to wearing a sling to steady his drinking hand.

Ned McLean might not have known a Linotype from a letter to the editor, but he certainly knew Palm Beach from Palm Springs. Evalyn hobnobbed with the world's richest and most famous, while Ned hunted and tended to his thoroughbred horses and his beloved flasks of whiskey. The McLean name became so well-known to society editors and gossip columnists that in 1934, when Cole Porter wrote his hit musical, *Anything Goes*, he put them right up there with the Vanderbilts, Whitneys, and Roosevelts in the lyrics of his title song:

When Mrs. Ned McLean
(God bless her)
Can get Russian Reds to
"yes" her,
Then, I suppose,
Anything goes.

Where the good life was concerned, for Ned and Evalyn, anything went. As the income rolled in, Ned found his niche as a big spender. They alternated between his country estate, "Friendship," and her house in town, and the farm in Virginia. Ned bought himself toys — fast cars, race horses, and hunting dogs. For Evalyn, he bought the fabled Hope Diamond (and its supposed curse, as well; soon after he bought it, their toddler son was hit and killed by a car in front of their Washington home).

'ENQUIRER' ON TIME SEVEN TIMES

The *Enquirer* was not only a newspaper, it was a race horse, as well, for a time. Baseball was just becoming popular following the Civil War, and the important sporting events were horse races or boxing matches.

Horse racing was the biggest sport of all. In 1868, a Gen. Abe Buford of Tennessee bought a Louisville-foaled colt at a yearling sale and named it "Enquirer" in honor of his friend, Washington McLean.

"Enquirer" raced 11 times, won seven, never finishing worse than fourth. As a three-year-old, the horse won six straight in Lexington and Cincinnati, Monmouth, N.J., and Saratoga, N.Y.

Then in 1871 he broke a leg in training, and was retired to stud in Nashville. His descendants won more than $2 million, in an era when that was

prodigiously big money.

"Enquirer" died in 1897. The paper's publisher, John R. Mclean, had a monument erected over the horse's grave at Nashville's Belle Meade Stud farm, and invited readers to a dedication ceremony, complete with military band.

Evalyn was no slouch when it came to consumption, either. Her father, a Colorado prospector who'd found fabulous silver deposits, had moved to Washington hoping something would rub off on his daughter, and it did. When not at Friendship, they lived in town with two dozen servants in her father's 50-room Washington mansion, which later became the Indonesian embassy. She kept llamas and a monkey as pets and taught her parrot to cuss. They spent tens of thousands on fabulous little "intimate" dinner parties, once decorating the table with $4,000 worth of flowers from England.

Among the McLeans' closest friends were the Warren Hardings. Ned and the future president met at a poker party in 1916 when Harding was a senator from Ohio and had become fast friends by the time the Hardings moved into the

White House in 1920. They remained close when revelations of moral and political corruption rocked the administration, culminating in the notorious Teapot Dome scandal. That Ned McLean escaped taint was probably because everyone knew he was too rich to be crooked and too naive to be involved.

The friendship led to what may be Ned McLean's only lasting influence on *The Enquirer*, because when Harding won the Republican nomination in 1920, Ned McLean made it very plain that neither *The Enquirer* nor the *Washington Post* would print anything that might hinder his chances of election. It marked the metamorphosis of the historically Democratic *Enquirer* into the conservative, Republican newspaper it has been since. Ironically, Harding's Democratic opponent was Gov. James Cox, an Ohio newspaper publisher who'd gotten his start in the trade as a reporter for *The Enquirer* in the 1880s.

After Harding won, The McLeans were constantly on the fringes of his "Ohio Gang," and were friends as well of that other Ohioan, Nicholas Longworth, Speaker of the House, and his charming wife, Alice Roosevelt Longworth, Teddy's daughter.

The McLeans were so intimate with the Hardings that after Florence Harding all but caught Warren and his secretary, Nan Britton, *in flagrante* in the Oval Office, Evalyn let them use "Friendship" for their trysts. Then, when Harding died, Evalyn atoned by letting Florence use her home as a sanctuary.

In a *Washington Post* review of Evalyn's book, *Father Struck it Rich*, writer Anthony Sforazza saw common elements in Evalyn and Florence: "They shared sordid upbringings and had both improved themselves no end by marriage. Florence had had a child out-of-wedlock as a teenager, and supported herself as a piano teacher before meeting Warren; Evalyn had grown up in a mining town amid drunks and whores, moving to Washington only after her silver-miner father had struck it rich."

In 1923, in the wake of the Teapot Dome scandal, the

Three powerful Ohioans with ties to the McLeans, from upper left: Nicholas Longworth, James Cox and Warren G. Harding. Cox also had become a press magnate.

sordid turpitude and corruption of the Harding administration burst into public view. First, a former Veterans Bureau official, suspected of bribery, shot himself in the Hardings' home. Then Florence Harding's fashion coordinator blew his brains out in the apartment he shared with Harding's Attorney General, Harry Daugherty. It turned out that Daugherty had been the White House bootlegger and his companion ran a

Justice Department permit-fixing ring — secure in the knowledge that Daugherty would never expose him.

On a nationwide tour to seek public support in the aftermath, Harding got sick and died. Forced to vacate the White House to make room for Harding's successor, Vice President Calvin Coolidge, Florence moved into "Friendship" with Evalyn and spent weeks going through Warren's

private letters, destroying those she wanted to remain private.

Wrote Evalyn in her autobiography: "Money is lovely to have, but it does not bring the big things of life — friends, health, respect — and it is apt to make one soft and selfish."

Evalyn and Ned McLean had three children besides the son who was killed in childhood. Their sons Ned Jr. and John R. II, lived a sort of Palm Beach-to-Washington-to-Saratoga-to-Texas social whirl, attending the right tracks, playing the right golf courses, visiting the right friends. By the time the fortune had trickled down through the third generation, it was diluted beyond recognition and the McLean family faded away into the attics of memory.

In 1937, not to long before their father died a lunatic, Ned's two sons were

Continued on page 78

Evalyn Walsh McLean framed by the estate "Friendship" and her Hope Diamond.

Above, John R. McLean III, the last family member to work at the paper. Right, Ned Jr., left, and John R. II, sons of Ned and Evalyn McLean.

SYMPHONY MEMBER COUNTERS MARCH BY SOUSA

In the fiercely competitive years of the late 19th century, newspapers promoted themselves tirelessly, and in many, many ways. *The Enquirer* even had a carnation named for it around 1900 by a Delhi Township florist named Richard A. Winterstaetter, known in the trade as the "carnation king."

Music figured much more prominently in the promotional schemes of aggressive publishers like John R. McLean, who owned and ran *The Enquirer* from 1872 to 1916. It was not uncommon for newspapers to commission composers. You may have thought all along, for example, that John Philip Sousa named his classic "Washington Post March" for a military installation in Washington. Not so.

It was commissioned in the 1890s by a former publisher of the *Washington*

Composer Louis W. Brand and his 1895 composition.

THE ENQUIRER CLUB March.

Post to honor his newspaper.

The idea that *The Enquirer's* sister newspaper would be commemorated in a march distressed some folks in Cincinnati. So they set about, so to speak, to even the score.

In 1895, a Cincinnati Symphony

musician named Louis Brand composed the "Enquirer Club March" for the paper. It was first performed in August that year by John C. Weber's Band, for a readers' gathering outside the building on Vine Street. They were marching to an *Enquirer*-sponsored outing.

In 1950, the paper's radio critic, Magee Adams, came across Brand's score in the files and persuaded bandleader Paul Lavalle to have his Band of America play the "Enquirer Club March" on NBC network radio. Sixteen years later, music critic Henry Humphreys re-scored it for performance at the WKRC Pops concert at Coney Island by the Indiana University Symphony Orchestra. Humphreys called the march "pleasant but rather bland" and changed it radically. "I decided," he said, "that the era of Mantovani and Mancini called for a 'swinger.'"

photographed in white tie and tails with various *Enquirer* editorial chieftains when the paper's Washington bureau chief, Ed Gableman, was installed as president of the Gridiron Club. The two young men seemed plainly ill at ease and out of place among the white-haired editors and publisher W. F. Wiley.

Periodically thereafter, they would appear on the society pages, be photographed on the golf links at the Greenbrier or in the grandstands at the races. The family had little or nothing to do with *The Enquirer*, and the name was all but forgotten until 1952, when the McLean estate's trustees put the paper up for sale, and the employees bought it.

In an ironic epilogue, the family's last connection with the paper was in 1958, when John R. McLean's great grandson, John R. III, then about 20, worked at *The Enquirer* as a copy boy. On his employee biography he listed John R. McLean as his father and New York as his birthplace. Under residence he wrote, "Cincinnati Club."

He didn't stay long. His photo — with a pipe in his hand— remains in the newspaper's files. He had been hired by Brady Black, the editor, and may have been the only copy boy hired by the editor himself since the young man's great-great-grand-father, Washington McLean, had taken his son John on as a copy boy in 1868.

WILEY TRANSFORMS ENQUIRER

> *"He believed every good paper had one, strong leader astride both the news and business sides, and on Vine Street, he was it."*

In 1898, a young man named William Foust Wiley, in tiny Tarleton, Ohio, was facing a tough decision. He wanted to teach but had been rejected because he had once clerked in a cigar store while he was in college and therefore posed a moral risk.

With this blot on his otherwise good record, he either had to leave Tarleton or resign himself to working on the railroad that passed through town.

He decided to leave, and asked the advice of his congressman, Dr. James Norton. Wiley's cigar-store past didn't bother Norton, and Norton knew it wouldn't worry his friend in Washington, John R. McLean, either. When the congressman asked, McLean wired back that he would give young Wiley a two-month trial on his newspaper, the *Washington Post*.

Wiley started at $20 a week. He was on probation, but McLean took active, personal interest in what seemed to be a bright, young man, and liked what he saw. Within four weeks, Wiley had earned a permanent spot and a raise to $25 a week.

Two and a half years later, McLean still liked what he saw in Wiley. He was less happy with what he saw at his paper in Cincinnati, where a succession of timid, cautious managing editors at *The Enquirer* had earned his disfavor. McLean, who had become publisher of *The Enquirer* himself when only 24, believed in able, ambitious young men, and he told Wiley he was going to send him from the *Post* to Ohio to run *The Enquirer*.

Wiley protested that he lacked experience.

"Nonsense," McLean told him. "All you have to do is open the mail and throw it away."

In his first few years, Wiley was tested by fire — a lot of fire, including the assassination of President McKinley and the rise of Teddy Roosevelt. He reorganized the news staff, spent long hours learning the mechanical and business sides of newspapering, and concluded that too many newspapers lacked character. *The Enquirer*, he decided, would have its own character.

He despised professional publicists — at one point banning them and their press releases from the premises — and refused to rely much on syndicates and outside news-gathering organizations, as *The Enquirer's* sister paper in Washington seemed to do. McLean had already built a strong network of *Enquirer* correspondents in major cities across the country, and Wiley strengthened it, especially in the Midwest. *The Enquirer* was such a regional power that the states of Ohio, Indiana, Kentucky and West Virginia became known as *"The Enquirer* Confederacy."

As John R. McLean grew older and more distant from Cincinnati, Wiley's

Continued on next page

Publisher W. F. Wiley and his office in the 'new' building at 617 Vine St.

grip on *The Enquirer* grew stronger. When McLean died in 1916 and left *The Enquirer* in trust for his playboy son, Ned, the first thing the trustees of his estate made sure of was to keep Wiley in charge. While Ned McLean took the title "editor in chief," his father's name remained on the masthead for two years. Even when Ned's name replaced his father's, no one ever doubted who was in charge on Vine Street.

Wiley became general manager in 1918, and later — after Ned's incompetence had become obvious — the trustees named Wiley publisher as well.

He believed every good paper had one, strong leader astride both the news and business sides, and on Vine Street, he was it. Although his heart remained in the newsroom, he knew every corner of *The Enquirer*.

Wiley became a giant in the industry, especially after World War I when he persuaded the McLean trustees to build a new Enquirer Building at 617 Vine St. It would have state-of-the-art color presses and a paneled, fifth-floor publisher's office far more luxurious than anything John R. Mclean ever had on Vine Street. The trade publication, *Editor & Publisher*, covered construction of the new building almost brick-for-brick.

Just before the staff moved in, Wiley wrote a story for the employee publication, *The Little Enquirer*, likening the new building to a "perfect hybrid rose" that "gratified the eye" but was "absolutely without fragrance." The building, he said,

WILY MR. WILEY ALWAYS GETS THE APPLE OF HIS EYE

Enquirer people have always been keen observers of what goes on on Vine Street, even the former, great general manager himself, W. F. Wiley. From his fifth floor office he'd spy out bargains at the fruit market across the street at the corner of Vine and Gano Alley. The market would put produce out on sidewalk stands and Wiley kept a pair of binoculars to look them over each morning. When he spotted, say, an apple that looked particularly good, he would send a secretary or copy boy over. "Buy the third one from the left," he would say, "fourth row down."

In the early 1920s, Wiley took to publishing a series of rather stuffy page one editorials, which he called "Credos." One day shortly after the last one ran, some reporters were standing around on the Vine Street sidewalk watching progress on the massive excavation for the new Enquirer Building. A passerby asked, "What are they working on?" and one of the reporters replied: "Oh, they're burying the credos."

wouldn't become a newspaper until the staff moved in.

"The real heart of *The Enquirer* is the company of men and women engaged in its daily preparation and presentation. It is they, and not the noble structure within which they work, that must make *The Enquirer* a fragrant and blessed institution to the people of Cincinnati. . . ."

Wiley left an indelible mark on the American calendar as well as on *The Enquirer*. Late in the Depression years of the 1930s, he persuaded President Franklin D. Roosevelt to change the date of Thanksgiving from the traditional last Thursday to a week earlier. The idea had come from Fred Lazarus, owner of what was then Shillito's department store, who argued that the change would help lengthen the pre-Christmas shopping season and give the depressed economy a boost.

In 1917, soon after John R. McLean's death, Wiley addressed a group of Ohio publishers and foresaw issues still on the American agenda today. It was just before Prohibition, and his subject was a proposed law to ban liquor ads in pub-

lications that use the mails, such as newspapers. Naturally, he was against it.

"Our right to devise as to the brand of varnish with which to paint the alimentary canal is about to be withdrawn. . . .I am not here to make a defense of the liquor traffic. I am personally opposed to some phases of it. . . .But I am more strongly opposed to the insidious effort. . . to repeal or emasculate Article 1 of the Amendments to the Constitution of the United States, which provides that there shall be no abridgement of the freedom of the press.

"The fight for censorship," Wiley warned, "will not stop with attacks on liquor advertisements. . . .Several states now prohibit the manufacture or sale of cigarettes, [and] in nearly every state it is unlawful to carry a pistol. . . ."

In a sense — and this is not said pejoratively — Wiley was an imperial publisher. He was widely known in business, political and social circles. But he was a good emperor and knew his way in the newsroom as well.

When he died in 1944 — in a Buffalo hospital after becoming ill on a train — the outpouring of sentiment was as genuine as it was extensive. His hometown newspaper had editorialized in 1935 that "for 31 years he and *The Enquirer* have been synonymous in Cincinnati." On his death it seemed that he and the city itself were one. He had guided the newspaper through one world war and almost through another, through the tumult of Prohibition and the pall of the Depression. He had thrown the paper behind civic projects, and had made it and the city perennial breakfast-table friends.

The Enquirer was still owned by the McLean trust, but the trust had few family ties left. Ned McLean had passed from the scene. The trust had sold the *Washington Post* in the 1930s, and Wiley, the last major link to John R. McLean, was gone as well.

OFFICIAL VICTORY!
THE CINCINNATI ENQUIRER

WEATHER—CINCINNATI AND VICINITY: Partly Cloudy, Cooler And Less Humid Today And Tonight. Predicted High, 84.

WEATHER REPORT, PAGE 1 AND 16.

WEDNESDAY MORNING, AUGUST 15, 1945 — 20 PAGES — FOUR CENTS — FIVE CENTS

WAR ENDS AS JAPAN QUITS

TODAY, THURSDAY ARE LEGAL HOLIDAYS

CELEBRATION WILDEST IN HISTORY OF CITY

U.S.S. Indianapolis Lost; All Aboard Are Dead, Missing Or Injured

HAD ATOMIC BOMB ROLE

Cruiser Carried Explosive To Guam Base Before Sinking With 1,196

WAR CONTRACTS Are Swept Away.

Cincinnati Writes Off $286,000,000—Loss Of Jobs Portended.

Four States Mark Total $40,000,000 List,

BANKS OPEN TODAY

Tears, Cheers, Whistles, Paper Mark End Of War As Cincinnatians Celebrate Peace

World Beats Peacemakers To The Punch; Torn Paper, Prayers And Noise Mingled

PETAIN GUILTY, Condemned To Death.

Clemency For Marshal Is Urged from MacArthur.

—French Vichy Leader Is Sentenced To Indignity.

Anami Ends Life; Jap War Minister

Glory Be To God!

MacArthur Is Appointed To Accept Surrender, President Says

HIROHITO IS ALLIED TOOL

All Man-Power Controls Are Removed—Draft Calls To Be Cut

MIKADO LACKS POWER.

DRAFT CALLS CUT

FAMOUS FRONTS

The words "OFFICIAL VICTORY!" appeared in red type. Color headlines were very rare but justified the significance of V-E Day.

JAMES GARFIELD STEWART, Mayor.

MARION DEVEREUX: 'TSARINA'

From late in the 19th century onward, *The Enquirer* was where Cincinnati's fashionable society read about itself. Society was a bit less egalitarian in those days, and many a nervous mother lost sleep worrying about whether her precious young daughter's name might (or worse, might not) appear on *The Enquirer's* society columns.

These columns were a window to the realm of social prominence, providing a chronicle of the dinners, teas, balls, weddings and travels of the city's rich, famous and well-connected. The potentates sent by the McLeans to rule this realm were the society editors. First, there was the doughty Clara Devereux, followed by her even more doughty daughter, Marion Devereux, and her successor, Jane Finneran Farrell. They called the tune to which society danced in Cincinnati for seven decades.

Their blessings could bring comfort and happiness, their disfavor anguish. Theirs was the power to thwart social ambition, unmask pretense, reward propriety. They de-manded, and got, obeisance to the unswerving rules that *The Enquirer* got the news first, and no young lady was considered a debutante unless the society editor called her one.

These women were approached with caution by subjects and editors alike, the only difference, perhaps, being that other editors called them by their first names. To the public, regardless of marital status, they were always 'Miss.' Miss Devereux. Miss Finneran. Jane Finneran's married name, Farrell, never appeared in copy.

As writers, Jane Finneran was by far the clearer, the more succinct. It wasn't hard, however, to out-succinct Marion Devereux, for she was the queen of excess. As one contemporary commented: 'Her sentences are longer than human thought usually runs without a period.'

In 1962, outdoor writer Dave Roberts, of all people, wrote a reminiscence:

"The streams of society copy which flowed from the typewriter of that tireless and outstanding society editor, Marion Devereux, never was marked for its purity of style. Yet during the 30 years in which she commanded *The Enquirer's* society department, few lines ever were changed."

When, on rare occasion, some copy editor had the temerity to alter a single Devereux line, the roof trees of the old Enquirer Building trembled and strong men grew pale. Miss Devereux was tiny, but when her temper flared, she had the power of a thunderbolt.

Miss Devereux thought it wise from time to time to intersperse her prose with bits of French. Young folks didn't set out for a honeymoon, they departed on a *lune de miel*. Her chosen people never were distinguished, always *distinguee*.

For all the glamour, pathos was with her to the end. It lay not alone in the reluctant messenger boy walking her home to her Hotel Sinton apartment after the final edition had gone to press, or in the fact that there was little room in her life for romantic love. It was best seen in Spring Grove, when her body was laid to rest. Only two of her friends, out of the thousands who once sat at her feet, were at the graveside.

Miss Devereux died of a heart attack on Oct. 10, 1948, at the age of 75, after a decade's illness. She had retired on March 27, 1939, simply by leaving the office after complaining of not feeling well. She never returned, and Jane Finneran, her assistant since 1932, took over. *Time* magazine referred to Marion Devereux as Cincinnati's "social tsarina," but the real truth, as

Clara Devereux

WEBSTER'S WRONG AGAIN

Marion Devereux, the domineering — call her formidable, if you want — society editor from 1904 to 1939, had a very free hand to write what she wished, as she wished. Perhaps it was because she was in charge of social prominence, a commodity prized by *Enquirer* publishers ever since John R. McLean himself. What Marion Devereux wished was to over-write. She was famous for overblown syntax, fake French phrases, and an exaggerated style. A managing editor named Jack LaRue once discovered her authority to err when he chided her about her frequent misuse of some word or other and produced a dictionary to show her the definition.

"Just another example," she replied, never skipping a beat, "of Webster being wrong."

her obituary put it, was that she was quite "a character"

"As persons intimate with her realized, she found it useful to be so, she found it profitable to be so, and it amused her to be so. She created a role for herself, she studied it and she played it with aplomb. . . .

"Not even the disgruntled aspirant to social position could call her anything but a lady, though a cruel one . . . . Not the most irate, space-hungry subeditor could call her anything but a newspaperwoman who knew her public. . . .

"Her endless sentences compelled the awe of the shop girls and dowagers. The spangles of phrases in French and exquisitisms in English added dazzle to opulence. But behind the gaiety and prattle. . .worked a shrewd, sensitive, self-driving woman."

Marion Devereux

Marion Devereaux was born July 8, 1873, in New York City, daughter of Gen. and Mrs. Arthur Forrester Devereux. General Devereux brought his family to Cincinnati in the early 1870s, and Murat Halstead, editor of the old Cincinnati *Commercial Gazette*, was their neighbor on East Fourth Street.

He hired Mrs. (Clara) Devereux as his society editor. She quit in 1897, and later *The Enquirer's* city editor, James Faulkner, and managing editor, Charles W. Hodges, persuaded her to take over *The Enquirer's* society column.

When Clara Devereux died in 1910, her daughter, Marion, inherited the job.

"Through much of her career with *The Enquirer*," her obit read, "Miss Devereux made her home at the Hotel Sinton, often beginning work there in early morning, going on to the office later and not returning until after midnight. During the social season, her exercise was a daily walk over the Suspension Bridge. She had few recreations except her enjoyment of the events she covered day after day. Between seasons, she took long annual vacations, usually going abroad."

In 1974, *Cincinnati Magazine* published a piece about Marion Devereux by the *Cincinnati*

Post's Polk Laffoon, and prompted *Post* TV columnist Mary Wood to produce a little reminiscence of her very own:

"My father, Lee Hawes, was a member of *The Enquirer* editorial staff during the '20s and '30s, and he and Miss Marion were great friends. She often came to our house for dinner, and he would frequently escort her from *The Enquirer* to the Sinton Hotel, where she lived. But I'm sure the dear lady never knew what boundless hilarity her column brought into my father's life.

"'Listen to this, Ida May,' he would say to my mother at the breakfast table, as he perused the *Enquirer* society page, 'Miss Minnie Tracy was seen having intercourse in the corridors at the symphony last night.'

"Miss Minnie Tracy was a former opera singer who had settled in Cincinnati after what we were led to believe was a glorious operatic career in Paris. She was cross-eyed and so stout that in order to attend the Symphony, she bought two adjoining season seats and had the arm between them removed.

"To Marion, each debutante was a 'rosebud' and all were equally ravishing. She hand-picked her 'rosebuds,' and they were precious to her even with buck teeth, limp hair and left-over baby fat.

"There were times when a few members of Cincinnati's elite

rebelled against Marion's dictatorship, but not for long. Suddenly, one of the rebellious ladies would find herself described as wearing 'the gown which has graced so many occasions' or in 'a black toilet with a silver chain.'

"One of Miss Marion's more memorable columns concerned a socially prominent widow and widower who, very late in life, had wed. 'The bride and groom will honeymoon in Mexico where they will explore old ruins,' reported Miss Marion. She added that the groom's wedding gift to the bride was an 'antique pendant.'"

Columnist Wood ended her reminiscence by recounting a story her father told one night after escorting Marion Devereux home: "'It was like walking the

Society editor Marion Devereux ruled Greater Cincinnati society from this elaborate office .

last mile,'" Wood remembers her father's saying. "'Miss Marion asked if I'd walk her down Vine Street to the Sinton, but first she wanted to stop off in the ladies' room.

"'Well, she came out of the ladies' room trailing about a mile of toilet paper from under her skirt. Hell, I couldn't tell her, so there we went, three blocks down Vine, with a festoon of toilet paper like a damn train behind her.'"

"'"Did anyone notice?' I asked."

"'Notice?' he replied. 'They were laughing like hyenas all up and down Vine Street.'

"'What did Miss Marion say?' I wanted to know."

"'She said, 'Lee, those people have no breeding. Their names will never appear in my column.'"'"

Marion Devereux's successor as society editor was less a matriarch, more a newspaper-woman. "Where Miss Devereux

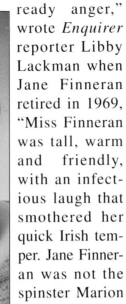

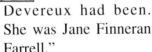

Jane Finneran Farrell

was a cold but diminutive woman with killing drive and ready anger," wrote *Enquirer* reporter Libby Lackman when Jane Finneran retired in 1969, "Miss Finneran was tall, warm and friendly, with an infectious laugh that smothered her quick Irish temper. Jane Finneran was not the spinster Marion Devereux had been. She was Jane Finneran Farrell."

But as Miss Finneran, she wore the mantle of Social Directress of the city for 30 years. "Jane Finneran's calendar," wrote Lackman, "kept thousands of social events from running into each other. As had her predecessor, Jane Finneran virtually dictated the dates of important balls, dinners, weddings and cultural events. Debutante parties, especially, were her preserve. Mothers often reserved dates 17 years into the future just to be sure their newborn daughters would

be properly introduced to society when the time came."

Jane Finneran also carried on *The Enquirer* tradition—unique in journalism — of carrying society stories first or not at all.

One tradition Jane Finneran disposed of, as Lackman reported, "was Miss Devereux's florid and ostentatious style, tangled syntax and overuse of fancy French phrases. Finneran retained a drawing room style, but it reflected her interests in flowers, fashion and travel."

Each year, she made sure she traveled abroad to keep up with the people whose lives she covered; each summer, she'd make tours to report on what Cincinnatians were up to at the fashionable summer resorts of northern Michigan and New England. Her society pages frequently won awards from the Ohio Newspaper Women's Association, an organization of

Eleanor Adams

which she was elected president three times. She frequently addressed press seminars on covering society.

Born in Newport, Ky., Mrs. Farrell lived in Pleasant Ridge most of her adult life. She lived 20 years in retirement and died on July 19, 1989, at 85.

Her successor, Eleanor Adams, was as much a lady as Marion Devereux had been a martinet. Gentle, kind, sweet, Adams also was much more a newswoman. She applied modern standards of objectivity and fairness to the society columns and got the paper out of the awkward business of dictating who was who in society, a business it never belonged in to start with.

After her retirement, society coverage centered on community volunteerism.

FACT

The words "FINAL EDITION" first appeared on page one on Oct. 2, 1922.

'BLUE BOOK' BECOMES BIBLE FOR BLUE BLOODS

Contrary to some long-held beliefs, the very first *Blue Book of Cincinnati* — long the definitive directory of polite Cincinnati society — was not published by a society editor, by someone named Devereux, or even by a woman. It was was published by a bookstore owner named Peter G. Thomson, and called *Cincinnati Society Blue Book and Family Directory*. The year was 1879, eight years before the New York-based Social Register Association produced its first list of America's supposedly "acceptable" families.

Thomson, whose store was at 179 Vine St., later founded the Champion (Coated) Paper Co. and built a mansion in suburban College Hill he named "Laurel Court" that was a miniature copy of the *Petit Trianon* at Versailles.

In 1887, a newspaper, the *Graphic Press*, produced a new edition, titled *The Graphic Blue Book and Family Directory of Cincinnati*. It included illustrations of the homes of various fashionable and/or prominent Cincinnati families, including "Rookwood," the Longworth Mansion on Grandin Road. It listed socially proper families in Covington and Newport along with those in Cincinnati, and indicated the "Reception Day" when each family

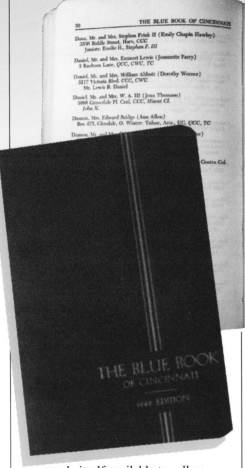

made itself available to callers.

The *Graphic*'s book included advertising and, in a section of "Rules of Cincinnati Society," specified protocol for such events as debutante teas, dances, weddings and introductions. It also outlined correct manners for gentlemen, gave the rules

of such fashionable games as hearts and whist and showed seating charts for places the city's rich and famous might go — such as The Odeon Theater and Heuck's Opera House.

Perhaps appropriately, lest any of its subscribers get too carried away by social position, the book's final page had an engraving of the entrance to the city's most socially acceptable cemetery, *Spring Grove*.

In 1892, *Who's Who, a Society Register for Cincinnati* appeared, published by Olive M. Avery and

C.A.R. Devereux. The latter was Clara Anna Rich Devereux, society reporter for the *Commerical Gazette*. Clara's first *Mrs. Devereux's Blue Book of Cincinnati* appeared in 1894 and was supplanted by newer editions every few years. Marion was listed in the 1906 edition as her mother's assistant editor.

Along with the society column, Marion Devereux inherited the *Blue Book*, but she never dropped her mother's name. From beyond the grave, Clara Devereux appeared to be its co-editor until Marion's final *Blue Book* in 1937.

While the books had appeared every two years from the turn of the century until 1929, there were gaps during the Depression. Marion Devereux's assistant, Jane Finneran, took over as society editor at *The Enquirer* when Devereux retired in 1939, but didn't resume the *Blue Book* until after World War II, in 1949.

That 1937-38 Devereux book was "offered to its subscribers and the public with the conviction that it will be found indispensable to the woman of fashion, and constantly useful to the man of business." And if Marion Devereux wrote so, it surely must have been so—at least for women of fashion.

"She was a brilliant woman," Jane Finneran once remarked, "but she pushed the whole city for 29 years."

62 KILLED IN FIERY CRASH OF JET AT BOONE AIRPORT

—Enquirer (See Free) Photo

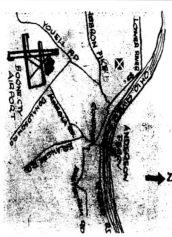

... X shows spot where Convair 880 went down

Firemen Fight Smoldering Remains Of Crashed Airliner

... 44 of the 79 aboard were reported killed

79 Aboard On TWA Flight

A Trans World Airlines jet crashed at Greater Cincinnati Airport Monday night. A reported 62 persons were killed.

There were 79 persons aboard the TWA plane which crashed here Monday.

They were en route from the Los Angeles to Boston plane, including a crew of seven.

10 From Here Aboard Plane

At least 10 Greater Cincinnatians were known to have been aboard the TWA plane which crashed here Monday.

They are:

Dr. Frederick A. Wolf, general practitioner, and his wife, Mrs. Paula Hoffman Wolf, 32, who live at 7464 Willow Brook Ln., Amberley Village.

A young woman, possibly a daughter, Tracy Smith, 5629 Eileen Ave., Pleasant Ridge, and her grandmother, Mrs. Alfred Helfrich, Dr. Oakley.

Mr. and Mrs. Alfred Helfrich, Silverton. The city directory lists an Alfred V. Helfrich, retired, and his wife, Clarie, as of 7023 Ohio Ave., Silverton.

Burning, He Carries Child

By BILL CARLSON
Of The Enquirer Staff

In the eerie floodlit haze of debris-strewn orchard, amid pieces of aircraft and the stench of fire, Thomas Dickman told this story:

"WE WERE the first ones here," said the captain of Hebron's life squad.

"We saw and heard two explosions on the way up here. There was one and dense black smoke all over.

"We passed one man lying face down in the field (about 75 yards from the bulk of the crash). He was dead.

"Then we came to a man carrying a child in his arms. He was badly burned — no hair, skin hanging off, his cheeks. Dr. said his face, his ears, feet, Get in there and help those that need it."

Dickman said two passengers were not badly hurt and even helped bandage some victims.

One passenger, on the way to the hospital, said there was a two-hour and 20-minute delay on the plane because of weather. The plane would not close properly.

Dickman related that when the stewardess gave instructions for landing and then apologized because the plane was not as scheduled.

Bidding To Be No. 1?

Lindsay Snaps 'No'

© New York Times Service
WASHINGTON—Mayor John V. Lindsay Monday disclaimed in the strongest terms yet any national political ambitions.

Prefacing his comments with, however, about published reports that Gov. Nelson A. Rockefeller had told associates that he thought Lindsay had begun his own campaign for the 1968 Republican presidential nomination.

THE QUESTIONS continued, and the governor said, "Have regular meetings," Lindsay said. "We're good friends and I have great admiration for him. What you've been reading about is just plain nonsense."

The Weather

Cloudy and not so cold today. Occasional rain likely. Low in mid-30s. High in low 40s.
Details, Map on Page 42

This page betrays how quickly the staff had to react to the crash. The map was drawn freehand.

Holiday Dining

Where to dine out for Thanksgiving? Check the special pre-Thanksgiving Restaurant Guide in today's Enquirer.
Picture, Stories on Page 23

BUREAUS DELIVER DIVERSITY

Until the late 1870s, *The Enquirer* spoke with one voice, and there were few, if any, bylines. Readers assumed, correctly, that whatever appeared in its columns was the proprietors' product. The exceptions were letters — usually from political allies—on issues of the day. Such correspondence was usually published over the writer's name.

An example appeared, in fact, in the very first issue of *The Enquirer* — a signed letter from a state legislator explaining his vote on a controversial banking bill. The correspondence was from James J. Faran, who later became mayor of Cincinnati and partner in *The Enquirer* for almost 40 years. He was, quite literally, *The Enquirer's* first "correspondent."

Most editors, in those days, took highly partisan positions. The Democratic *Enquirer*, like most papers, had its trusted acquaintances in the state capital who would mail regular reports and comment. But these "correspondents" were unpaid, their work unsigned. The editors themselves took full responsibility for whatever was published.

Around 1850, after the telegraph had become the medium for communicating news, old-fashioned "correspondence" by mail was reserved for less hurried commentary. About the same time, *The Enquirer* and other papers began paying their correspondents. Most of the early correspondents were political observers, but some were expert in other fields, such as finance, drama and art.

When John R. McLean took *The Enquirer's* helm in 1872, he gave it a flavor that was far less predictably partisan, because he wanted more circulation than any one-party paper could provide. One of his moves was to encourage writers who had other points of view. To make sure the readers understood whose opinions were whose, he had them write under their own bylines.

The device had a desirable, circulation-building effect: It encouraged reader loyalty to individual correspondents. Early in the McLean era, commentators and columnists became known among Cincinnatians for their individual interpretations of events, rather than for voicing the paper's "official" position. Some agreed with the publishers and some didn't, just as the views expressed today by, say, Pulitzer-prize winning cartoonist Jim Borgman don't always agree with editorials that share the page.

Many of the early columnists wrote under pen names, although their identities were well-known; easily remembered pen names served as promotional devices. Among the correspondents whose regular contributions made the Victorian-era *Enquirer* distinctive were the likes of George Alfred Townshend (who

Continued on next page

wrote as "Gath"), Felix L. Oswald ("Savyard") and D.J. Edwards, a highly regarded financial correspondent who wrote as "Holland." Olive Logan, a late 19th-century writer for *Harper's,* was among the *Enquirer's* early correspondents.

"Gath," *The Enquirer's* political correspondent in the 1880s, was a Washingtonian and a nationally known figure. It was always a special event when he passed through the city for a lecture and dropped in at *The Enquirer* to exchange greetings. Gath was an uncompromising Republican, and his column

was anathema to many dyed-in-the-wool Democrats who simply couldn't understand why John R. McLean was so determined to break with the partisan traditions established by his father, Washington McLean.

John R., of course, was no less a Democrat (he later ran for both governor and vice president), but he was determined that *The Enquirer* would offer something for all readers, and the popular "Gath" Townshend was a part of the strategy — a typical product of the genius of McLean.

Every so often, some powerful Democrat would storm into McLean's off-

ice demanding that he fire Gath for his heresies. For precisely such moments, McLean always kept two stacks of letters ready.

"These," he would say, indicating one pile, "are letters from those who, like you, refuse to read his views from the other side and don't want any one else to do so.

"And these," he would go on, waving his hand at the much larger stack, "are from those who seem to like them and urge me to continue their publication. You can see for yourself which stack speaks the louder to a man who is publishing a real newspaper."

In making *The Enquirer* a journalistic power in the Midwest during the 1880s and

'90s, McLean stationed correspondents in major cities from New York and Washington to St. Louis and Des Moines, and many smaller towns in between. Every major town in Ohio and Indiana had an *Enquirer* man, as did all Midwestern capitals. Obviously, there wasn't space enough for all those correspondents to have bylined columns, and being a "correspondent" lost much of its cachet except for the men in Washington or Columbus.

Most of the bureaus that survived the exigencies of the first World War disappeared in the reality of the Depression, until *The Enquirer's* only bureaus dur-

Members of The Enquirer's bureau in New York City in 1941 were, from left, J.C. Muma, John Wheeler and Peter Egan.

ing World War II were in New York, Washington and Columbus, Ohio. The New York bureau was closed after correspondent Lee Evans died in 1950. The Washington and Columbus bureaus remained. The correspondents there were given the title "bureau chief," which gave them a certain autonomy, and they built audiences all their own with their signed reports and columns.

As Cincinnati grew and its influence spread in southern Ohio, the bureaus in nearby towns grew in importance. The Hamilton, Ohio, bureau is one of these, and at *The Enquirer's* 150th birthday its correspondent, John Clark, has been with the paper 52 years, longer than any current employee. Outside the courthouse in Hamilton is a plaque honoring him. The Columbus and Washington bureaus were folded into the Gannett News Service when the paper joined Gannett 1979.

MOST PAPERS SNUBBED HISTORIC SCOOP

Reporter Harry P. Moore didn't even work for *The Enquirer*, but it was one of the few papers that printed his story about one of the 20th century's most amazing events. In 1903, Moore was working for the *Norfolk Virginian Pilot*. In an interview 25 years later to commemorate the scoop, he retold the story of his story.

A Coast Guardsman had come into a Norfolk restaurant in September that year, he said, and told him of a recent visit to the beach at Kitty Hawk, during which he said he had come upon "two looney Yankees down there who are trying to learn how to fly."

Moore's checked and learned that the "two looneys" were brothers from Dayton, Ohio, named Wright. He began keeping track of them and persuaded a Coast Guardsman near Kitty Hawk "to promise to let me know if those two birds happen to get up in the air or get killed."

On December 17, one of those birds

Only six newspapers initially ran the story of Orville (upper left) and Wilbur Wright's first flight.

did, indeed, happen to get up in the air: Orville Wright kept their flimsy craft aloft for 12 seconds and flew 120 feet. On subsequent days, as the Wrights conducted longer flights, the Coast Guardsman contacted Moore. Moore, years later, still remembered his informant's words: "One of them just flew around like a bird. I never did think they could fly, but darned if they didn't do it this morning. They put a gasoline engine in the thing and after chasing it down the hill along a wooden track, it went up and flew all over the place . . . . They must have flown three miles. I got out of breath trying to keep up. . . ."

Moore's story began this way: "The problem of aerial flight without the use of a balloon has been solved by Wilber (sic) and Orville Wright, of Dayton, Ohio, who today, at Kitty Hawk, on the coast of North Carolina, successfully navigated a flying machine of their own invention for three miles in the teeth of a twenty-one-mile gale . . . ."

Moore sent queries to other papers offering them the news. Few even bothered to reply. One Ohio editor who did said, "We do not want any such wild story as that." Not so John R. McLean's papers in Cincinnati and Washington. *The Enquirer* and *Washington Post* were among five which did buy it. (Others: the *New York American, Chicago Inter-Ocean* and *Philadelphia Inquirer.*)

FOOTSTEPS ON MOON!

In this drawing, Apollo 11 Spacecraft Commander Neil Armstrong scoops lunar soil sample into pouch held by Lunar Module Pilot Edwin Aldrin. About 50 pounds of rock and soil are to be brought back to Earth.

Eagle Lands, Astronauts Take Lunar Walk

SPACE CENTER, Houston (AP) — Man landed and walked on the Moon Sunday, July 20, 1969.

Two Americans, Neil A. Armstrong and Edwin E. Aldrin Jr., 240,000 miles from their home on the planet Earth, settled to a dusty landing on the Moon's alien soil at 4:17:42 p.m. (EDY) and some six hours later Armstrong made the first footprint on that strange globe.

In a bulky suit that gave him the life-sustaining environment of his planet, Armstrong climbed laboriously down the nine steps of a ladder at the side of his spaceship.

Aldrin, his companion on this trek of history, waited inside the ship Eagle to watch Armstrong before venturing down himself.

They had been impatient to be here.

They'd spent a millennium of dreams and a $24-billion effort that opened the world of the universe.

SPACE CENTER, Houston (UPI) — For SEVERAL LONG minutes, the Moon Sunday at 4:17:42 p.m.

The landing by Neil A. Armstrong (Buzz) Aldrin Jr. in a spaceship named ...

At 220 feet: "Coming down nicely."

At 75 feet: "Looking good."

At 30 feet: "Picking up some dust."

Then finally at 4:17:42 p.m.: here. The Eagle has landed.

At the time of the landing the Moon was about 238,548 miles from Earth, Michael Collins, the third astronaut of the Apollo team, kept the command ship Columbia in the command ship orbiting the Moon at an altitude of 69 miles while Armstrong and Aldrin eased their way down.

Collins was poised to swoop in and rescue his colleagues, had anything gone wrong. But now that they are on the lunar surface, they are beyond his reach.

After giving their landing craft systems a quick check, Armstrong and Aldrin simulated a countdown for their blastoff Monday.

As Eagle neared the surface, its computerized automatic pilot sent the ship toward a rock-strewn rocks and boulders in the projected land site in the Moon's Sea of Tranquility.

Armstrong grabbed control of his ship, steering it clear of certain disaster and put it down four miles from the original landing point.

THE LANDING SITE was on the lunar Sea of Tranquility, almost exactly on target. It kicked up a large number of rocks. Many were "extremely rough craters and a large field sized crater with a large number of big boulders and rocks."

"Very smooth touchdown," confirmed Aldrin.

Ground Controller Charles M. Duke told Collins in the command ship:

Eagle is in Tranquility base.

"He has landed. Tranquility base, got you down. You've got a bunch of guys about to turn blue. We're breathing again."

Moments later, the Eagle's hatch swung open and Armstrong stepped onto the lunar surface.

Eagle Lands, Astronauts Take Lunar Walk

Armstrong reported, "I'm at the foot of the ladder. The LM footpads are only depressed in the surface about one or two inches, although the surface appears to be very, very fine grained as you get close to it. It's almost like a powder."

Armstrong stepped onto the Moon's surface and said: "That's one small step for man, one giant leap for mankind."

WHILE THE APOLLO fliers were ...

Red's Luna Shadowing Eagle

From Enquirer Wires

JODRELL BANK, England (UPI) —Russia's Luna 15 satellite Sunday dropped into a 9.9-mile-high Moon orbit that carried it above the landing site for America's Apollo 11 astronauts, the Jodrell Bank Observatory reported.

Although the new orbit was announced by the Soviet Union as well as being tracked here, there was still no clue to the exact mission of the Soviet satellite.

"We don't know whether it is going to land, or explore the nearMoon space, which could include close reconnaissance of the American landing site," said Sir Bernard Lovell, director of the observatory.

Lovell said the 40th orbit of Luna 15 varied the descent of the Moon's Sea of Tranquility at the same time the U.S. astronauts were making a landing approach in their lunar module.

The Soviet news agency Tass announced the new orbit level Sunday in a brief dispatch, which described the Luna 15's mission only as

"scientific exploration." Tass said the new orbit ranged from 9.9 miles to 68.2 miles above the Moon's surface.

APOLLO 8 astronaut Frank Borman received a cable Saturday from Soviet academician Mstislav Keldysh, chairman of the Soviet Academy of Science, advising him of an earlier change in Luna 15's orbital path.

The space agency said Keldysh told Borman, who recently returned from a trip to Russia, that Luna 15 was in an egg-shaped orbit ranging from a low of 128 degrees in relation to the Moon's equator, compared to an angle of 128 degrees in relation to the Moon's equator, compared to the Moon's equator.

The message fulfilled a promise made by Keldysh in an earlier cable when he promised to keep the astronauts advised of any change in Luna 15's path to assure Apollo flight controllers it would not interfere with America's lunar landing mission.

Saturday's cable made no mention of Apollo and only listed the

Rain Delays City's Soap Box Derby

Greater Cincinnati's Soap Box Derby was postponed Sunday until 10 a.m. today on Ault Park's Observatory Avenue hill. The boy-high in mild tonight and Tuesday drivers are to report to the track's top-side at 8 a.m.

Rain delayed the pre-race parade 40 minutes but on-and-off downpours throughout Sunday afternoon finally caused a postponement at 4 p.m.

The boys will be ready to race Sunday boys.

Derby director Jerry L. Stickley or co-chairmen Bob Bridges (522-0154) or Barry Paul Bridges (522-8292) or Barry Paul specific information. Today's 6:30 p.m. derby awards banquet in University of Cincinnati's Great Hall.

The Weather

Mostly cloudy and mild today with the chance of showers in the morning. Partly cloudy this afternoon with a low in the upper-60s. Partly cloudy Tuesday.

Details, Map On Page 14

Index

More . . Pages 2 and 26

ERA OF THE EDITOR EVOLVES

> " *What followed was the ideal editor — a man who ran the paper with a cool head and a firm hand — Charlie Hodges. Hodges had done it all . . . .* "

Until after the Civil War, at least one of The Enquirer's owners also was its editor, supervising the gathering, writing and placement of news in the paper. For most of the early years this role fell to James J. Faran, co-owner with a variety of partners.

Following the Civil War, Faran continued as "editor," in that he was responsible for the Democratic paper's politics and editorials, but in the later 1860s Washington McLean installed an energetic young man named John B. McCullagh as his managing editor to run the news side.

In 1872, McCullagh went on to the *St. Louis Globe-Democrat*, but before he went, he hired as a reporter a talented young man named John R. Cockerill. Between them, these two men just about invented much of modern journalism, starting while they were at Cincinnati and later, as editors in St. Louis and New York.

Cockerill, a printer's apprentice in 1860, had become a colonel in the Civil War. After the war he returned to the only trade he knew, and in

1868, was hired on at *The Enquirer*.

When McCullagh departed, John R. McLean had just taken over his father's interest in *The Enquirer*. He quickly demonstrated a skill that distinguished him all his life as a publisher — a skill for picking talented young men and giving them big responsibilities. He gave McCullagh's job as managing editor to young Cockerill.

It was Cockerill, more than anyone, who carried out John R. McLean's strategies to transform the cautious, predictably partisan *Enquirer* into a lively, popular paper with truly mass appeal. He, like his boss, hired talented young writers, such as Lafcadio Hearn, and aggressively pursued stories that people wanted to read regardless of politics. It was a style of journalism unheard of in its day, but it would probably be more than casually familiar to anyone who reads today's supermarket tabloids.

In 1878, Cockerill was hired away by a brand new Democratic daily in Washington, *The Post*, as its first managing editor. Later, he landed at Joseph Pulitzer's *St. Louis Post-Dispatch* and then at the *New York World*, where the sensational style

he'd invented at *The Enquirer* developed into the even more progessive format that became "yellow journalism" in the 1890s.

When Cockerill left, the aggressive John R. McLean was already the clear winner in his campaign to overtake the rival *Commercial* and *Gazette*, and in the early 1880s, he bought out old Faran's interest and became sole proprietor of *The Enquirer*.

Then, in search of a broader stage, he moved to Washington, D.C. He remained "editor in chief" as well as publisher, but left the hands-on

Continued on next page

supervision of the news operations in Cincinnati in the hands of a managing editor, who inherited McLean's old second-floor office over Vine Street.

None of the first three managing editors — Chauncey Newton, Robert Criswell and Samuel Johnson — lasted very long. Newton was cautious and quiet, Criswell a bit bookish, and Johnson a former political writer more at home with editorials than news. They were hardly suitable stewards for the assertive— and success-

Charles Hodges, left, and John R. Cockerill.

ful — style Cockerill had given McLean at *The Enquirer.*

In search of more flair, McLean turned to yet another: Allen O. Myers was one of the stormiest editors ever to grace *The Enquirer.* He came from a paper in Pickaway County, Ohio (and had used "Pickaway" as a pen name for his columns of biting commentary). He began his brief reign as managing editor by passing out loaded cigars to everyone in the newsroom. "Though he kept the staff in constant turmoil," wrote one *Enquirer* historian some years later, Myers "got out a paper that sparkled with originality."

That strong a personality, however, would sooner or later clash with the equally strong McLean, who eventually demoted Myers. Myers went to

another paper as a columnist and for a while frequently attacked his old boss in print. But it helps to remember that those were days of fierce, bare-knuckle, name-calling competition among papers, and some of that might have been mere show; when McLean ran for Governor in 1896, Myers (who was an eloquent speaker) campaigned for him.

The young man who replaced Myers was Alexander C. Sands, Jr., who first distinguished himself as a tireless, thorough police reporter nicknamed "Dead-to-rights" because he so often used that term in his copy and headlines. Sands, also nicknamed "Eck," was promoted to city editor, then managing editor, where he demonstrated that the expert reporter's eye for detail is often a hindrance as a manager. He fretted over every detail of every department and, as one colleague later explained, "worried himself into a nervous

collapse over the impossibility of getting news of happenings of 4 in the morning into the edition that went to press at 8 the night before."

Sands' successor in the "front room," was Morton L. Hawkins, who had served with distinction in the Union army during the Civil War and at its close became a reporter on an afternoon paper before moving to *The Enquirer.* Hawkins was city editor when he was elected sheriff of Hamilton County in 1882, which turned out, unfortunately for him, to be just before the courthouse riot of 1884. After one term, he returned to newspaper work, replacing Sands as managing editor of *The Enquirer.*

He found, however, that newspapering, McLean style, had changed too much in his absence, and his military mind was unsuited to the new way. He didn't understand, one friend later said, "how to maintain discipline without lessening the efficiency of the staff."

What followed was the ideal editor — a man who ran the paper with a cool head and a firm hand — Charlie Hodges.

Hodges had done it all: reporter, exchange editor, telegraph editor, city editor.

As managing editor he was the taciturn, thoughtful pro, literate and tolerant, and tough when need be.

"When news broke fast and others went up in the air," wrote a colleague after Hodges died in 1915, "it was then that Charlie Hodges refilled his ever-present pipe, puffed a few clouds of smoke and issued terse instructions which restored normalcy and caused the machinery of the paper to resume its efficient functioning. . . .Firmly grounded in the best traditions of his profession, skilled by long service. . . Hodges did not explode over trifles, and in emergencies was always in full grasp of the situation."

The staff loved him. Even the youngest called him "Charlie," and, as one colleague explained, "There was no disrespect . . . merely a feeling of love for this man."

"If he had an enemy in the world," said another, "it was the enemy's fault."

The Little Enquirer, an in-house organ, carried a posthumous profile of him in 1928 by William W. Morris, who wrote: "He loved a good joke. . . and while he was most firm and exacting in everything pertaining to the paper, no one ever saw him lose his temper or appear unduly ruffled. The more serious the situation.. . the calmer Charlie Hodges appeared."

Hodges, Morris wrote, had a marvelous memory for details, and was an intent listener. As a reporter he seldom made notes, except for scribbling an occasional name or address or significant date, and he seldom had to refer to those, even for long stories. As an editor he had uncanny news sense. "If it was news," Morris wrote, "Charlie sensed it immediately."

No one seemed to know the cause, but in 1901 Hodges had a falling out with McLean and was demoted to exchange editor in favor of Charles Alfred Williams. Hodges, one colleague remembered, "calmly clipped exchanges" for a few years until Williams, too, was fired. His successor in the front office, W. F. Wiley, brought Charlie back up front as city editor, where he stayed until he died in 1915.

George S. McDowell

He had one habit that fascinated all who worked with him. When events were breaking fast and he had hard, quick decisions to make, he always would pick up a pair of scissors while he listened to reports from the field and begin slicing pieces of copy paper into confetti. The magnitude of the event could always be measured by the depth of the confetti around his desk.

Charles Alfred Williams, who followed Hodges to the "front room," was an unconventional sort, forever experimenting with unconventional ways to enliven the paper. Williams had lost one eye years before in a fire, and kept a festoon of brightly colored strips of paper on his desk, which he often stopped to stare at for minutes at a time. This, he explained, relieved the strain on his one good eye from reading fine print all day.

Most of his experiments were failures, and in 1901 John R. McLean replaced him with another of those bright, talented, young men. This one, named W. F. Wiley, stayed long enough to survive McLean himself, and run the paper as editor, editor in chief, and general manager and publisher, through one World War, through the Roaring '20s, through the Depression, and through most of the Second World War.

Wiley was the last occupant of that old "front room" on the second floor at 617 Vine St., and the first of the new, paneled, fifth-floor suite that still serves as the publisher's office in the Enquirer Building. Inevitably, change came when John R. McLean died in 1916. He considered himself to be without a suitable heir and left his paper in trust for the benefit of his son, Ned. Wiley continued to run the paper and the only thing about its hierarchy that changed was the titles. Wiley became "general manager" in 1918, and the title of — managing editor" was devalued and applied to the editorial executive immediately under him — in this instance, Horace Potter.

L ater, after the reality of the playboy publisher Ned McLean's role as "publisher" had become obvious to the bankers responsible for the paper's success, Wiley took that title, too, and the titles changed again. The "managing editor" ran the editorial side, the "general manager" the business

side. It set a pattern that lasted almost 60 years.

Potter was followed in 1926 by George S. McDowell, and

Everett Boyd

when he died in 1932, John W. LaRue became managing editor. In 1943, a year before death ended Wiley's long regency as publisher, the editorial deck was shuffled wholesale, as the highly popular, veteran city editor, Lee Evans, was sent East to be New York correspondent, and Everett M. Boyd was ap-

pointed managing editor. He briefly shared the title with Ken Doris, who was named city editor to replace Evans but for a

Glenn Thompson

while was called "night managing editor" as well.

Boyd's successor in 1956 was Glenn Thompson, who continued his career in Dayton, Ohio, as editor of the *Journal-Herald*. He retired in November, 1968, and maintained a presence in that newspaper as a frequent contributor to the

letter-to-the-editor column.

Thompson's successor on Vine Street was an ambitious young reporter who'd worked his way up from cub reporter to Columbus correspondent, Brady Black. He became executive editor in 1959 and remained in the editor's office, until he retired in 1975 after 35 years at the paper. He was also a vice president of the paper.

B rady Black, who died in 1991, had come to *The Enquirer* in 1940 from Ashland, Ky.'s *Independent*. At *The Enquirer* he worked for a while as a copy editor, then as local politics reporter, assistant city editor, Kentucky correspondent, Ohio bureau chief, managing editor and editorial page editor before becoming vice president and editor. At one point in the 1960s, he was on the board of directors, and even after he retired, his column was a fixture in *The Sunday Enquirer* Opinion Section.

Black had been one of the

founding leaders and the first secretary of the paper's editorial union called "EEEPA," Enquirer Editorial Employees Professional Association. (The Newspaper Guild is now the bargaining agent for most newsroom employees.) One of his main concerns was a pension plan, a concern he never lost even when he became editor and found himself negotiating on the management side of the table. As one later union leader remembers, "Even all the time that I negotiated against him, he was adamant about getting a new pension plan brought in. He thought it was incredibly unfair for *The Enquirer* to have such a lousy pension plan . . . when old-timers retired, he insisted that they come back for one day a week, if only to say hello to friends, and he paid them $25 for that one day, and it really supplemented that old pension plan."

Only one retiree refused the offer. That was Henry Eddy, an artist. Another artist, Stan Kohn, came in once a week to retouch a few photos until he was over

Brady Black

80. "Stan just couldn't do it anymore," remembers Elmer Wetenkamp, who was art director at the time. "I remember visiting him at the hospital and telling him I was keeping his desk open for him, and he cried. "When Brady left," Wetenkamp recalls, his special, one-man retirement supplement

system "went kaput."

The meaning of the titles changed again when Black retired. Although the new own-

Luke Feck

er, financier Carl Lindner, called himself "publisher," it was William J. Keating, a former congressman, whom Lindner installed with the title "president and chief executive officer." He later became publisher and, when Brady Black retired and moved onto a teaching position at Ohio State University, briefly

assumed the title of "editor." He dropped it when Luke Feck became executive editor.

Feck was graduated from St. Xavier High School and joined *The Enquirer* as a copy clerk while a senior at the University of Cincinnati in 1956. He left for several years to start a publication of his own, *Dimension: Cincinnati*, and to operate a printing business. It wasn't stimulating enough, he eventually decided, and he returned to Vine Street.

His colleagues more than once needled him about being the only *Enquirer* editor to reach the top without experiencing an extensive hard-news background. He'd been TV editor, local columnist, assistant features editor and magazine editor, before becoming news editor and then managing editor.

His successor in the paneled office on the fourth floor was George Blake, who unabashedly says that what distinguishes him among 150 years' worth of *Enquirer* editors is, "I'm the tallest." Blake, at 6 foot 5, certainly is. He is what is known at *The Enquirer* as a "Gannettoid," a transplant to Vine Street from another paper in the Gannett company, which bought *The Enquirer* in 1979. Blake came from the Ft. Myers, Fla., *News-Press,* which had been voted the "Best of Gannett" twice in his three years as editor. He has since seen *The Enquirer* designated Gannett's best newspaper as well, in 1984.

With the advent of Gannett's corporate culture on Vine Street, titles proliferated, often taking on yet more new meanings. The title "managing editor" under John R. McLean in 1885

meant "runs the paper," and the ME was in charge of everything on Vine Street. Today there is still just one managing editor (although Jim Schottelkotte and Sheryl Bills shared the title for a brief time in the early 1980s) and several deputy and assistant managing editors. They report to the managaing editor, but many of them manage departments and operations larger and more complex than the entire paper in McLean's day.

George R. Blake

Santa Claus Hangs Around Copy Desk On Secret Visits

On a daily paper someone has to work on holidays. So, on days such as Christmas, the newsroom becomes its own family — and observes its own family traditions.

Sometime in the 1960s, late one Christmas Eve, a big drawing of Santa Claus appeared, pasted on cardboard and hung from the ceiling over the big, horseshoe-shaped copy desk. Under it on a card was written: "Merry Christmas to the Copy Desk, from the Copy Desk." No one knew where it came from. After Christmas, the picture vanished.

No one gave it a moment's thought until the next year, when it reappeared. Year after year, Santa would mysteriously appear over the copy desk at Christmas time, hanging from the ceiling on the same big, unbent paperclip. After Christmas he'd vanish just as mysteriously. No one ever saw anyone hang up Santa, or take him down. It just happened. Not only did Santa reappear yearly, for a few years a second Santa showed up, with a bandage on his nose and a caption saying, "Punch a friend for Christmas."

In 1977, veteran copy editor Frank Adams died, and, in cleaning out Adams' desk, editor Luke Feck found Santa tucked in a drawer. He realized he'd discovered the truth . Feck

learned that artist Ed Carr, by then retired, had drawn Santa and hung him up the first time. Adams, apparently, had appointed himself secret custodian thereafter. Adams was a crusty old-timer, given to two-martini lunches each evening at the Cricket Tavern. He was a superb copy editor but hardly a sentimentalist. Keeping his secret was an amazing feat, for Adams' colleagues could be working at almost any hour. For only a few hours, after the last papers are off the press, is the newsroom empty. And that, apparently, was when Frank Adams would sneak in, each year, to put up, and take down, Santa.

Feck kept the secret, and began sneaking into the office in the pre-dawn hours before and after Christmas to keep Santa in service. When Feck resigned in 1980, he entrusted the secret to John Kiesewetter, who passed the tradition on to someone else when he became radio/TV critic. One year in the 1980s, a managing editor declared the "punch-a-friend" caption offensive and ordered both Santas removed. But the next year, that editor was gone and the Santas reappeared.

The identity of Santa's current keeper is a secret again. Each year, Santa appears overhead with his greeting to — and from — the copy desk.

CITY EDITORS: CHARACTER AND CHARACTERS

"Editor" is not an exact term. Some managing editors don't manage anything. For that matter, some editors don't even edit. At the beginning level, a copy editor — about the same level as a reporter — edits copy, just as the title implies. But the higher one goes as an "editor," the less time one spends editing and the more one gets involved with things like payroll, scheduling, recruiting. It's like the Army. A general may call himself a "soldier," but his working day seldom involves shovels, rifles and chow lines.

The best of both worlds belongs to the one who has minute-by-minute contact with the reporters on the street and still sees the big picture, the city editor.

For 60 years until 1926, the city editor's province at *The Enquirer* was on the second

The city editor's office overlooking Vine Street in 1926.

floor at 617 Vine just behind the editor's office, which overlooked Vine Street. Here, in "the middle room," the city editor and his assistants gave out assignments each morning and later received and edited the local copy. The city editor, in classic newspaper lore, is the cigar-chewing veteran with armbands and a green eyeshade whose word is law to every reporter and cub. However fair or unfair this characterization, there's no denying there have been some characters in the job at *The Enquirer.*

In the 1880s, *The Enquirer* had a city editor named John T. McCarthy, who was known to the staff as "Whispering Mac" because he was forever conducting whispered, conspiratorial conversations that spread an air of mystery over the middle room. Even for the most routine assignments he would summon a reporter to a far corner of the room and give his instructions in whispers. As one contemporary later wrote, it was "as if the matter were fraught with the utmost consequence. Sometimes it was, but there was no telling from the city editor's manner. . . ."

Not all city editors were general news reporters. John B. McCormick had been a sports writer in the 1880s before becoming city editor, and when he moved on later to a paper in New York, he continued sending back a weekly column on boxing to *The Enquirer.* Many a city editor went on to bigger jobs, becoming managing editor.

One city editor who held the job but briefly late in his career was so respected throughout the state for his earlier work as Columbus correspondent that when he died, his colleagues on papers statewide established the James W. Faulkner Memorial Fund, "for the aid of worthy recruits to the newspaper profession."

Another, more recent city editor, Lee Evans, was not only a keen newsman but even better known for the way he taught and encouraged young journalists. He began as a reporter on the *Cincinnati Commercial Tribune* in 1909 and moved to *The Enquirer* in 1914 as City Hall reporter. He became city editor in 1933 when Charles Bocklet, city editor since 1926, resigned to become postmaster.

Evans' decade as city editor was marked by new emphasis on local news, which seldom appeared on page one before 1933. Evans fought tenaciously to get space for his staff, and was supported at every turn by managing editor Everett M. Boyd.

'THIS IS GOD. I SEE WHAT YOU'RE DOING...'

One of former city editor Jack Cronin's favorite stories was about Ken Doris, the man who preceded Cronin as city editor in the 1940s. It seems there was a dentist who had an office in the building directly across Vine Street from *The Enquirer* and one night, some *Enquirer* staffers looked over to see the dentist engaged in some very serious hanky-panky with a young woman. All hands gathered around and watched for a while, and then—as they watched— city editor Doris picked up a phone and dialed the dentist's office. When the interrupted dentist answered it, Doris intoned: "This is God. I see what you're doing, and I don't like it."

∞   ∞   ∞

On Feb. 24, 1975, an obituary appeared in *The Enquirer* reporting the death of Ken Doris, a memorable man at 617 Vine St. because of his amazing way with statistics and calculations and his uncanny memory for data.

"Kenneth Doris," it said, "a former *Enquirer* managing editor who was probably best known for his uncannily accurate predictions, died Sunday of leukemia at Christ Hospital. He was

Ken Doris served as city editor and managing editor of the paper.

80. Doris came to *The Enquirer* in 1917 and worked as a reporter, copy reader, city editor and night managing editor.

"He also was the newspaper's unofficial chart maker, because of his penchant for sorting percentages and figures. The predictions he made were based on mathematical laws and history, Doris said. When a flood was just beginning in Cincinnati in 1937, he correctly forecast it would become

the worst in local history. He forecast Cincinnati City Council election results to within 1%, and foretold stock market fluctuations.Once, the *New York Times* did a feature on his predictive sense, calling him a "prophet," and bringing him offers from national magazines and tabloids to predict the outcome of elections and movements of the stock market.

He turned them down.

Evans was so beloved by his staff that half a dozen of them named children after him. One reporter, frustrated because his child was a daughter, named her

Lee, anyway.

In 1943, when Evans became New York correspondent, *The Enquirer* threw an immense going-away party at a hotel, and

some years later, when he died in New York, his contemporaries set up a special scholarship fund in his name. The idea arose at lunch sessions Cincinnati journalists took to having at the Cricket Tavern which came to be called the "Lee Evans Roundtable." The regulars met for lunch weekly for many years, long after they stopped giving individual prizes and turned the scholarship funds over to the University of Cincinnati.

When Evans went to New York in 1943, Ken Doris succeeded him. Jack Cronin, who followed Doris, was city editor in the 1950s when the employees bought the paper from the McLean estate, and was fired in 1955 as a key supporter of a newsroom rebellion against top management.

In the 1960s, reporters began clamoring to write everything "in depth." *The Enquirer's* top brass, however, believed in high "story count" and preferred many short stories to a few long ones. City editor Bob Harrod, feeling the pressure, decreed in a memo one day that no story could run longer than 40 typed lines without his written OK. Well, as any newspaper person knows, it just doesn't always work that way. A day or so later, a reporter was churning out a hot-breaking piece on deadline and wasn't quite finished when he came to the end of 40 lines. But Harrod was in the composing room or something, unavailable to authorize more, so the reporter halted in mid-sentence and filed his copy in the city desk basket, then went down to the Cricket for a schnapps. He knew better than to go home, however, and sure enough, a few minutes later, came the call authorizing another few lines. Happily for reporters, editors and readers, the policy soon was allowed to die quietly.

By the time Jim Myers succeeded Harrod, the title had changed to "metro editor," in line with the fashion among newspapers in the 1960s. Myers had been a country correspondent for a Dayton paper and then *The Enquirer's* state editor. He was a paraplegic, the result of an accident as a youth, and not until his very last years did he swap crutches for a wheelchair. Each day, he'd drive to Cincinnati from his home in Lebanon, Ohio, and sometimes spend equally long waiting for a parking spot near *The Enquirer's* entrance. He'd circle the block over and over until a parking meter opened up, then dash for it. One of the regular copy clerks'

The city room in 1941 overlooked Vine Street. Reading clockwise, are: H. L. Brown , Jr., (pencil on paper), Joseph Garretson , Jr., Fred E. Morgener, Bentley Stegner, Glenn Thompson, Philip E. Lawwill, Paul R. Lugannani, James T. Golden, Jr., and Andrew G. Foppe.

chores was to keep track of the time, get change from Myers, and go down to the street to feed the meter.

No one — especially Jim Myers — thought of him as particularly heroic. What his colleagues said of him was mainly that he was a good newsman who happened to favor news from the rural areas where his career had started.

Myers' car broke down one rainy night in the 1970s on the expressway toward Lebanon. He managed to get his wheelchair out and propel himself through the storm to an exit but wore himself down and wound up in the hospital, exhausted from the ordeal and from the illness no one at the paper knew he had. Everything just gave out at the same time. The funeral at his church in Lebanon looked like a newspaper convention.

The editors who actually edit copy are the ones reporters fear most. Reporting and writing are very personal work, and egos — often very sensitive egos — are on the line. Reporters pride themselves on fine use of language, and many say they write for their editors more than for the public.

No newspaper worthy of the name is without its competent, professional wordsmith-arbiter, and often at *The Enquirer*, this role has fallen to an assistant city editor. The assistant city editor is not unlike

Clockwise, from top, are former **Enquirer** *city editors Lee Evans, Bob Harrod and Jim Myers.*

the career veteran non-com or grizzled Navy chief. He's seen it all, been through combat, is cool under fire, and knows how everything works. One of *The Enquirer's* first such editors was James Gardner. "Arriving punctually" each mid-day in the 1890s, one colleague described him: "Jim laid out his working tools meticulously, donned his long, black sleevelets and churned his paste pot. All this done to his satisfaction, he lighted his pipe, tackled the great stack of accumulated local copy and began making English of it, 'heading it up' and noting on its various units guide lines for the benefit of the composing room.

"Gardner was a hard worker and a stern critic. A growl, not unmixed with profanity, a pencil slash, and the room knew that some pretty bad stuff was getting what it deserved. Choice horrible examples were read aloud, with no concealment of authorship. . . ."

It was ever thus, and the principal differences between Gardner and his modern successors are the pastepot and sleevelets.

THE RACE TO YOUR DOORSTEP

In the composing-room, eighty compositors are busy getting the matter into type and one hundred and thirty of Edison's incandescent electric lamps furnish the light. At four o'clock three huge presses are at work printing and folding twenty thousand per hour each. As fast as the papers are struck off, an elevator takes them up to the mailing-room, where fifteen clerks are kept busy wrapping them in time for the early trains that take the papers to outside towns. . . ."

So wrote an upstate Ohio subscriber in 1884 after spending a June evening at *The Enquirer*. He probably considered *The Enquirer* his local paper. By those days, *The Enquirer* had been distributed by rail for years throughout Ohio, Indiana and Kentucky. It was so strong in the region that those states, and West Virginia, were called "The Enquirer Confederacy" for years.

Deliveries by rail to Louisville, for instance, began in the 1860s. "The Enquirer in Louisville" read the announcement under the masthead on page four. "The ENQUIRER will be delivered promptly to subscribers in Louisville upon the arrival of the morning train. J. A. Melville, 170 Fourth Street, is the agent and will receive orders. It can be had, too, for sale at W. Scott Glower's bookstore."

But rival papers could use ordinary trains, too. And ordinary trains ran at times convenient to travelers, who seldom wanted to be traveling when *The Enquirer* was coming off the presses at 3 a.m.

So, in November, 1884, when competition among Cincinnati's morning papers was keenest, the aggressive John R. McLean invented the "Enquirer Train." The first Enquirer Special ran up the Cincinnati, Hamilton and Dayton line to Toledo, to carry papers to towns along the way and (via connections at Toledo) to Chicago, Cleveland and New York. It was the start of an institution that lasted for 40 years. The train left Cincinnati at 4:18 a.m., stopped twice for water but otherwise merely slowed to unload bundled papers, and reached Toledo in time for a late breakfast minutes after nine.

These were fast trains. A few days later, the inaugural Enquirer Train to Louisville covered the 127 miles in two hours, 28 minutes, the fastest anyone had ever traveled between the two cities. Each time a new route was added, *The Enquirer* trumpeted speed records. The fastest of all was the one put in service to Columbus on August 25, 1886. Former *Enquirer* librarian Harry Pence wrote of the inaugural run in a Sunday feature years later:

"A line of wagons waited outside of *The Enquirer* office. With marvelous speed they took on their loads and rattled away. The distance to the Little Miami Railroad station (at Pearl and Eggleston) was covered at the best pace horses could make.

Continued on next page

"A tall-stack locomotive, coupled to two light baggage cars, was waiting in the yards. The papers were thrown into the cars. The conductor swung his lantern, giving the 'high-ball' to the engineer. . .and The Enquirer Special was on its way at 2:54 o'clock in the morning. Two hours and 11 minutes later the train arrived in Columbus, Ohio. It had covered a distance of 119.7 miles in 2 hours and 8 minutes plus a three-minute stop at Xenia where the locomotive took on water.

"The locomotive that pulled The Enquirer Special was of the old type with high smokestack, small firebox, four driving wheels. . . The cars were tiny wooden affairs. . . probably 40 feet. . .

There also was the chance any train had to take in the days before electric block systems. The only signals received by Engineer Pat Golden as he drove his engine into the dark-

ness were from lanterns in the hands of station masters. Despite the dangers, the train carried a staff writer and staff artist of *The Enquirer* and a group of politicians. Arrangements had been made in advance to try to set a record. The

best previous time between Cincinnati and Columbus had been 2 hours and 20 minutes, and it had been accepted as. . . the extreme limit of speed for a steam locomotive.

"Golden was chosen as being among the most fearless engineers and for his long experience. Kelly was recognized as a fireman who had made his work a science. Conductor Runyan and the brakemen were selected because of their thorough

knowledge of the road. . . .The train reached Pendleton in six minutes. The [Miamiville] bridge over the Miami River, 17 miles from the Cincinnati station, was crossed at 3:12

o'clock. At 3:23 the train streaked through Loveland. Foster's Crossing, 27 miles from the start, was reached at 3:28. . . and Morrow was passed nine minutes later. Between Corwin and Xenia, 14 miles, the maximum of 83 miles an hour was reached. . . ."

Circulation work isn't quite that breathtaking nowadays, but the logistics are every bit as tricky, even with urban expressways and interstates. The Enquirer Trains, some of which later also carried passengers, remained in service until the government nationalized the railroads during World War I. In just a few years, after the war's end, it was clear that the highway was the way of the future.

The Enquirer's circulation at birth, on April 10, 1841, was about 1,000 daily, 2,200 including subscribers to the weekly and triweekly versions. The rival *Gazette* was at least twice that size, by most accounts, but even

In 1902, P.M. Wolfe and his crew of newsboys delivered and sold **The Enquirer** *and the* **Commercial. The Enquirer** *was the dominant paper.*

that wasn't as large as such papers as the abolition-minded *Philanthropist* and the *Western Temperance Journal,* which circulated 6,000.

In the beginning, the paper was sold either at the printing office in Cincinnati or through agents in such outlying places as Columbia (the Lunken Airport Playfield area today) and Covington. Many subscribers received it at home by mail, on the day of publication.

The Enquirer was an afternoon paper at first, when most readers were within a few miles of Fifth Street. But things were changing, with growing numbers of readers in outlying Ohio, Kentucky and Indiana. In 1843, the publishers, John and Charles Brough, discovered that in order to get the paper into the day's mail in time to reach readers on the day of publication, they had to print it earlier in the day. *The Enquirer* became the morning paper it remains today.

The Civil War boosted circulation, as readers thirsted daily for news from the fronts.

The Enquirer took unpopular, anti-war positions and, after the war, circulation grew slowly, but until the 1870s the *Enquirer* always lagged behind its competitors, especially the *Commercial.*

The turning point came in 1872. The long-time publisher of the *Commercial,* Murat Halstead, insulted John R. McLean. He retaliated with sensational reporting, gossip and scandal, cuts in price, contests and promotions and within 10 years had forced the *Commercial* to merge with another paper and eliminated it as a serious rival. *The Enquirer* finally overtook the wounded *Commercial* around 1880, and by 1900 was printing

Lt. Al Williams would fly editions of The Enquirer from Washington D.C., to President Calvin Coolidge, when the president was away from the White House.

40,000 copies a day.

While trains carried the paper to distant points, and the mail still served some, most papers in Cincinnati had come to be delivered to the neighborhoods and homes by independent carriers who would queue their wagons before dawn in Battle Alley behind *The Enquirer* to await their papers.

One such hardy veteran, known to everyone at the paper, was August Rahn. From 1884 until 1909 he served almost the entire East End, from downtown to Red Bank, where Fairfax is now). When he died, in the 1920s, his obituary recorded how he had traveled

with his horse the entire length of Eastern Avenue, out and back, every day for 25 years.

World War I provided another boost, even though it killed off the Enquirer Trains, and by 1926, circulation was 63,000 daily, nearly 170,000 Sunday. These numbers grew rapidly through the Roaring '20s and peaked at 90,000 daily, 188,000 Sunday, just after the Crash of '29. Then the numbers fell. In the worst days of the Depression daily circulation was down to 86,000, Sunday to 177,000. Late in the 1930s, however, the paper had made up the lost ground, driven by publisher W. F. Wiley's tireless attention to circulation.

Realizing that many Cincinnatians hardly had five pennies to rub together, he cut the price from five cents — where it had been for 40-odd years — to three. And he hired a delivery boy who would spend the next 46 years building circulation as he rose to vice president and circulation director. A. Robert Oehler was nationally recognized as a newspaper leader in increasing circulation when he retired in 1976.

Most papers have reached

readers' homes via independent carriers for more than 100 years, but until the 1950s thousands of copies were also hawked every day on downtown sidewalks by *The Enquirer's* corps of newsboys (many of whom were far beyond boyhood). Their cries of "Getcha EN-kwi-yuh PA-puh!" when the bulldog edition (an early evening edition discontinued in 1973) hit the streets was as familiar a Cincinnati street sound as the grinding of streetcar wheels.

Wiley took good care of the newsboys. In 1934, the paper's 65 streetcorner "boys" were the paper's guests in a special, reserved section at the Reds' Opening Game. Once, they were treated to dinner at the Hotel Gibson and a double feature at the Palace. In 1939, *The Enquirer* took 115 newsboys to the Indianapolis 500. The next year, they were feted at a dinner and musical revue at the Gibson Hotel's Roof Garden.

Recognizing that home delivery was the backbone of circulation, Wiley courted the independent carriers as assiduously as any manufacturer ever wooed its key dealers. In 1939 he entertained 200 at a party in *The Enquirer* auditorium. The paper hired movie stars to entertain at carriers' luncheons. In 1939, top carriers had an all-day outing at Coney Island, including a boat trip on the *Island Queen,* clubhouse dinner and evening fireworks.

It wasn't all hugs and kisses. In the midst of the Depression, in June, 1935, one struggling carrier was having chronic trouble paying for his papers and *The Enquirer* dismissed him. The next day, instead of papers, many other carriers delivered copies of a letter demanding his reinstatement. The day after that *The Enquirer*

responded with a strong message of its own on page one.

"If your *Enquirer* was not delivered Friday morning, it was the fault of the carrier you have been patronizing. He failed and disappointed you and broke his personal contract with us. His purpose in doing so was to compel *The Enquirer* to reinstate a carrier who was discharged for insubordination and repeated and prolonged failure to pay his bills for his newspapers. . . .

"**Y**ou have probably received a circular letter from these malcontents saying it is the purpose of *The Enquirer* to displace 150 men carriers with 500 or 600 boys. This statement is without a grain of truth. . . ."

The government told the carriers' union the strike was illegal, cooler heads prevailed, and the brief strike was but a wart on the

nose of progress. In two years, daily circulation surged 30,000, topped 100,000 for the first time, and reached 116,000 in 1937. Before dawn on Dec. 7, 1941, while the Japanese prepared to attack Pearl Harbor, more than 200,000 Sunday *Enquirers* came off the presses, and before the war was over, the daily *Enquirer* had 130,000 readers. Postwar, sales really leaped ahead. The daily was at 140,000 by 1946, despite a price hike back to a nickel a copy, and passed 200,000 in the early 1950s.

The Sunday *Enquirer* peaked at 301,000 in 1970, and moved above that mark in 1985 to stay. Today it is 346,620. And in March, 1991, daily circulation reached 201,006 for the first time since the recession of 1961-62.

These 1932 **Enquirer** *delivery trucks advertise six days of the paper for 15 cents. A single copy cost three cents.*

CALAMITY CREATES NEWS NEED

Newspaper people have always responded to calamity, crisis and disaster, knowing that at such times the public is most in need of hard, timely information.

For instance, after the infamous 1884 riot which left 45 dead and the Hamilton County Courthouse a charred ruin, the demand for news knew no limit. The presses rolled until the paper ran out, and for years afterward, everyone at *The Enquirer* knew the story of Harry Shafer.

His older brother Ollie, a young reporter, had died, and Harry had found a job in the mail room. In mid-morning on the day after the fire, publisher John R. McLean arrived at the paper to find Shafer still bundling papers for delivery. He was half asleep, his fingers bleeding where they'd been cut by baling twine. McLean gave him $10 and sent him home with instructions to report to McLean in person Monday. On Monday, McLean made him a reporter. He covered police news and was a fine newsman, and eventually became city editor.

Newspaper lore is heavy with such stories, but the cub reporter doesn't always go on to great things. An *Enquirer* cub named George F. Hayman rushed to cover a story on Jan. 10, 1911, and never came back. He heard the fire alarms and dashed to the scene, the Chamber of Commerce Building at Fourth and Vine. Just as he ran into the building, the upper floors collapsed in a tangled heap into the basement, carrying Hayman to his death with five other victims.

In an 1884 article an *Enquirer* editor called the paper's 14 reporters "a nervy set. . . right to the front where bullets fly or fires burn they go, into the lowest slums where man's life is worth next to nothing, thinking of but one thing, and that is an item."

An item. It's what they used to call a news story.

The biggest item in *The Enquirer's* 150-year history was the 1937 flood. Quite an item it was: An entire region of the country was under water and millions of lives were disrupted for weeks as the Ohio River rose far beyond any historic level. Nearly 150 died, 50,000 were homeless, and property losses were too vast to count. It was international news with Cincinnati at center stage. When it crested, the river had risen nearly to Fourth Street and ran 80 feet deep under the Suspension Bridge — the only span open on the Ohio. The city lost its waterworks, electricity was rationed, streetcar service was halted.

For two weeks, the river dominated all *The Enquirer's* news pages. Headlines were bigger and blacker than ever before in peacetime. The river level was reported daily on the front page, as measured hourly to the

Continued on next page

hundredth of a foot. News from the rest of the world was summarized in a column on page two as *The Enquirer* spent all its energy telling readers what was happening at home, where to go for drinking water, how to get typhoid shots, and what the forecasters thought tomorrow would bring. The day after burning fuel from a ruptured storage tank swirled through flooded buildings in the Millcreek Valley, *The Enquirer* ran an entire page of night time news photos of the fire. It was unprecedented coverage. Like all disasters, it finally ended and passed into history, leaving behind an entire generation of Cincinnatians who still speak of events in their lives as having happened before or after The Flood.

Before The Flood, the words "The Flood" meant 1913, which was another pretty good item. Unbelievably heavy rains —10 inches at Hamilton, Ohio, seven at Columbus, 11 at Bellefontaine —triggered horrifying flash floods in an era with neither flood-control dams nor modern warning procedures. Fast-rising streams caught whole towns off guard. The Great Miami rose 15

The front page of Jan. 26, 1937, announced **The Enquirer's** *intention of providing free drinking water to citizens.*

feet overnight at Hamilton, the Olentangy 20 feet at Columbus. Virtual walls of water uprooted trees, swept away homes, washed out bridges. Hundreds died in Dayton, which also suffered a terrible fire. Officially, the toll in the Ohio Valley was 356, but relief and rescue workers knew it was much higher—probably in the thousands.

The editor who led *The Enquirer's* team in Dayton, Ohio, during the flood of 1913 was no stranger to disaster. He'd gotten his start because of one. He was Harry Shafer, the mailroom boy who had become city editor. The flood was his last big story

The Enquirer had begun printing news photos only a few years before, and the '13 flood was the first local story that warranted multiple photos on the front page. It was hardly sophisticated coverage by today's standards, but quite an advance over the way the paper illustrated the Great Flood of 1884. That year *The Enquirer* sent "news artists" out to depict the scene. One panoramic drawing of flood-stricken Law-renceburg, Ind., ran seven col-

Knowlton's Corner was innundated during the 1937 flood.
The front page is from 1913 as is the rescue on Second Street.

umns wide on the front page of February 17, 1884.

The Flood of '84 cut rail lines into town, posing problems for *The Enquirer*, which was distributed far and wide by train. On Wednesday, Feb. 13, headlines reported "Another Night of Rain and The Waters Still Advance,"and on page one with all the other news, *The Enquirer* indulged in a little self-promotion. Don't worry, it said, a little flood won't stop us. "A skiff loaded with *Enquirers* went to Lawrenceburg and Aurora, where the Ohio and Mississippi Railroad was sup-

plied with papers for St. Louis and the West."

People in river towns take a perverse sort of proprietary interest in their floods, which is what has always made them a big item. But there have been many other types of big disaster stories to cover in *The Enquirer's* 150 years.

None posed more difficulty for journalists than the rioting in Cincinnati's black neighborhoods in June, 1967, and April, 1968. Reporters accustomed to the familiar hierarchies

of government and commerce suddenly found themselves dealing with new "leaders," all purporting to speak for the angry citizens who had begun burning and looting their own communities. These were communities where reporters had few contacts and little experience at a time when ugly and frightening rumors were rampant and hard facts were treasures. It put tremendous burdens on what few black reporters there were at the time, such as *The Enquirer's* Allen

Howard. In 1968, the former aide to Sen. Robert Taft Jr. — used to covering orderly government processes — suddenly found himself in a virtual war zone trying to make definitive sense out of frightening ambiguity. *The Enquirer,* like most papers, covered the violence first, then groped for a long time to sift the genuine from the phony, the reliable from the spurious, and get a handle on the causes and issues. Reporters found themselves floundering in a sea of organizations they'd never dealt with, run by people they didn't know — SNCC,

The 1974 tornadoes hammered Sayler Park and Mack. Top, the intersection of Goodrich and Sayler Avenues in Sayler Park. Below, a station wagon in the 6500 block of Bridgetown Road.

CORE, NAACP, SCLC, ACC, Welfare Rights Group.

It was much the same with the campus disorder of the Vietnam era, and a lasting effect of those tumultuous years of ghetto riots and anti-war protests was an alienation of journalists and civil authorities. Long virtual teammates, they soon were the adversaries they remain today. The riots, like war, were frightening aberrations — politics run

THE CINCINNATI ENQUIRER

62 KILLED IN FIERY CRASH OF JET AT BOONE AIRPORT

79 Aboard On TWA Flight

Firemen Fight Smoldering Remains Of Crashed Airliner

Burning, He Carries Child

Bidding To Be No. 1? Lindsay Snaps 'No'

THE CINCINNATI ENQUIRER

JET LINER CRASHES IN BOONE; 58 PERSONS DEAD, 4 SURVIVE

Craft Hits Hillside In Storm, Explodes

Tail Assembly Of Crashed AA Astrojet

Eyewitness To Disaster

'Plane—It's Going To Crash!'

No Time For Grief

Baby Blanket...Coffee Pot... Pillows...Tell Of Life That Was

Top Of The News

amok. But in direct effect — death, injury, property damage— they were small potatoes compared to the Courthouse Riot of 1884, and even less next to such aberrations of nature as the tornadoes of April 3, 1974, which crammed incredible destruction into just a few minutes' time all across the Midwest and South.

The twisters hit Greater Cincinnati in late afternoon, a time when morning papers are fully

Above, the Nov. 22, 1967, TWA crash; below an Air Canada DC-9 caught fire June 2, 1983, and 23 persons died; lower right, the Nov. 8, 1965, American Airlines crash.

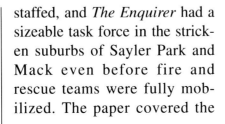

staffed, and *The Enquirer* had a sizeable task force in the stricken suburbs of Sayler Park and Mack even before fire and rescue teams were fully mobilized. The paper covered the

damage in Cincinnati throughly, but took an entire day to catch up with the even greater damage just up the road in Xenia.

The tornadoes were not unlike the air crashes of 1965 and

1967— so swift and unexpected that all the damage was done before the first reporter was even dispatched. The difference was that air crashes are preventable, and leave behind years of stories about aviation safety issues. The air crashes also kill far more people. The first, on November 8, 1965, was an American Airlines jet that plowed into a hillside approaching Greater Cincinnati Airport on a squally

Rescue workers search for survivors as Beverly Hills burns.

evening. The crash killed 58 of the 62 aboard. Reporters and photographers tried to maintain their composure as authorities sifted the smoking wreckage for body parts just two years later when a TWA jet hit the same hillside about the same time on Nov. 22.

In terms of the sheer body count, neither of those disasters compares with the calamity at Northern Kentucky's Beverly Hills night club on May 28, 1977, that left 165 dead. The fire started about 9 p.m. on a Saturday, and the newsroom's first inkling of a big story came minutes later. It was a bad time for big news because the city desk had only its customarily small weekend team at work. *The Enquirer*, its defenses down, had but an hour or two to cover a truly huge story with a skeleton crew. Neena Pellegrini, today's ex-

ecutive news editor, was the reporter who wrote the lead story. She was so new to the paper that the copy desk misspelled her byline.

Metro editor Kerry Klumpe, then a reporter, was on a date, and when he heard of the fire, he rushed to *The Enquirer*. His formally dressed date spent the evening pressed into service at a newsroom desk, answering the phones.

By the next day, *The Enquirer* had recovered its balance, presented stark aerial photos, explanatory drawings, grisly chronologies, lists of victims, and heart-rending yarns of valor and pathos. It took four inches of space just to list the names of the 42 reporters, photographers, editors, columnists, artists and free-lance contributors who worked on the story.

PI LINES BRIGHTENS WAR YEARS

Newspaper people like nothing more than having a lot of news to handle, so 1941 must have been a grand year. At year's end, *The Enquirer* ran its annual editors' list of the year's top 10 stories, and the news that Germany had invaded and conquered Greece was in 10th place. It was a very newsworthy year.

The bombing of Pearl Harbor topped the list, of course. The rest of 1941's top 10: 2) Hitler invades Russia; 3) Congress approves Lend Lease of weapons to England and Russia; 4) Germany's Rudolph Hess makes mysterious flight to Scotland; 5) Churchill and Roosevelt meet in mid-Atlantic, proclaim Atlantic Charter; 6) Mineworkers' leader John L. Lewis calls strike in defiance of government; Army takes over aircraft plants; 7) Nazis attack American ships; 8) Germans sink British battleship *Hood*, British sink Nazi battleship *Bismarck*; 9) Charles Lindbergh opposes war with Germany; 10) Germany conquers Greece.

Before World War II ended in 1945, 179 *Enquirer* employees had served in the armed forces and four had died. The first to die was Bill Donaldson, a Covington police reporter who, spurning a sportswriter's suggestion that he join the Navy, joined the Marines because, he said, he wanted to "be where the action is." He was killed in the invasion of Tarawa in the Pacific in 1943.

Louis Weiskittel, an apprentice pressman and son of pressroom foreman Sidney Weiskittel, joined the Marines in 1942 and was an aviation machinist on a Navy plane that crashed in the Caribbean in February, 1944. Andrew G. Foppe, assistant business editor when he was drafted in 1943, was killed in infantry action in Germany in October, 1944. And Hugh Dennedy, an apprentice printer and former copy boy, joined the Marines a year after Pearl Harbor, came through two years of action in the Pacific, including the invasion of Saipan, without a scratch, only to be killed during the invasion of Iwo Jima in March, 1945, five months before war's end.

Many from the paper were decorated during the war, including Ran Cochran, 10 years an *Enquirer* photographer before the war, and chief photographer for years afterward. He won two bronze stars as a combat photographer during the invasion of Leyte in the Philippines in 1944. Reporter Charles Vandergrift also won a bronze star in the Pacific, as a combat correspondent on Saipan and Tinian. One of the war's more interesting assignments fell to music critic Frederick Yeiser, an accomplished linguist, who served in the American military mission with Marshal Tito's anti-Nazi partisans in Yugoslavia. After the

Continued on next page

> "With each week, as the dark days of the war were being recorded, Pi Lines *became more important. Many members of the* Enquirer *organization requested a copy....*"

war, he went to Vienna and married the Austrian countess with whom he had fallen in love as a music student in 1931.

Not long after *Enquirer* people began going off to war, the International Typographical Union's chapel in *The Enquirer's* composing room named a Military Affairs Committee to stay in touch with them. At first, the plan was simply to be sure they got mail with news from Vine Street. But these were printers with access to state-of-the-art printing equipment, and they soon were publishing a newsletter.

It was named *Pi Lines*. A "pi line" is the printers' term for a line of nonsense type used to fill space, usually as a reminder to compositors that a revision was coming and room had to be saved for it. (The usual "pi line" consisted of the letters ETAOIN SHRDLU, which happen to be the 12 letters produced by running a finger down the two end rows on a Linotype keyboard.)

The name set a perfect tone, and a nearly endless succession of volunteer guest editors and typesetters saw to it that *Pi Lines* brought news of home to

This plaque commemorating employees who died in WW II hangs in the lobby of 617 Vine. The victory edition of Pi Lines *appeared Sept. 15, 1945.*

the paper's men and women in uniform — including all the latest jokes and *Enquirer* gossip, and news about who was serving where.

Pi Lines appeared monthly for three years. The printers worked overtime without pay to write it and set type, and dug into their own pockets to pay mailing costs. Two jokesters named Shober and Swope were among the first editors and contributed wit all through the war, often in ads for "Swope and Shober Jokes, Inc." Their ad in the final issue of *Pi Lines*, in September, 1945, read "Going out of business!"

Printer Clifford Druck produced a monthly review of Cincinnati news and sports items, condensing each to a line or two to conserve paper. He reported on everything from streetcar collisions and deaths of prominent Cincinnatians, to the reappearance of new cars in dealer showrooms at war's end. The final issue appeared in the closing weeks of the 1945 baseball season. The Reds, Druck reported, were "firmly entrenched in seventh place." During the war, *Pi Lines* reported receiving a letter from ad salesman Tom Hamilton in the South Pacific which had nothing on the envelope but a clipping of a drawing by the paper's sports cartoonist, Harold Russell in which Russell's favorite character, Danny Dumm, was saying "Make my next stop Cincinnati." He knew that Postmaster Charles Bocklet had once been city editor, and would see to it that the mail went through.

Pi Lines specialized in little items like these: "Tom Hennessey sent a package from Naziland containing a cap, armbands, money, postage stamps. . .and other things to Frank Meichert. . . ."

"The sons of M. F. McDonough, who are in the Pacific, met on Iwo Jima several weeks ago. Francis, who has seen action on Guadalcanal, has been overseas 42 months. His younger brother, Larry. . . was a gunner on a B-29. . .[and] he had a 45-minute layover on Iwo Jima . . . ."

"Bill Mauntel takes a dayside situation, starting Monday, Sept. 17. The change was brought about by the moving of Harold Seilacher, apprentice in the ad room, to the night side. . . Mauntel will be able to take up bowling four nights a week now. . . ."

In its final issue, the editors printed an honor roll of all *Enquirer* employees who had served and published valedictories from several guest editors. In his valedictory, printer Lee Daniel told the whole story:

"As I remember the first edition, the total circulation was only 15. One extra was posted on the bulletin board. . . .Bob Allison did most of the work. . ." With each week, as the dark days of the war were being recorded, *Pi Lines* became more important. Many members of the entire *Enquirer* organization requested a copy just to see

'THE VOICE' GOES TO KOREA

During the Korean War, in the 1950s, the in-house publication that brought news of *The Enquirer* to employees in uniform (and vice versa) was the *The Voice of the Enquirer*. In 1951, an issue carried a letter from Tim Meehan, who finished his career in the 1980s as a business writer and copy editor. Meehan reviewed food on his troopship (" . .the worst I'd ever eaten.

. . .") and reported that he was a supply-clerk at a depot for maintaining flame-throwers.

Another issue reported that young Pfc. Albert Schottelkotte had just gotten married and was an instructor at Ft. Knox, Ky. Schottelkotte went on to become a columnist ("Talk of the Town"), then news anchor at WCPO-TV and news vice president for all Scripps-Howard TV stations.

what the printers were saying. . . The committee worked for and with everybody. Even Pete Grimm stayed after 'time' setting type. . . .

"Every day the economic conditions were beginning to pinch, and *Pi Lines* struggled onward."

First, he said, "the stereo-typers and pressmen sent copies to all their friends in the service." Then managing editor Everett M. Boyd endorsed the project. Next thing the boys in the composing room knew, their project was being mentioned by the likes of nationally syndicated columnist and radio commentator, Walter Winchell. A best-selling author sub-

scribed, saying he planned to include *Pi Lines* in his book on home-front activities during the war.

By war's end, *Pi Lines* was circulating in Europe and the Pacific, in England and Ireland, in North Africa and India, and Alaska, Australia and Singapore.

In closing his postwar vale-dictory, Daniel wrote: "Now all this has come to an end, and I, for one, have a sort of empty feeling about its ending, and yet a satisfaction in knowing that *Pi Lines* is needed NO MORE."

Pi Lines wasn't the only internal communication eng-endered by the war. The *Little Enquirer,* an in-house employee

publication which had appeared and disappeared often in the prior 20 years, reappeared.

It told of *Enquirer* people in uniform and of coping with wartime censorship and short-ages. One in 1943 reported:

"ORCHIDS—Lit-erally, we seldom get them. But W.F. W. (William F. Wi-ley, the publisher) voluntarily wrote this Memo recently: 'That was a fine ex-clusive on the new radio station. I am one of the old-fash-ioned newspaper fellows that glories in scoops. I think they have a very decided effect on the reading public, provided they come with some degree of frequency. Hope we'll be able to get more.'

"Well, that story was about the new 750-kilowatt station for WLW. Some 10 staffers, and several others outside this office, were responsible. . .after a month's effort, despite necess-ary censorship regulations. Although credit is due to everyone I am citing only two names, JACK CRONIN who came in with the first tip, and CHARLIE DEAN who cracked the Office of War Information no sooner than he took over in the Wasington Bureau.

"C'EST LA GUERRE—Add war-wrought staff changes since May 1: Assistant society editor Bibbie Chatfield has gone to New York for preliminary training for overseas service with the American Red Cross. Assistant financial editor Andy Foppe is an infantry private at Camp Shelby, Miss. Also a private is copy boy-reporter Henry Hauenstein.

"STYLE BOOK—Something as little used as Webster! But it will be used in the future, if only we agree. . .that it is Adolf (not Adolph) Hitler. . . .

"MISCELLANY— Certain newspapers haven't conserved 10% on newsprint or 50% on zinc. . .WE HAVE. . . .But don't let down. . . .Continue to trim on all stories and zinc. . .E.B. Radcliffe reviewed the new Broadway shows, after attending a war conference of the amusement industry.

"BREVITY—A survey by Everett M. Boyd, managing editor. . .shows some rather interesting data about the trend

REPRESENTING ALL DEPARTMENTS OF THE CINCINNATI ENQUIRER.

Akin, Joseph	Ford, William	Marshall, Richard	Sanders, William D.
Angi, Margaret	Forest, Edward	Mason, Wilmer	Sauer, Frank
Ashton, Raymond	Franke, Glen	Massari, Pete	Schaber, W.
Auskamp, Vincent	Fuchs, Ralph	McCarren, Wilbur	Schaefer, Albert
Bacon, Emery	Gardner, William L.	McEwen, S. G.	Schatz, Frank
Becker, Don	Garretson, J. Jr.	McLay, Lloyd	Schmarr, W. F., Jr.
Beinecke, Virginia	Gilligan, Andy	McNary, Samuel	Schmidt, Leo
Bell, William	Golden, James Jr.	McMillan, Allen	Schneider, Joseph
Berghger, Robert	Gormley, Thomas	McGee, Elwood	Sennett, Jack
Biggerstaff, Howard	Goshorn, A.	Meehan, Charles	Shelton, Claude
Bitzer, Robert	Grannen, Walter Jr.	Metzger, Halpin Jr.	Shook, Verrell
Bizzari, Mike	Grannen, William	Mitchusson, Fred	Snyder, Orville
Bohne, Robert	Gray, Thomas	Moorman, Robert J.	Spence, C.
Britt, Charles	Griffith, Vernon	Morgener Fred	Spinks, Charles
Brown, Arnold E.	Gross, Philip Jr.	Murray, James	Starkey, William H.
Brown, Harry	Grossman, Earl	Neace, Samuel	Stigers, Robert E.
Brown, H. L. Jr.	Hagedorn, Jack	Nelson, George	Stone, Robert
Brune, Rey	Hamilton, Thomas	Norris, Larry	Sturm, Donald
Butler, Neal	Hand, Edward	Norris, Richard	Thoman, Robert
Byrne, Robert	Harp, Arnold	Ochs, Charles	Thomas, Edward
Campbell, Maurice	Hauenstein, H.	Ormand, John	Thomas, Robert
Campbell, Thomas	Healy, James	O'Regan, John	Thompson, Glenn
Carr, George	Heaton, Highland	O'Rourke, Clarence	Thompson, Wm.
Carraher, Charles	Heim, Arthur	Parsley, Earl	Toppin, Robert
Casey, Robert	Hennessey, Thomas	Patterson, Ralph	Uhl, John H.
Casey, Wm. J.	Hessler, William	Pflanzer, Gordon	Vandergrift, C.
Cassady, R.	Hills, James	Pirrung, Joey	Reypen, Ralph Van
Chadderton, T.	Hizer, Elbert	Potraffke, Edward	Varn, John C.
Chambers, Russell	Imsande, Lemoine	Powell, Harry	Vincent, Glen
Chatfield, Elizabeth	Imsande, Wilfred	Pratchard, G.	Volkering, B. J.
Chicoine, Martin	Johnson, A. W.	Price, Winston	Walker, Joseph F.
Clark, John R.	Jordan, Jerry	Pulsfort, Joseph	Walker, Robert
Clark, Kenneth	Jordan, Leonard	Purdy, J.	Walsh, William
Cochran, Randall	Juengling, L.	Questel, W. L.	Warnick, Charles
Collett, Lloyd	Jung, Fred	Ragland, Harvey E.	Weaver, Floyd
Cooper, Durrell	Keith, Harold	Rankin, Robert	Webster, Robert
Crawley, Calvin	Kennedy, William	Ransohoff, Jerry	Weiskittel, Louis ★
Davis, Thomas	Kirkpatrick, R.	Ratliff, James H., Jr.	Weiskittel, Ralph
Deem, David	Klein, John	Rebel, Joseph	Weiskittel, Raymond
Delaney, Walter	Kloecker, Geneva	Reed, Clifford	Weiskittel, Robert
Dennedy, Hugh Jr. ★	Kramer, Melvin	Reese, Robert	Weiskittel, Sid., Jr.
Dollriehs, Edward	Kuprion, Albert	Renk, William A.	Wellinger, Carl
Donaldson, Wm. C. ★	Landers, Jack	Reynolds, Mark	Wieland, Jacob
Dowd, John	Langelield, August	Rhodes, John P.	Wilcox, Edwin
Dudley, Jack	Lawwill, Philip ★	Rineair, E.	Wiley, William U.
Eggert, William	Logan, V. H.	Roan, Robert	Wilshire, Peter
Eten, Herman	Lueking, Richard	Rogers, J.	Wills, Earl
Etsinger, Charles	Lugannani, Paul	Rohan, Rodney	Wilz, Ed
Flaig, Ed	Macke, James	Rosing, Frank	Wisner, Robert
Flanigan, Robert	Madden, Robert	Ross, Wm. B.	Witte, Paul
Foppe, Andrew ★	Mairose, Lawrence	Rowland, Robert	Yeiser, Fred
Forbes, Richard	Maley, John	Ryan, Jack	Young, Wayne

★ Killed in Action or in Line of Duty

All Served in the Armed Forces of the United States in World War II.

toward shorter stories in *The Enquirer*. . . .In an 18-month period from December, 1941, to June, 1943, the average length of local stories dropped from seven inches to four inches. . . . With the white paper situation what it is already, and what it is going to be, we have to make 'em even shorter.

"SOLDIERS' PHOTOS— Relatively few soldiers' pictures will be used in Roto in the future. A page or part-page once a month is the plan. This is because each picture requires a separate plate and photo film is getting scarcer all the time."

FERGER: IMPERIOUS PUBLISHER

Roger Ferger, like so many publishers, was not a journalist. He was an advertising man. Born in Cincinnati on Jan. 5, 1894, he attended Whittier School, was graduated from Franklin Preparatory School in 1912 and attended the University of Pennsylvania. He worked briefly in his father, August's, hay and grain business in Cincinnati before a four-year fling with his own ad agency, Ferger & Silva, from 1916 to 1920. In 1920, when Ferger was 26, W. F. Wiley, the general manager of The Enquirer, asked him to take over the advertising department.

Ferger ran the ad department until 1933, when he left to become director of sales for the Pacific Railways Advertising Co. in San Francisco. In 1936 he became assistant to the publisher of the Milwaukee *Sentinel,* and in 1939 he went to Pittsburgh as business manager of the *Post-Gazette.*

Ferger returned to Cincinnati as assistant publisher and general manager in 1940, and four years later, when Wiley died, was named to succeed him as editor and publisher by the American Security and Trust Co. of Washington, trustee of John R. McLean's estate.

He presided over the paper through the tumultuous 1950s when *The Enquirer's* own employees raised $7.6 million and snatched the paper out from under the nose of a would-be buyer from across town, the Taft family's *Times-Star,* only to wind up owned by E.W. Scripps, publisher of the other afternoon paper, the *Post.*

Ferger retired in September, 1965, and Francis L. Dale succeeded him.

Ferger was popular in Cincinnati business and social circles; he was a member of a dozen corporate boards, member, officer and trustee of a dozen professional and civic organizations. He belonged to the right clubs — the Cincinnati Country Club and Queen City Club — and lived on posh Garden Place in suburban Hyde Park. And he ran the paper with a firm, Republican hand.

Roger Ferger was not universally popular among the employees, especially the independent-spirited editorial employees. He seldom visited the editorial offices or welcomed rank-and-file to his fifth-floor domain, and he was regarded by many as imperious and aloof.

Nonetheless, he remained as publisher even after the employees bought the paper from the McLean trust, and later when the E.W. Scripps Co. acquired it from the employees.

And *The Enquirer* prospered during his tenure. When he retired, he was able to boast: "In 1940, *The Enquirer* was a poor third in a three-newspaper town. Today it is one of the most successful papers in the country." (Statisticians may note here that even though a trend was forming, the daily

Continued on next page

Enquirer's circulation didn't surpass the afternoon *Post and Times-Star's* until well after Ferger retired.)

"The fifth floor, that was his tower," remembers one veteran editorial employee who started as a copy boy about the time Ferger became publisher. "You never went up to the fifth floor except when you were summoned, and very few ever were summoned.

"He only came off the fifth floor but once that I can remember," recalls the same veteran employee, "and that was when the employees bought the paper and he was probably worried about losing his job."

Elmer Wetenkamp, a staff artist and former art director of the newspaper, is nearing retirement after more than 45 years with *The Enquirer*. He recalls Ferger as "very aloof . . . He stayed upstairs and seldom came down, and he grew very rich by the standards we had in the 1950s."

Ferger ran *The Enquirer* for the trust that owned it, but he and his wife owned two papers of their own as well — society-news weeklies in Southampton, Long Island, and one in Florida

Roger Ferger

called the Palm Beach *Illustrated*. Wetenkamp remembers *Enquirer* artists being asked to design ad layouts for them "gratis, of course."

He also remembers well the one time he saw Ferger in the art department. A bronze bust of Ferger had been commissioned for display on the fifth floor.

"He came into the art room with the sculptor one day, because he had a photograph of the sculptor and himself with the bust in the middle. He wanted this sculptor to sign the photograph, and he had bought this little bottle of white ink and wanted to know whether artist Henry Eddy had a pen that this guy could use. Well, it worked, and he signed it. And everybody beamed and smiled."

Ferger was no populist Democrat. Moses Dawson would never have understood, although John Brough might have. In the years after World War II, when McCarthyism was running wild and the Cold War was just beginning, Ferger put *The Enquirer* squarely in the conservative camp. There it stayed for decades, earning the enmity of Democrats, Charterites and liberals, and providing a forum for conservative thought on such matters as fluoridation, communism, Barry Goldwater, Eugene McCarthy, George McGovern, test-ban treaties and Vietnam. When Roger Ferger retired in 1965, an *Enquirer* news story characterized him as "a Republican and a conservative."

EMPLOYEES BUY PAPER FOR $7.6 MILLION

The American Security and Trust Co. of Washington controlled *The Enquirer* for more than 35 years after John R. McLean's death in 1916.

It was the bank which made W. F. Wiley publisher, and the bank which authorized him to build the building at 617 Vine St. where *The Enquirer's* editorial, advertising and business offices are today.

Bank trust officers avoid risk and prefer comfy precepts about not putting too many eggs in any one basket. It made McLean's trustees nervous to have so much in a newspaper, especially since the *Washington Post* had all but failed in the Depression. In 1933 creditors had forced a receivership auction that had fetched only $825,000 — less than a sixth of what they'd been offered a few years before.

So, after World War II, they decided to unload *The Enquirer* as well, saying that it tied up too many of the trust's assets. There was a ready buyer: The Taft family's afternoon Cincinnati *Times-Star*.

Talks had gone on for some time before the city's third paper, the *Post*, broke the news in a three-paragraph story on Jan. 5, 1952, that a sale "might be completed this week" of *The Enquirer* to the *Times-Star* and that the price was $7.5 million.

Although *The Enquirer* hadn't been first to report the negotiations, publisher Roger Ferger had been in on them and favored the sale. In an unusual, signed editorial on Jan. 6, he confirmed the *Post's* story, said he was "confident" the sale would go through, and seemed to speak for *Times-Star* management in promising that *The Enquirer* would continue as an independent paper under *Times-Star* ownership.

By mid-February, the *Times-Star* had signed a contract to buy *The Enquirer* from the McLean estate for $7.5 million, and *The Enquirer* reported that while

*James H. Ratliff, Jr. and a copy of the check used to buy the paper. The calendar sheet is in **Enquirer** files*

Jubilant **Enquirer** *employees crowd onto the second-floor balcony to celebrate their purchase of the newspaper on June 6, 1952.*

the papers would "function independently," *The Enquirer* would eventually move to the Times-Star Building on Broadway.

The only thing remaining was approval of the deal by a federal judge in the District of Columbia, where the McLean estate was administered. Managements of both papers regarded the sale as a *fait accompli*.

But the working folks had their own ideas about that. *The Enquirer* and *Times-Star* were bitter rivals, and to rank-and-file

veterans on Vine Street, the idea of suddenly becoming employees of the Tafts over at 800 Broadway didn't sit very well. Many feared — probably accurately — that they'd lose their jobs, and the unctuous editorial pledges of independence for *The Enquirer* may have been intended as much for an audience of 1,000 on Vine Street as for the city at large.

As luck would have it, court approval wasn't swift. John R. McLean's heirs objected to the sale, saying the bank wasn't

getting enough for the paper. The ensuing wrangle gave *The Enquirer's* employees time. They seized the moment.

On March 20, *The Enquirer* reported formation of an employee committee to try to buy the paper. The man behind it was columnist James H. Ratliff, Jr., who persuaded his colleagues that the sale was not inevitable, after all, and that they could prevent it. All they had to do was come up with $7.5 million to match the *Times-Star's* offer. They had

one month to get organized, because a court hearing was scheduled April 28 in Washington on the *Times-Star* deal.

A groundswell of sentiment swept Vine Street. The employees consulted financial and management experts, formed subcommittees, and within two weeks they had pledges of $800,000 — a 10% down payment on what they hoped would be an $8 million offer.

On April 28, Ratliff appeared in court in Washington and submitted an offer on behalf of the employees. By this time, Ferger had sensed the strength of the employees' resolve and realized they might just succeed. Perhaps he didn't want to work for the Tafts after all. He accompanied Ratliff on the trip to Washington. With them, representing the employees' group, was a young attorney named Francis L. Dale, from *The Enquirer's* law firm, Frost & Jacobs. The court didn't accept the employees' offer but granted them time to seek more backing.

A cliffhanger then developed as an employee campaign was cobbled together, then snowballed. It took on all the enthusiasm and fervor of a crusade. Pledges poured in from employees, their families and friends, and other Cincinnatians who wanted to own a part of the hometown paper. Employees took out personal loans and second mortgages to buy stock. Many pledged their life's savings.

One of the first to step forward and subscribe was a former copy boy, Henry Berne. He had always wanted to be a newspaperman and later ran a weekly paper in Madeira. He had begun

Ohio industrialist Cyrus Eaton bought **The Enquirer** *and held it until the employees could raise the money they needed to buy it.*

as a copy boy at *The Enquirer* in the 1940s. What the editors who tipped him nickels and dimes for fetching their coffee didn't realize was that he was the grandson of Barney Kroger, founder of the supermarket chain, and he didn't really need the tips. His desire to learn newspapering was so earnest and sincere, however, that not once while he worked at *The Enquirer* did anyone have an inkling of that truth. Many

discovered who he was for the first time when he appeared at city editor Jack Cronin's desk with a check for $100,000 to buy stock.

"Freedom Is Everybody's Business" read the headline in an ad on May 11, 1952, asking readers to subscribe to buy stock. The ad appeared in both *The Enquirer* and the *Times-Star*, and the *Times-Star* ran an editorial the next day disputing some of *The Enquirer* employ-

ees' claims. The *Times-Star's* sports editor, Nixson Denton, wrote the first of many carping, sarcastic columns bitterly attacking *The Enquirer* and its management and belittling the employee campaign. He made fun of readers who pledged to buy stock and referred derisively to *The Enquirer* as "our esteemed morning contemporary."

Denton's was a minority view; *The Enquirer* story made national news and captured imaginations coast-to-coast. Its erstwhile sister paper, the *Washington Post*, editorialized its "warmest commendation" to *The Enquirer* employees for trying to "maintain the independence of a community institution which has been a force in Ohio life for more than a century."

While most employees worked around the clock to get pledges, others sought big-time financial backing. They got it from J. Harold Stuart, a Chicagoan who delighted in outmaneuvering the New York hotshots; his brokerage house, Halsey, Stuart & Co., agreed to underwrite $6 million in bonds.

On May 16, Ratliff, Ferger and

Dale met with the bank in Washington and offered $7.5 million for *The Enquirer*. It was no more than the *Times-Star's*

offer, but it would be all cash; the *Times-Star* had offered only $1.25 million cash and the rest over 12 years. The bank told the court the *Times-Star* bid was better; however, the judge, Bolitha Laws wasn't convinced. He gave the employees more time.

"Last Ditch Attempt Is Made To Raise Cash," read the *Enquirer* headline May 29. "New Delay Granted By Court" was the next day's headline. Time was plainly running out.

Then a miracle happened: Ohio financier Cyrus Eaton came to the rescue of the employees. Like Stuart, he was a maverick who had made himself unwelcome on Wall Street by befriending liberal mine-workers' union boss, John L. Lewis. Through one of his companies, Portsmouth Steel Corp., Eaton

agreed to buy *The Enquirer* and hold it for the employees until they could sell shares and buy it back. All he asked was a 3.33% commission — $250,000. He even agreed to let the employees committee name a majority of the new company's board of directors.

That clinched the deal. Ratliff, Ferger and Dale went back to Washington with a bid of $7.6 million in cash — $100,000 more than the *Times-Star's*. The bank accepted. The heirs agreed. And on June 6, 1952, Judge Laws approved the deal.

The Enquirer belonged to its employees.

Joyful pandemonium erupted on Vine Street. Ratliff was greeted on his return from Washington like a conquering hero. The employees swarmed onto the second-story balcony overlooking Vine Street for a panoramic group portrait that remains a classic in *The Enquirer's* family photo file.

"We are not greatly put out," said *Times-Star* editor Hulbert Taft, explaining that he doubted *The Enquirer* was worth the $7.5 million his paper had

offered in the first place.

By Labor Day, state and federal securities regulators had approved the details and stock — $10 a share — was being sold to raise the money to buy the paper back from Eaton. Employees were licensed by the state to sell securities and staffed a booth in the lobby at 617 Vine, where buyers were photographed signing checks. New booths went up in the paper's Kentucky offices as well. Promotional stories appeared daily. "Enquirer Stock Is Purchased By Steady Stream Of Buyers," read an Aug. 18 headline. A mother bought a share for her 12-year-old daughter but only after the daughter had been assured that the comic strip, "Blondie," would remain in the paper.

The campaign was short and successful. On Sept. 30, *The Enquirer* gave Cyrus Eaton a check for $7.6 million. Another month was enough time to raise the $250,000 commission. *The Enquirer* had 2,900 new owners.

The grand experiment in corporate democracy was pure success at first, and Vine Street

was one, big, happy family. Employee committees studied other employee-owned companies and expanded the board of directors to include experienced, influential outsiders.

The new corporation — The Cincinnati Enquirer Inc. — had Ferger as president, business manager Eugene S. Duffield as executive vice president, Fred J. Barnes as treasurer and Ratliff as vice president and secretary. The employee-owned shares went into a voting trust, and five employees were chosen to vote them: Ferger, columnist Ollie James, and Patrick Madden a pressman, Albert Otto, a printer and Barnes.

But reality soon began reasserting itself, and it was business as usual on Vine Street. Directors directed, managers managed, supervisors supervised, editors edited. Workers worked. Owners or not, employees were still employees. When the new company paid off its debt to Eaton, the man photographed handing him the check wasn't Ratliff. It was publisher Ferger.

'CIVIL WAR' ENDS EMPLOYEE OWNERSHIP

Employee ownership proved to be a difficult arrangement, however, and by 1955 the paper was embroiled in a sort of civil war, with Ferger on one side, flanked by most of the outside directors and by his own lieutenants from the business side of *The Enquirer* — Eugene Duffield and Charles Staab. On the other side stood several editorial employees, led by Ratliff and two loyal colleagues, city editor Jack Cronin and reporter Hal Metzger.

The central issue was where *The Enquirer* drew the line between employees' rights as employees and employees' rights as shareholders. Within 18 months of the employee campaign's triumphant conclusion, corporate director Ratliff began questioning board decisions. In particular, he seemed to decide that Ferger and other top brass were overpaid, were padding expense accounts, and — worse — were trying to gain control of the paper by means of stock options the board (including Ratliff) had approved just after forming the employee company.

In November, 1955, the dispute broke into open conflict when the directors ousted Ratliff as vice president and secretary. The afternoon papers reported it

Jack Cronin, center, and James Ratliff, Jr., right, were fired in December, 1955, during the squabble with management. Hal Metzger, a Ratliff ally, was elected to the board.

two days later, and *The Enquirer* finally reported it in two paragraphs on the third day.

City editor Cronin and several other editorial colleagues sided with Ratliff. Ratliff called an employee meeting; management forbade the use of company property and refused employees time off to attend. Charges flew back and forth, orally and in written press releases.

The *Times-Star* — particularly Nixson Denton — reveled in *The Enquirer's* internal agony. "It is quite possible," he wrote, that the strife would end "the halcyon era of employee ownership," which he called "specious, spurious ballyhoo."

Top management rented the Cox Theater and called for a mass meeting of employees on Dec. 5. Then, just hours before the meeting, Ferger dropped a bomb: he fired Ratliff and Cronin, the heroes of the employee-ownership campaign.

At the meeting, long-winded statements from both sides were accompanied by gripes, grievances and bills of particulars. Ratliff demanded that shareholders be given access to the company books. Ferger accused him of damaging *The Enquirer's* reputation and airing dirty linen in public. "Jim is inspired," said one outside director, in praise for his past leadership, "but, God help him, he gets off on tangents." It was one of the mildest of the statements from either side.

The firings stood. Some employees — mostly editorial — formed a new "Committee to Save The Enquirer Again." Its chairman was reporter-columnist Al Schottelkotte. Employees in the business offices countered with their own " United Employees Committee for Continued Success of the Enquirer." Outside stockholders held their own meetings to decide what to do. Some, led by former copy boy Henry Beirne, demanded that Ratliff and Cronin be rehired; others supported Ferger. Nixson Denton accused his bitter rival of not covering its own story. For once he was right. Most of the news, beyond "official" statements appeared in the afternoon papers.

The showdown came over elections to fill three seats on the board of directors — seats reserved for employee-shareholders. Two Ratliff-camp candidates won — assistant city

editor Hal Metzger and Loren White from the composing room. The third was the Ferger loyalist, Staab. Charges and countercharges reverberated less and less frequently, and eventually subsided. Ratliff and Cronin went on to other jobs. And the burning issue of whether Ferger was or wasn't trying to gain control of the paper soon became moot.

Later in 1956, Halsey, Stuart & Co. announced it would sell $2.5 million in convertible debentures it held. Again, representatives of the *Times-Star* bid, and again they were outbid, this time by the E.W. Scripps Co., owners of the Scripps-Howard papers and the *Times-Star's* esteemed afternoon contemporary, the *Post*.

Scripps had slowly been buying up *Enquirer* stock, and when it converted the convertible bonds to common shares, it and not Ferger, had firm control of *The Enquirer*. Ferger remained as publisher for eight more years, and most of his management team survived — as employees of E. W. Scripps.

To avoid attention from federal antitrust watchdogs, Scripps held its *Enquirer* stock in a non-voting trust, which kept *The Enquirer* independent of the rest of the Scripps chain.

The final irony came in 1958 when Scripps-Howard's bought Taft's *Times-Star* and, with about half a day's warning, sent telegrams to the employees — Nixson Denton included — telling them they were out of a job.

PROUDFOOT BEQUEATHS A VERY BITTER LEGACY

In the early 1960s, just before Roger Ferger retired, *The Enquirer* hired a management consulting company named Alexander Proudfoot to study *The Enquirer*.

Proudfoot had never studied a newspaper before, knew little of the news business and tried to apply ordinary standards of office production efficiency to a staff that dealt daily with the imponderable and unpredictable.

Efficiency experts stationed in the newsroom would ask reporters questions like, "How many calls do you make to get the news every day?" and "How long does it take to write a story?"

Anyone who ever spent a day in a newsroom knows there are no set answers to questions like these. Gathering, reporting and writing and editing news are tasks not easily quantified. But "The Proudfeet," as they came to be known, persisted. Library clerks were timed to see how long it took to clip the day's paper and paste the clippings on file cards. One artist remembers being watched as he did rough sketches, trying to work up a cartoon for the next day's paper. "What are you doing?" the

efficiency expert asked. "Thinking up an idea," the artist answered.

"How much time does it take to formulate an idea?" the expert asked. That did it.

"Put down six hours," said the artist, getting up from his easel. "I'm going for a walk."

One November day in 1964, management announced that people who'd be let go would be notified at 4 p.m. the next day. An advertising artist surreptitiously made and put up posters reading "Stay Alive 'til 4:05."

Just before the staff cuts were announced one editor called a meeting of his staff and told them, "Anyone fired in this department will be fired over my dead body." When the list came out, the editor's name was among the first. Another executive was told by a vice president to make a list of people to be let go, and when he submitted the list, watched as the VP picked up a pencil and added the executive's own name to the top of the list.

Another long-time editor emerged from his meeting in tears, having just informed his wife, a veteran reporter, that she had lost her job. It was a bitter period, a time of purges and vendettas, and is still remembered with ill feeling. The *Columbia Journalism Review* later ran a story by a former *Enquirer* staffer about ithe experience titled "Living a Nightmare."

CRITICS CHARM AND CHASTISE

"Cincinnati was one of the first cities with a commercial radio station — WLW — and The Enquirer was one of the first newspapers with a radio critic."

Frank E. Tunison was an able reporter with a flair for words who wrote music reviews in the 1880s, and one day he used the word "cacophonous" to describe a symphony performance. In an era when the newspaper was the only mass medium, critics held the success of theatrical or musical performances in their hands and did not use such words lightly. While musicians gnashed their teeth, Tunison's colleagues looked the word up. They called him "Cacophonous Tunison" ever after.

In those days, when John R. McLean was battling the rival *Commercial* head-to-head for morning dominance, there was great team spirit at *The Enquirer*. In 1882, Cacophonous was one of 14 on the news staff who posed for a group photo that hung for years in *The Enquirer's* library. Tunison went on to become an executive for a company called General Motors. In 1929, while passing through Cincinnati, he called on another of those 14, Ed Anthony, who was then working in the auto-license office at the courthouse. They laughed about the good old days and organized a reunion at the old Sinton Hotel. Five of the 1882 staff attended.

As critic in 1882, Tunison had a demanding audience. Cincinnati knew its music. It was, the city of *saengerfests* and Music Hall. In 1878, on a visit to the city, the paper's nationally known, Washington-based political commentator, George A. Townshend, wrote: "I have been most impressed with the real understanding, intelligence and taste here . . . . The young girls, the farmer-like boys, the middle-aged, the poor and the opulent, seem pervaded with a musical refinement . . . . Everybody knows who Gluck is, what a symphony is not, the difference between music and harmony, and the meaning of *Stabat Mater*."

Soon after the turn of the century, the paper's theater critic was Al Thayer, whose nickname was "Ah, There." Less of a stickler than, say, Cacophonous Tunison, he had a reputation as an easy mark for press agents. Their handouts often made the paper unedited, and Thayer's Sunday column, "Lobby Chatter," was known among the staff as "Sloppy Chatter."

Probably the best remembered theater critic *The Enquirer* ever had was E. B. Radcliffe. He reigned over the city's theater—stage and—film for a quarter century, in the 1930s, '40s, '50s and '60s. Rad, whose full given name was Ellis Brownell, was born in Massachusetts, worked his way through Ohio Wesleyan University. He began newspapering in Florida and moved to the *Cincinnati Commercial Tribune* before *The Enquirer* bought it and closed it in 1930. The next year *The Enquirer* hired him.

He called himself "Old Dad," and when he retired in 1969 he calculated he had reviewed 1,200 plays and

Continued on next page

4,000 movies. He worked tirelessly to promote legitimate theater in Cincinnati and energetically supported the Playhouse in the Park.

Radcliffe was widely acquainted in the world of theater and film. "Rad was forever getting visits from these famous actors and actresses," one contemporary recalls. Whenever one of them came to town, usually for a play at the Shubert or something, they'd make a visit to Rad's office."

Enquirer artist Elmer Wetenkamp remembers two such visitors very well, from the days when the art department was next to Rad's office."

"One day, we were sitting there about 5:30 in the evening, and who walks in but Cary Grant. He said he'd been in earlier to see Radcliffe and had seen this painting we had hanging on the wall of a guy with a pipe reading *The Enquirer*. He wanted to buy it for his collection and asked for a price.

"Henry Eddy was the chief

E.B. *Radcliffe used to order complimentary tickets for friends by telling the theater his "cousins from the east" had dropped in. He used the same line hundreds of times.*

artist in those days, and he was in his glory because he was able to tell Cary Grant he couldn't have that painting at any price.

"Once in the late '50s," Wetenkamp continued, "Erroll Flynn opened here at the Schubert in a period play, and Radcliffe had totally bombed it in his review. It was bad. Flynn was bad. The show closed the very next day it was so bad. We were on the fourth floor at that time, and we didn't have a receptionist, and the next day

the elevator opened and there was Erroll. His face was puffy. He was overweight. I guess the years of high living and boozing really took its toll. He looked terrible, but he still had that charm and charisma about him. And he wanted to know the office Radcliffe was in. I told him, and then I thought, '*Uh-oh, here comes all hell now.'* "Afterwards I went in to see Rad and asked if he got punched, and he said, 'No, he said he had read the review and

I was right. He stank. The play stank. Everything was bad. It convinced him he was not a stage actor.' The play was Flynn's last role. He was only about 50, but he died soon afterwards."

Radcliffe died in 1977 at a daughter's home in Connecticut.

Changing times mean changing jobs, and *The Enquirer* now has critics for popular as well as classical music, TV as well as theater. For some reason, while they compete hotly for advertising dollars, newspapers seem not to regard the electronic media as journalistic competitors, but as performances to be covered, reviewed, criticized. Cincinnati was one of the first cities with a commercial radio station — WLW — and *The Enquirer* was one of the first newspapers with a radio critic. Jack Snow's column began appearing in 1924, when "tube sets" were less common than "crystal sets."

Snow's column, "With the Radio Reviewer," dealt with both the technical and aesthetic aspects of this brand new medium.

"We learned with great joy during the past week," the column began on Sunday, March 1, 1925, "that WSAI was going to broadcast the WEAF concerts. Now, there is no need to shudder at static or fear the loss of a single one of these beautiful treats. Static means very little to WSAI. Besides making the concert very listenable to everyone with tube sets, WSAI is perform-

Fredrick Yeiser

ing a wonderful service to crystal set owners. . . .The idea of broadcasting special musical programs . . . puts the question in our mind of repeating of concerts. Everyone who wishes to hear a certain program cannot conveniently always arrange to be at the dials at the appointed hour.

Of course,

the only answer to this question, that has just begun to face broadcasters, is the repetition of the particular concert. Perhaps in the future not far distant, we shall hear radio programs repeated nightly for, it may be, two or even three nights."

One of the most influential critics *The Enquirer* ever had wasn't a critic at all, but a financial reporter and, later, city editor— Lee Evans. Evans was a keen student of both music and drama, and the paper's regular critics often sought his opinion before reviewing a performance they knew that he, too, had attended. Jack Cronin, one of Evans' successors as both financial editor and city editor, remembers that in the late 1920s Evans always attended Friday afternoon Symphony performances with music critic William Smith Goldenberg, and then, "almost as if it were a ritual, late in the afternoon Bill would drop into the financial department and compare reactions with Evans

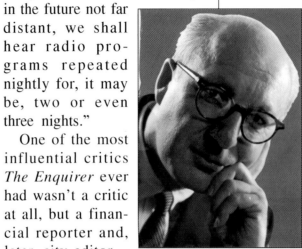

Henry Humphreys

before he wrote his review."

When Evans was sent to New York as correspondent in 1943, he won distinction there reviewing plays. He once even reviewed a fashion show for the women's pages — comparing it to a good burlesque show.

It was an era of versatile newspapermen. When Frederick Yeiser joined *The Enquirer* in 1936 as music critic, for instance, he had already graduated from Princeton, studied music in Vienna, been a businessman, and a teacher at the American University in Beirut. During World War II, he served with the OSS in German-occupied Yugoslavia. After the war he returned to Vienna and married Sylvia, the countess he'd fallen in love with as a music student in 1931. They'd been engaged 15 years, prevented from marrying by distance, bureaucracy and war. Back in Cincinnati, he settled down at *The Enquirer* again as book editor, editorial writer and art critic.

"I've enjoyed them all," said the tall, cultured Yeiser of his many roles upon his retirement in 1968, "but books and art more than music." Music, he explained, his pencil-thin mustache twitching, presented the same fare season after season. "But you get to do a new book every week."

He and Sylvia retired to Austria in 1968. They died in 1975, she July 21, he 13 days later.

Yeiser's illustrious successor as music critic was a colorful critic named Henry Sigurd Humphreys. Born in Vienna into a musical family, he grew up in Evansville, Ind., and as a teenager in the 1920s worked as an organist in silent-film theaters. He had graduate degrees in music from the Cincinnati College of Music and in German literature from the University of Cincinnati, and was a student of Greek and classic antiquity. Well-known as a lecturer as well as a critic, he also served many small Cincinnati churches without pay as organist and music director. He was music and drama critic at the old *Times-Star* before moving to *The Enquirer*. He died in 1990.

SHARP SPIKES BOW TO SAFETY

Before computers and word processing, just about everyone had a spike on his desk—a stiff coat-hanger wire anchored in a base of heavy type-metal, and filed to a needle-sharp point. The spike was used for old galley proofs and carbon copies, and most veteran editors were keenly aware of the dangers it presented. Every so often, someone would sit on a spike, or jab his hand and draw blood. But most were so practiced that they safely spiked copy without even looking. One who was especially fast with his spike was a telegraph editor, Bill Waters, who would jam copy onto his spike, hard, without looking up, while he reached with his other hand for the next take. One evening he was working his way through a stack of copy, and the inevitable happened. He skewered his finger all the way through and it required hospital attention. Next day the order came down, and from then on, all spikes were bent over so editors had to spike copy upwards, and with care.

But Humphreys was much more attuned to music than to newspapering, and the nitty-gritty details of the trade often eluded him. He seemed to live in a world of his own, and his colleagues treasured their pet yarns about what they called "Henry in Humphreyland."

The early edition, printed around eight at night, was called the "bulldog," but Humphreys always called it "the doggie." In his day, copy went from the fourth-floor editorial offices to the third-floor composing room in a pneumatic tube, and before sending down his copy, he would always put his mouth to the tube and shout, "My copy for the doggie is coming down now!" He never quite understood that there wasn't someone down at the other end in the composing room, listening.

To Humphreys, if it wasn't music, it wasn't news. Accompanying the Cincinnati Symphony on a world tour, he once called the city desk from somewhere like Bangkok and announced, "I won't be sending you a story today. The orchestra's plane got lost and landed in the wrong city."

Then he hung up, leaving the poor city editor gasping for more information but without a clue to where Henry had called from.

Another time he arranged with the Symphony to get a photo of the entire orchestra on stage at Music Hall, in full dress even though it was only a rehearsal night, for a feature of some kind. The orchestra showed up, in full regalia. Henry showed up. But the photographer didn't. They all waited, and waited while Henry grew more embarrassed by the minute. Finally, fuming mad, he phoned the city desk, which was responsible for dispatching photographers.

"What happened?" Henry demanded. "I've got the whole symphony here on stage, all dressed and ready to go, and there's no photographer."

"Did you put in a photo order?" asked the unruffled night city editor.

"Well!" humphed Henry. "You can't expect me to think of *everything.*"

MR. WHIG, DIES, RISES AND, ALAS, DEPARTS

Some of the most charming characters to grace the pages of *The Enquirer* over the years have been utterly fictional. Attila, the killer roach arose from the fertile mind of the late humor columnist, Bob Brumfield, and John Q. Public was the all-purpose Everyman of L. D. Warren's editorial cartoons.

Neither of these fictional characters outlasted the mustiest of them all, Mr. Whig. This pontificating old Washingtonian was forever fearing for the future of the Republic in the Sunday Opinion Page columns of editorial-page editor Thomas Gephardt, who was nearing retirement on the *Enquirer's* 150th birthday.

We would have preferred a report from Mr. Whig's creator on his origin, but none is available because his creator is, alas, dead. Editor Gephardt, however, tells us the story here in this charming reminiscence of a man who has edited more than one fifth of all the editorial pages ever

printed by *The Enquirer:*

It's hard for me to imagine myself one of the old-timers around *The Enquirer*, yet precisely 31 years have elapsed (as of March 14) since I went to work. Joseph W. Sagmaster, editorial page editor, was leaving to become the first general manager of WGUC at the University of Cincinnati, and editor Brady Black had

advertised in *Editor & Publisher* for a replacement. Several letters and one personal visit preceded my hiring — first as an editorial writer and then, after a few months' trial, as editor of the page.

I was not only the newest member of the editorial page department, but also the youngest.

Most celebrated among my new

colleagues was Ollie M. James. Ollie was widely known for his humor column, which he produced an extraordinary seven days a week. But he was also chief editorial writer and wrote most of the paper's major editorials. He did so with a flamboyant style that delighted those who agreed and outraged those who did not. One of his classics was a piece on the United Nations entitled 'U for Useless.' Ollie had an intense interest in such specialties as the space program (then in its infancy), but he had an encyclopedic insight into very nearly everything in the news. He was always in terrible health and traveled, I'm told, with a briefcase full of pills, potions and other remedies. His work schedule did not enhance his health. One day he'd come in at 4 p.m. and work until after midnight. The next he'd come in at 7 a.m. and work until mid-afternoon. No constitution could take that rigor very long, but his did.

Another colleague was William H. Hessler, who was billed as *"The Enquirer's* foreign news analyst." Bill wrote several signed columns a week and most of the editorials on foreign-policy issues. He was always at odds politically with *Enquirer* management, but that didn't keep him from being a prolific editorial-writer.

A remote member of the department was the picturesque Forrest Davis, stationed in Washington and the author of several columns weekly and a number of editorials. A sometime ghostwriter for Sen. Joseph R. McCarthy and an intimate of a number of celebrated conservatives, Forrest was also the creator of Mr. Whig, a venerable Washingtonian whose memories of Washington dated back to the early days of the Republic.

Forrest Davis died in a fire in his apartment, but after a decent interval I resurrected Mr. Whig, changed his style somewhat, and made him the centerpiece for Sunday columns for quite a few years, until the publisher confided a few years ago that "people laughed at the whole idea." Mr. Whig has made few appearances since.

On my first day on the job I was ushered for a welcoming into the presence of publisher Roger H. Ferger, who managed to give his office the aura of a cathedral—with its fireplace, its dark paneled walls, its oriental rugs. Dressed almost always in black, with his Sigma Chi pin on his shirt, Roger Ferger had presence. Unfailingly self-possessed, he never failed to impress visitors. I remember the first occasion I sat in on a meeting with a delegation protesting one editorial posture or another. At the conclusion of the presentation, Mr. Ferger declared, "We make no claim to infallibility, but we

accept responsibility with accountability, etc., etc." It struck me as exceptionally eloquent for an extemporaneous response, and the visitors accepted it with good grace. Only later did I learn that it was a speech he had memorized and used on one such occasion after another. I don't know how many times I heard it after that.

There was a wave of byzantine intrigue after his retirement as publisher in 1965, and from it all emerged Francis L. Dale. He had a dynamic vision of what the publisher of a Cincinnati newspaper should be, and he rose fully to the image. Indefatigable and imaginative, he liked to be a part of every worthwhile movement in Cincinnati — from the Reds and the Bengals and Riverfront Stadium to the workings of city government. He inspired a lot of long, thoughtful, essay-like editorials, suggesting the subject and the drift.

Carl H. Lindner was his successor as publisher, but William J. Keating functioned as publisher even before he had the title. Bill Keating has keen

Forrest Davis

Thomas Gebhardt

interest in public affairs, having been a participant on several levels, and enjoyed sharing his experiences and insights, which proved, along with his knowing nearly everyone in Cincinnati, to be of immense value to the editorial writers.

Keating's promotion within the Gannett family brought Gary L. Watson to Cincinnati from Rockford, Ill. He wanted *The Enquirer* to have a vigorous editorial board but had no aspirations as a local king-maker. He, too, was moved to a higher position within Gannett, and his successor, John P. Zanotti, took a more personal hand in editorial positions until he left *The Enquirer* and Gannett for a publisher's position in Phoenix. His resignation brought Bill Keating back.

The Enquirer has changed in many ways in 31 years. The most obvious changes have been visual — new printing techniques, an abundance of color, shorter and more streamlined treatment of the news. The editorial line has changed remarkably little.

MR. WHIG FEARS FOR REPUBLIC

Mr. Whig's homilies were distinctive because of the style Gephardt adopted. Here is a sample from a column which appeared May 17, 1981.

MR. WHIG SAT for a long moment gazing into his roaring fire, seemingly unaware that Clarence Dill had shown me to my usual chair.

"Ah, Gephardt" he finally rasped, scarcely above a whisper. "You find me, my boy, gripped by fear."

"But surely — "

"You are quite right, my boy. I should be fairly leaping with joy at the enthusiasm with which the Congress has embraced Mr. Ronald Wilson Reagan's economic prescriptions."

"Yes, and — "

"It goes without saying that I am delighted. And yet, my boy, my high expectations are haunted by the fear that the American business establishment — upon whose energy, dedication, initiative and ingenuity Mr. Ronald Wilson Reagan is banking so heavily —may not be capable of embracing the challenge."

"You mean —"

"Alas, my boy. I recognize that my sentiments are tinged with heresy, which is why I utter them in the strictest confidence. But my fears are no less real. . . ."

THE TALK OF THE TOWN

One of the longest-lasting institutions ever to grace the pages of *The Enquirer* was a column that evolved over more than 80 years, made celebrities out of such writers as Joe Garretson and Al Schottelkotte, and eventually came to be known only by the name of its last author, Frank Weikel.

It began as "Talk of the Town" soon after the turn of the century, but went at various times under more names than a chameleon has colors. It sometimes seemed to have a life of its own, combining and recombining with other columns, spawning spinoffs and mergers, and sometimes living a double life as more than one column.

Not only did it not have a regular name, for much of its life it didn't have a regular place or author either, and its frequency varied as well. Sometimes it ran daily, sometimes weekly and sometimes just every once in a while. But for all its years, the format was the same: a brisk read of brief, gossipy, offbeat items.

The column first appeared in the paper on July 31, 1901. It might not be coincidence that this was the year publisher John R. McLean dispatched a young reporter named W. F. Wiley from the *Washington Post* to be managing editor of *The Enquirer*. We are careful not to say it was Wiley's idea to start the column, but at many points in his 40 years as manager and publisher, Wiley showed unusually keen interest in this column. In internal memos and employee newsletters of the 1930s and 1940s, Wiley not only urged staffers to contribute, he sometimes all but begged them to write (and heaped praise on ones who provided good material). At times during World War II he even wrote the column himself, although his name did not appear on it.

His concept was a daily compilation of short news items contributed by various staffers — interesting material too short to be full-fledged stories. The column ran for years with the business news and items were often business-related. Many were about visitors to town.

One 1901 column quoted a Methodist minister, passing through town on the way home to Danville, Ky., from a conference in England: "There is only one thing in which the British are superior to us, and that is in their honest, economical and admirable municipal government and the cleanliness of their inland cities."

The next item had Harry Manss, a young shoemaking company president, saying: "More people are employed, more capital invested, and a greater volume of business done on Sycamore Street between Sixth and Ninth than on any other three blocks of manufacturing industries in the city."

It is not always easy to get busy

Continued on next page

reporters to contribute items to such a column, and there are

many slow days, like the one in October, 1911, when the best the poor columnist could muster was three paragraphs about how Eugene Porter, the French consul in Cincinnati, wasn't surprised that France and Germany had settled their territorial differences in North Africa without war. Only in a city with a sizable German population could that be the "Talk of the Town."

By the late 1930s, "Talk" had split into two columns, "Talk of the Week" on Sundays and "Talk of the Town" on most Mondays (and occasionally on other weekdays as well).

For its first 44 years, the column was unsigned, so it's impossible to say whether it had regular authors. Not until the end of World War II did a regular byline appear: Joseph Garretson, Jr.

Garretson was one of those veteran reporters who knew

Joseph Garretson, Jr. was the first journalist whose byline regularly appeared on the column.

everyone in Cincinnati, and vice versa. He'd started at *The Enquirer* early in the Depression, when he was 32, and his byline always read "Joseph Garretson, Jr." to avoid confusion with his late father, managing editor of the afternoon *Times-Star* from 1899 to 1923. At *The Enquirer* in the '30s, Joe, Jr., had covered everything from police to politics, including the trial of Anna Marie Hahn, the infamous Cincinnati murderess.

In 1944, as Maj. Joseph Garretson Jr., he returned from the Army Air Corps and became a weekly columnist. His first "Talk of the Week" appeared on Sunday, March 18, 1945. It soon became a daily column titled "In Cincinnati," and in 1946 changed to "About Cincinnati."

Then came some of those mutations this column was famous for: In 1946, with Garretson's column a successful spinoff, "Talk" returned — unsigned — as a daily feature. However, in 1949 the two merged again as "Talk of the Town" with Garretson's byline.

Then, to confuse matters even more, Garretson had a heart attack late that year. While he recovered, "Talk of the Town" appeared under the byline of Mildred Miller, one of those versatile, wear-any-hat newspaper people who did just about everything but set type. In 1949, she had a woman's-page column called "Talk About Women," but on Nov. 30, 1949, her name appeared on "Talk of the Town" with an editor's note that Garretson was ill. When he returned, his column resumed as "About Cincinnati" and hers as "Talk About Women."

Garretson left *The Enquirer* in 1952 and became a columnist for the *Times-Star*, and the *Enquirer's* "Talk of the Town" carried on under the byline of a young man named Al Schottelkotte. He had started at *The Enquirer* in 1943 as a teenaged, cub police reporter. His brother Jim, still at *The Enquirer*, has been sports editor, news editor, and managing editor.

Excerpts from this Al Schottelkotte column published in March, 1960, typifies the "Talk of the Town" style he cultivated.

AL SCHOTTELKOTTE'S FIRST 'BIG STORY'

Al Schottelkotte, the "Talk of the Town" columnist in the 1950s, may have been the youngest full-time reporter ever at *The Enquirer,* if not at any big-city daily. He was hired as a copy boy on his 16th birthday in 1943 and promoted to reporter three months later. His first big story was so big that it landed him on NBC's popular radio series, "The Big Story."

What he did was help solve two northern Kentucky murder cases in 1944. Al was working at *The Enquirer's* Newport bureau when the first killing occurred, in Bellevue, Ky., and was assigned to the Covington office when the second happened there a few months later. Because he covered both, he was able to put together crucial clues the police had missed.

Both victims were cabbies, shot and robbed. Meager clues indicated a woman's presence in one of the cabs, but that wasn't much to go on, and for weeks the crimes went unsolved. Then, one day, Al noticed an AP dispatch about a man arrested in Miami for killing a cabby and a policeman. The suspect, dressed as a woman, had a draft card with a Cincinnati address. Al checked and found that no one at that address had ever heard of the man. So he called Miami police and suggested they check the card to see if it had been altered. They did, and it had been. Even more to the point, the card had originally been issued to one of the Kentucky cab drivers. Al notified Covington police , and tests showed the suspect's gun had been used in all three killings. It was some story for a 17-year-old kid.

"Don't blame the groundhog for all this late winter snow. It was Councilman Charlie Taft who was the jinx. Taft was at a Capital Improvements Committee meeting a few weeks ago and remarked that, 'I wonder what Mr. Wichman (then Public Works Director, later city manager) is doing with all that money he's saved because there's been no snow removal this year.' There hasn't been a day without snow on the ground since.

ᙍ ᙍ ᙍ

"Mayor Donald Clancy's suggestion that Colerain Avenue be reopened to connect with Millcreek Expressway near Central Parkway touches on a point which has had motorists wondering since the expressway opened. It would have eased much of the southbound pressure on Central Parkway if Colerain never had been shut off from the beginning . . ..

ᙍ ᙍ ᙍ

"Something for the town to talk about: Those new multicoin parking meters which take up to a quarter . . . Cincinnati Congressman Gordon Scherer's indignant defense of the Communist infiltration of churches charged in that controversial Air Force manual. . . ."

Al Schottelkotte had a long run, writing the column for nine years before departing in 1961 to become the evening news anchorman at WCPO-TV. When he left, the column had become "Talk of Our Town" somewhere along the way, and Schottelkotte had become a celebrity even without benefit of TV.

One story that put him in the spotlight was a 1960 expose in which he alleged that an employee at Cincinnati's auto safety lane had taken a one-dollar payoff to pass an unsafe car. The employee later committed suicide.

When Schottelkotte left *The Enquirer* for TV, editor Brady Black held a competition for the columnist's job.

The winner was TV editor Luke Feck. Feck produced the column for just two years before leaving the paper briefly to publish his own magazine.

The columnist who followed Feck invested it with so much personal identity that it soon was retitled simply, "Frank Weikel." It remained a fixture on the local news pages for 22 years.

Weikel started at *The Enquirer* as a copy boy in 1947, when he was a sophomore at Purcell High School. When he graduated two years later, he became a full-fledged reporter, covering the police beat. It was there, through the 1950s and early '60s that he made contacts that produced so many items for him after he became the "Talk of the Town" columnist. Like so many police reporters, Weikel always fancied himself a sleuth of sorts. Once, accompanying suburban Fairfax police on the case of a missing child, he crawled under the porch at the home of a teen-aged suspect and found the victim, a little girl. His story , of course, ran on page one.

A law-and-order conservative himself, and an elected Republican trustee in a Springfield Township, he gave readers a view of the town drawn from his daily contact with court-house cronies and Republican regulars. Amid the polarization of antiwar demonstrations, urban riots and Watergate in the 1960s and '70s, Cincinnati divided into Weikel-lovers and Weikel-haters. Even ardent detractors read his column, if only to see what they could be

A FRANK WEIKEL SAMPLER

A LITTLE MORE THAN eight years ago Mr. and Mrs. Carl Dappen sat in disbelief as police told them that a neighbor confessed murdering their four-year-old daughter, Debbie.

Last week that disbelief returned as they watched television and saw that the same youth who had killed their daughter had just been arrested in nearby Butler County on charges of attacking a housewife.

Carl Dappen called me Monday to express "horror and shock" that George Rickey had been returned to society.

Incidentally, I discovered Debbie's body hidden under Rickey's front porch and was the first person to confront him with the fact that the body had been found.

Rickey, then only 13, confessed and observed, "I'm sick."

I know the DAPPEN family is SICK over the manner in which the case was handled.

AN AREA HORSE BETTOR writes to say that he and some of his fellow bettors were a little suspicious about a raid on their favorite betting parlor.

Seems like a "hot horse won" and the bookie was going to have a big

payoff to bettors. Well, before the winners were paid the police raided the joint and took all the betting slips.

Our betting friend has a suspicious mind and believes that the bookie himself tipped the fuzz. It turned out the fellow paid a small court fine . .but because his records were gone as evidence he didn't have to pay his betting customers.

OBSERVATION DEPARTMENT: The always courteous Hamilton County Park rangers are wearing even broader smiles this year as they deal with the public using park recreation . . . Could it be that the needed park tax levy will be RETURNED TO THE BALLOT IN November?

From this desk it looks like a big YES.

TEN DAYS AGO this column called attention to the wide open prowling of prostitutes at the Ninth and Vine St. area.

Well, the vice squad has moved in and, as one officer put it . . . "Before we're done the area will be suitable for a church."

The improvement is noticeable and the vice squad boys get the credit.

outraged about that day. He threw "darts" at people he didn't like, awarded "flowers" to those he did.

Weikel was also the butt of many a copy-desk joke because, while he was a fine police reporter, he wasn't much as a writer, and the finer points of syntax, grammar and spelling often eluded him. Copy editors often threatened to expose this weakness simply by letting his copy go through unedited. Weikel would always take the threats with good humor. "Hey," he'd reply, "I don't spell 'em, I just tell 'em."

He finally got his wish to be a cop. When he retired in 1987 after 40 years at *The Enquirer*, he got a new job as public relations man for Hamilton County's Republican sheriff, Simon Leis Jr.

Weikel was gone, "Talk of the Town" was dead, and the copy desk sighed relief.

LUKE MCLUKE AMUSES NATION WITH 'BYPLAY'

James Syme Hastings, who became famous as an *Enquirer*-based, syndicated columnist under the pen-name of "Luke McLuke" in the first two decades of this century, arrived in Cincinnati without a promising history.

He had owned and edited a paper in Pennsylvania in his youth, but injected too much pepper into its columns for his simple, rural readers. When circulation and advertising vanished, he went to Boston as a reporter. There, according to an *Enquirer* historian in the 1920s, "his reports on the doings of a riotous Irish society so roused the ire of its members that his employers sent him to Canada till the trouble blew over."

He next found work on a Florida paper, but enraged local officials by exposing the cruelties of prison logging camps and phosphate mines. Lest they find a way to put him inside one of those camps, he came to Cincinnati in 1901 for what he once termed "a short loaf."

He stayed the rest of his life. At *The Enquirer,* he began as exchange editor, clipping items from out-of-town papers, and then found himself catering anew to rural readers as editor of *The Weekly Enquirer.* He bridled at these tasks and (he was brashly outspoken) longed for what he called "unrestrained liberty of expression" at the conservative *Enquirer.* He offered a compromise: He would continue his tame tasks if *The Enquirer* let him also produce a regular column of his own. Managing editor W. F. Wiley, ever receptive to fresh ideas, went for it.

Called "Bits of Byplay," the column first appeared in 1912. It offered a humorous style all its own and was well accepted, largely because "McLuke" had a way of quenching the serious fires of life with wit and clever phrasing. The column was so well accepted that other papers began reprinting parts of it without proper credit. *The Enquirer* copyrighted it, then offered it for syndication, and soon it was appearing in papers all over the country.

One of "Luke McLuke's" favorite subjects was Prohibition, and his brand was the best wry available. Poking fun at both the Wets and the Drys, he set the tone for the nation's irreverent attitude toward that Great Experiment. Soon after Nevada made Prohibition official in 1919 by ratifying the 18th amendment, for instance, McLuke led his column with

BITS OF BYPLAY
BY
LUKE McLUKE
COPYRIGHT 1921 BY
THE CINCINNATI ENQUIRER

this bit of doggerel, titled "Omar Turns Over in his Grave:

"They tell me that the land's no longer wet, That wine can not be purchased on a bet; That long-haired men and short-haired dames now rule, And near-beer is the best that you can get.

"Nut sundae parties fill the inns with gloom. The caravansary looks like a tomb. No more the mallet and the faucet reign, And men await a cheer-less, seltzer doom.

"They tell me now that wine and song are dead, And that the nights are hours of arid dread; What joy is there in life when every man, Must wake up every morn' without a head?

"Why should I long for life and be a slave? Alive I could not get the wine I crave; The land today is dryer than my dust. No wonder I roll over in my grave."

He larded his column with verse—usually his own but sometimes contributed by readers or colleagues—as well as one-liners, trivia and philosophical amusings:

"We have secured early closing of the stores and the factory, but early closing of the mouth is what is really needed.

"Well, fellers, Ohio is dry, and you'll have to make the best of it. And our wish, from the heart out, is this: May your cellar never be empty.

"Dr. H. I. Blood is located in Middletown, Ohio, and Dr. J. H. Death is located in Franklin, Ohio. Middletown and Franklin are only a few miles apart, and we do hope that Doctors Blood and Death will not form a partnership.

"There was a time when a story had to have a moral to make people read it. Nowadays it must have an immoral.

"The 'See-More' skirts demonstrate the fact that Nature often gets careless, and after developing the torso goes away and forgets all about developing the legs."

He once boasted proudly that in nine years of writing a daily humor column, "I never once resorted to printing a mother-in-law joke." Hastings was 53 when he died, on June 3, 1921, of complications from an appendectomy. It was probably nothing more than coincidence that, adjacent to his obituary in the next day's *Enquirer* was a news story headlined: "Dry Enforcement Fund Is To Be Provided By Congress."

KENTUCKY CONTRIBUTES TWO GIANTS OF HUMOR

Innocent Bystander

Ollie M. James

Only the good Lord knows what it is about Kentucky, but we know from the record that for nearly one-third of The Enquirer's century and a half of existence, its readers have depended on Kentuckians for daily laughs.

That's not the slander it might seem. The Kentuckians it depended on were just two in number: One was Ollie James, the other Bob Brumfield. They both came from small down-home towns; both their columns were alive with imaginary critters; both were learned, erudite men.

Here are some reminiscences about these Kentuckians, whose humor columns appeared opposite the editorial page in The Enquirer for four decades.

Ollie Murray James arrived at The Cincinnati Enquirer as an editorial writer and assistant managing editor in 1936. Between then and 1971, when he retired, he wrote most of the paper's editorials — which few readers realized — and generated a huge percentage of the city's daily laughs — which almost everyone knew.

Ollie, whose pen could generate the most learned editorials, was famous because of his humor column, "The Innocent Bystander," which appeared

Continued on next page

ANDREW HOPPLE, one of the big bongs at NuTone, contributes a groaner which has a great advantage — it's short. Are you ready, public? Lie down, or else put your head between your knees (this gives the brain a better blood supply). A baseball umpire was infamous for his foul temper on the field, but what the fans and players didn't know was that he was even worse at home. He would beat his wife, kick the cat and paddle his son — for no derned reason at all. Man, he was mean.

But one night he had a few drinks and went home in a loving and cheerful mood. He didn't beat his wife, he didn't kick the cat and he even asked his son to sit on his lap and listen to a baseball story. The boy refused. Which all goes to prove that the son never sets on the brutish umpire.

A pharmaceutical house announces the development of a wonderful new wonder drug. It doesn't cure anything, but it is entirely free of side effects.

WANT TO turn orange? The Journal of the American Medical Association tells about a 53-year-old man who ate a pound of raw carrots, washed down with a pint of tomato juice, every day for three years, and he turned a bright orange. This probably will knock him out of marching in the St. Patrick's Day parade, but it should make him a dandy conciliator in civil rights disputes. Think of the sobering effect it would have in a white-and-black controversy if a bright orange man walked in and said: "Now, what is the issue here?"

The only other colorful story we can think of at the moment is a report that a school child, asked to identify Lyndon Johnson, guessed that he was "The Jolly Green Giant."

WE DID NOT tell you on purpose. Week before last was "Clogged Nose Week." Come to think of it the baking soda industry backs an "Indigestion Week," after Thanksgiving. Give us time, and we'll be having Chronic Colitis Week, Weak Bladder Week, Fallen Arches Week, Infectious Dandruff Week, Continuous Crud Week — and it's going to be terrible on us right-thinking people who always aim to co-operate to the fullest during any special week.

HAVE YOU noted how nice and ROOMY Cincinnati looks with all the buildings in Block A of the Urban Renewel project torn down (between Fifth and Sixth, Vine and Walnut)? Paul Hodges suggests we just leave it as it is, and call it Debris Square.

DO ANY of you happy people remember when the Hopi Indian dances looked crazy?

in *The Enquirer* seven days a week from 1940 to 1970. That's remarkable, when you think about it. That he was as widely read and thoroughly enjoyed in 1970 as when he began, is even more remarkable.

The Kentucky town where he was born in 1908 was so small it later vanished. It was called Kuttawa (which James made sure everyone knew was pronounced "cut-away"). It vanished because it was flooded after the Army Corps of Engineers built the Barkley Dam (which, ironically, was named for Vice President Alben Barkley, who earlier had succeeded Sen. Ollie James — the columnist's uncle and namesake — as majority leader of the U.S. Senate).

Ollie went to the University of Kentucky, and got a job at the *Lexington Herald* afterwards. It was there that the man who later would be famous for his "Bullfrog Holler" columns wrote his first animal story—about Freddie, the pet rat at a Lexington firehouse.

He moved on to become Washington correspondent for the *Louisville Herald Post* during the Depression, then found himself jobless when the paper went bankrupt in 1936. As he once described it: "I had about 68 cents in the bank and company coming up from Indiana to see the Kentucky football game."

He sold a detective story to a magazine and the $110 it brought him lasted until he could find another job — writing editorials for *The Enquirer*. He and his wife moved into a home on the old Dixie Highway in Northern Kentucky, and the frog noises from the swampy backyard prompted James to name the place "Bullfrog Holler." The name stuck, and events in the holler amused Cincinnatians for decades. Years later, when James dumped 250 truckloads of dirt into the swamp to reclaim it as a backyard, he made sure he rescued all frogs first and provided them with a new pond.

James, who became the paper's chief editorial writer in 1944, was an astute observer of world events and constantly in demand as an after-dinner speaker. He did a radio show for a while called the "Bullfrog Holler Night Club." A voracious reader as well, he drew some of his best humor from bits of real news he'd pick up from out-of-town newspapers, obscure weeklies, and unused AP copy from the telegraph editor's spike.

He was the master of the risque double-entendre, and could weave uncommon prurience out of yarns of pure euphemism — in an era when graphic candor was hardly in vogue. And when he intended to write "hard whiskey," it somehow always came out "buttermilk" in print.

He was most adept at picking up on minor news items in which he perceived an amusing twist. In 1965, he wrote of a book of "facial isometric" exercises he'd seen advertised in the paper, which purported to do away with wrinkles and double chins. "We are telling you about it," he wrote, "because we want you to be forewarned if you happen to see a lady dilating her nostrils and flaring them out. This is Exercise No. 3 of the facial isometrics, and it may have nothing to do with what you have just said or done to her."

He had scouts all over town who would tip him off to amusing items. Many were readers, some were colleagues. In 1960, he wrote that "Brady Black, our peerless executive editor, reports he saw a `Panty Bar' in Shillito's, and he wonders whether it is for little dogs that are out of breath, or do you have to wear panties to get a drink there. We are checking with the Cincinnati Bar Association," wrote James, "because we hate to go right up and ask."

Ollie was a tireless worker, but sometimes unpredictable in his hours. Morning newspaper people tend to work odd hours anyway, since the main business of producing the paper occurs between 2 p.m. and 2 a.m. But, although editorial writers don't necessarily keep the same hours as normal people, no one ever knew when to expect Ollie. He'd work 8 to 5 one day, stay until after the final edition at 2 a.m. the next, vanish for a day or two, then show up at noon and work again until midnight.

Late in his career, Ollie James was plagued by ill health ("the punies," he called it). In June, 1971, he retired. The next Jan. 26, he died, at Holmes Hospital, at the age of 63.

In 1982, the home at "Bullfrog Hollow" was torn down to make way for an office building. The fate of the frogs is not known.

BRUMFIELD RAN ON RAGE, WON WITH WIT

Of all the reporters, editors and columnists whose words have graced the pages of *The Enquirer,* few have made themselves at home in their readers' hearts in the way Bob Brumfield did during his 16 years with the paper. Certainly, no one else ever parlayed writing weather forecasts into a daily column that ran the rest of his life.

The way he did it was by enlivening with humor what to him was a tiresome chore he had been given when he started at *The Enquirer* in 1964 as a reporter The weather report is one of the most colorless bits of copy in any paper.

Colorless, perhaps, but widely read — and that was Brumfield's secret to turning the tables and making *his* weather reports one of the paper's brightest corners. Eventually, Brumfield's humor edged aside the droning daily recitations of occluded fronts and low-pressure troughs. A typical early "weather" story would begin like this:

"Partly cloudy, high of 70. The forces of Mt. Adams launched an all-out offensive against Indian Hill yesterday, sending their legions through Mariemont and Madisonville in a pincers movement . . . ."

Cincinnatians began reading the weather report not because they wanted to know whether it was going to rain, but to see what outrageous things Brumfield had to say. Soon, he outgrew the weather and left it behind on page two, in someone else's hands, while he moved with his now-weatherless column opposite the editorial page. The column appeared four times a week and was marked by irreverence. He frequently made fun of military life as he remembered it from the Army. And he poked fun at his upbringing in Hopkinsville, Ky. He was at his best when writing of down-home characters who had peopled his own childhood.

Luke Feck, his colleague, editor and admirer, understood the love-hate relationship Brumfield had with his job.

"He loved and hated it at the same time. He enjoyed writing it, but hated what it took to write it," Feck once wrote. Feck is especially fond of a column

Brumfield once did about saying goodbye to a Volkswagen that had never seen an oil change.

Brummie's work was filled with imaginary characters — Floyd the crazy cat; Jackie, the seductive society jet-setter who was secretly in love with him and who, on dark and stormy nights, would come calling in his columns; Attila, the attack roach, who would communicate with Brumfield by scribbling on a chalkboard when he wasn't gnawing on a horse he'd just killed and dragged into the kitchen.

Brummie's relationship with his readers was the same as his relationship with the column itself. He was mightily impatient with stupidity, and wrote some of his funniest, most acerbic columns when in a fury. Robert Firestone, an assistant city editor at *The Enquirer* during Brumfield's career, was fond of saying that Brummie liked to give the impression he was against everything.

Recalled Firestone: "He was even tempered. Always mad." Co-workers always knew when Brumfield had a column he was particularly happy with, or one

BRUMMIE NAMES ATTILA'S NEW BABY

BOB BRUMFIELD

NEWS ITEM: The first adult royal goliath beetle in the world to be raised in captivity has emerged from its cocoon at the Cincinnati Zoo. The achievement represent years of waiting and a lot of experimentation and research at the zoo's Insect World.

"ATTILA, I'D like to talk with you for a minute," I said to my attack roach.

"What about?" he wrote on the tablet he uses to communicate.

"I think you know what about," I said.

"IF IT'S about that zebra haunch I left in the yard, I can explain that," he wrote. "I was just getting ready to . . . ."

"That's not what I want to talk about. I want to talk about that story in the newspaper."

"What story?" he wrote.

"You know very well *what story* I'm talking about," I said. "I'm talking about the zoo story; the one about the first royal goliath beetle to be born in captivity."

"WHAT DOES that have to do with me?" he wrote.

"Don't jack me around, Attila!" I exclaimed. "I'm serious about this!"

"Okay, I'll level with you," he wrote.

"It was just one of those things. Just one of those *crazy* things. A trip to the Moon on gossamer wings. Just one of those things."

"Oh, my God!" I moaned. "I knew something like this was going to happen. I knew I should have had a man-to-roach talk with you; explained a few . . . ."

"IT WASN'T your fault," Attila wrote. "We knew what we were doing. It happened at Insect World. She was an exotic foreigner from Ghana; I, a handsome, yet naive, young roach from the Midwest."

"Spare me the sordid details," I said. "At least you could have done the honorable thing, and . . . "

"I tried. I asked her to marry me, and . . . ."

"I didn't mean you had to be

that honorable," I said. "I simply meant . . . ."

"SHE TURNED me down," Attila wrote.

"*She* turned *you* down?"

"El flatto," he wrote.

" Well, I'll be . . . where does that cheap little baggage get off turning *you* down! She might be royalty, but she'll be lucky if she lands a dung beetle now."

"SHE'S GONE. Adult royal goliath beetles just live long enough to mate and produce eggs for a future generation," Attila wrote.

"Does the kid know you're his father?" I asked.

"No, he thinks he's all beetle," Attila wrote.

"You mean even the people at the zoo don't know you're his father?" I said.

"Why, I knew it the minute I saw his picture in the paper. And just look at the size of that cocoon. It's bigger than a football.

"DID YOU and the . . . his mother . . agree on a name for the little . . . *child*?" I asked.

"Yes, we decided to name him Volkswagen."

he knew would cause a ruckus, because he would pace the glass-enclosed hallway alongside the newsroom in an agitated, near manic, state.

What many of his humor-

column fans didn't fully realize was that Brumfield was learned in military history and aviation. When he was graduated from high school in his native Hopkinsville, Ky., in 1942, he

joined the Army Air Corps and was a B-29 bombardier in the Pacific and over Japan.

After the war, and a journalism degree from the University of Kentucky, he sold ads for the

Louisville Courier-Journal, then worked in TV news in Huntington, W.Va., Miami, Fla., and as news director for Cincinnati's WKRC-TV. He joined *The Enquirer* in 1964.

Bob Brumfield lived alone, a bachelor. He was but 56 when he died, of a heart attack, in 1981, in the house he rented in Indian Hill. He left a will naming editor Feck as executor, leaving a modest inheritance to a colleague — a woman he had secretly admired from afar — and directing that his ashes be scattered on Brookville Lake in Indiana, where he had kept his sailboat.

He had shared an office with columnist Tony Lang. The day after he died, Lang wrote:

"Brummie came on like Groucho half of the time, but he was too clever to let himself get pigeonholed that easily. You can't pigeonhole an original — an irrepressible honest-to-God character. He was Brumfield. And, oh, how I'm going to miss him.

"He loved to twit others but didn't spare himself. If he put on a little extra blubber, he was the first to call himself a 'beached walrus.'

"If he heard a new joke, he would scurry lickety-split around the fourth floor with a kind of impish, naughty-little-boy delight in passing the laugh around.

"A lot of days, *The Enquirer's* resident humorist ran on rage. It was his fuel. He raved and ranted because he cared so fiercely, too fiercely. No wonder he invented Attila the killer roach. He had his share of blind spots and hot buttons. Baboonery of all sorts could provoke the old bemedalled B-29 bombardier to start blasting away again in his columns.

"To him, *The Enquirer* was 'the Grand Old Lady of Vine Street,' and almost any change in it, or any other part of his life, he took as a personal slap in the face.

"He was a bachelor; his children were his columns. Desperate for a column idea almost daily, he'd mutter, 'I'd kill for an idea.'

"Aviation and military history books made up his library. He believed the victor in the next global war will win it from outer space. He could recite troop movements, even wind directions, at battles from Gettysburg all the way to Zululand. Fact. For a funny man, he cared mightily about getting the facts straight and threw fits over sloppy reportage by baby-faced journalism-school grads he regarded as 'greener than a gourd.'

"Try as they may, no one can come close to describing Brumfield better than Brumfield himself. Here's one of his early weather reports. It ran on July 3, 1967, under a headline that didn't even begin to hint at what lay beneath it. . . . The headline read:

'The Weather Cool and Cloudy.'
'By Bob Brumfield of the Enquirer staff

'I'm going to try again. I'm bound to get a forecast straight one of these days.

'Partly cloudy and cool, low near 60, high in the upper 70s. Tuesday outlook, fair and cool. About a 20% chance of showers today.

'My high school graduation class (Hopkinsville, Ky., High School, Class of 1942) held its 25th reunion last weekend at the Governor's Mansion in Frankfort.

'Ned Breathitt, Governor of Kentucky, is perhaps the most distinguished member of the Class of '42, but it also includes Dr. Merl Baker, chancellor of the University of Missouri branch at Rolla.

'Little old Hopkinsville High had only 600 students at the time I went there, so you can imagine that the senior class wasn't very large. But out of that class are several physicians, attorneys, successful businessmen, educators, prominent politicians, scientists athletes . . . and me.

'I didn't attend the reunion. I didn't have the guts to face them.

'I remember what they wrote under my photograph in the high school annual: 'He who loves not wine, women and song, remains a fool his whole life long.'

'But I outsmarted them. I loved wine, women and song my whole life long (although not necessarily in that order of preference) and still managed to remain a fool.'"

CARL LINDNER TAKES CONTROL

Just four years after *The Enquirer's* employees had succeeded in their dramatic campaign to "save" the paper from the hands of the afternoon *Times-Star*, it fell instead into the hands of the E. W. Scripps Co., whose Scripps-Howard chain owned the afternoon *Post*.

First, Scripps paid $4 million and change for $1.5 million worth of *Enquirer* bonds the investment firm of Halsey, Stuart & Co. had underwritten. They were convertible bonds, exchangeable for common stock. Next, Scripps began buying up shares of stock *The Enquirer's* employees had bought, or persuaded other Cincinnatians to buy, in their campaign to keep the paper out of the *Times-Star's* control. Before long, Scripps was the majority shareholder in *The Enquirer.*

As Scripps' stock-buying proceeded in the spring of 1956, the coverage was extensive in the *Times-Star*, which had lost its bid for *The Enquirer.*

When Scripps bought the bonds from Halsey, Stuart, the *Times-Star* accorded the story two lines of big, black capitals on top of page one. The *Times-Star* had bid, too, but its $2.3 million offer was far short of Scripps' $4 million. The *Times-Star,* now thwarted twice, told of *The Enquirer's* new situation in the sort of headlines usually reserved for war and peace.

Seeking reactions from Vine Street, the best the other media could get was from the newsroom. *Enquirer* publisher Roger Ferger was in New York at a publishers' convention when his paper was bought. The mood on Vine Street was dismal. "Newsroom Resembles Loser's Dressing Room," headlined the *Times-Star*. "The question now," said one *Enquirer* employee, "is, 'who's going to save us, and from what?'" The atmosphere, reported the Associated Press, "was full of anxiety."

If the *Times-Star* was pleased at *The Enquirer's* fall from independence, the pleasure was brief: Two years later, Scripps also bought the *Times-Star* and merged it with the *Post* to create the *Post and Times-Star.* This left Scripps as the only daily newspaper publisher in town.

In 1964, Roger Ferger retired as publisher and the directors chose Francis L. Dale as his successor. Closely involved with the paper since he represented the employees who bought it in 1952, Dale now saw his own opportunity to buy it. The federal government had filed an antitrust suit challenging Scripps' ownership of *Enquirer* stock, and it was creeping through the courts. Dale assembled a group of Cincinnati investors to buy the paper. His plan was not universally acceptable, and by 1967 a proxy fight loomed.

William J. Keating, nearing retire-

Continued on next page

ment as publisher of *The Enquirer,* remembers the day in 1967 when he was serving as chairman of Cincinnati City Council's Finance Committee and Dale asked that the city pension-fund trustees vote the fund's *Enquirer* stock in favor of Dale's purchase.

"Will McGrath and some other stockholders," recalls Keating, felt Frank Dale "was overcommitting financially." Keating favored the sale to Dale's group. "I thought the price was right and that Frank Dale should have had a chance."

His chance never came to pass.

Under terms of a 1968 court order from that antitrust suit, Scripps had to sell. In June, 1970, as the sale deadline neared, Scripps signed a deal with Dale's group to accept $35 a share for Scripps's 60% interest in *The Enquirer.* The minority shareholders went to court to block the sale, saying the price wasn't enough. That meant more delays, and they proved crucial. Not until early 1971 did the judge who was hearing the whole matter take it under advisement.

At that point, Scripps unexpectedly opposed what seemed a routine government motion to have the court extend the contract between Scripps and Dale's group. The next day, the reason became clear: Scripps had another offer. It was from the Omaha financier, Warren Buffett. The bidding was open again.

It was at this point that a hometown financial giant, Carl Lindner, stepped onstage, upping the ante to $40 a share. The other bidders fell away, and Lindner's bid was enough to satisfy the minority stockholders, the court, the government and Scripps. The next week, Scripps accepted.

What a difference 18 years made. *The Enquirer,* whose employees had captured the imagination of the nation in 1952 with their quixotic crusade to own their own paper, had become an investment property, a ward of the court, and then chattel — sold to the highest bidder to satisfy bureaucrats and minority shareholders.

Actually, it's oversimplification to say that Lindner bought *The Enquirer.* What happened was that American Financial Leasing & Services Co., a subsidiary of which 80% was owned by Lindner's American Financial Corp., (AFC) bought the 60% of *The Enquirer* that Scripps owned plus every share of stock outstanding. In the deal, $20,080,000 changed hands and Lindner owned *The Enquirer.*

In a May 7, 1971, story about its own sale, *The Enquirer's* business staff leaned heavily on official press releases. They quoted Lindner as calling his new asset "one of the great newspapers of the United States" and promising the people of Cincinnati "we will spare no effort to keep it that way."

Within 16 months of Lindner's buying the paper, Dale resigned as publisher and Lindner took the title for himself. Keating resigned from Congress to become president and CEO of *The Enquirer.*

Lindner, as Keating explains it today, bought *The Enquirer* because "he wanted to keep the ownership in the hands of Cincinnati people." In 1975, when Lindner "sold" *The En-* *quirer* to a Phoenix, Ariz., TV and billboard company called Combined Communications Corp. (CCC), he maintained some control, because what the "sale" amounted to was Lindner's using *The Enquirer* as the wherewithal to buy a large, minority stake in CCC. "The transaction," reported *The Enquirer,* involved payment by CCC of "$30 million in cash and $16 million in secured notes to AFC in addition to the equity securities. The total price received by AFC approximates $55 million, based on the current market price of CCC securities. The announcement was made by Carl H. Lindner, president and chief executive officer of AFC, and by Karl Eller, president and chief executive officer of CCC."

For the first time since the end of the McLean trust *The Enquirer* had an absentee owner. Not long after it acquired *The Enquirer,* CCC bought the Oakland, Calif., *Tribune,* and for the first time since the forced sale in 1933 of the *Washington Post, The Enquirer* had a sister paper.

Somewhere along the way, however, local ownership had

waned in importance, and the last vestige vanished in 1978 when Combined, at Lindner's urging, merged with the Rochester-based Gannett Co., Inc.

Gannett owned dozens of daily newspapers and, among other things, prided itself on a principle of local autonomy. Editors were offered the support of the corporate staff but were encouraged to make their own news decisions based on their evaluation of their readership.

Lindner was plainly more a businessman than a newspaperman. The *Enquirer* story announcing his ascension as publisher had dealt far more with business accomplishments than journalistic philosophy. The new publisher, it said, "heads the giant Cincinnati-based AFC, which has resources totaling almost $2 billion. . . ."

This is not to say that Lindner was distant or disinterested. Quite the contrary. He took a keen, personal interest in the paper and its employees, and in four years earned a reputation at 617 Vine as a benevolent owner. He ardently courted the employees and took an almost familial interest in them. By the time he

Carl H. Lindner

had taken control of *The Enquirer,* stories about his loyalty to employees who had stood by him when he was struggling in the dairy business were legend.

"He is a very kind man," remembers one former editor. "He gave all his employees a nice Christmas party with big-name entertainers every year, and gave each one five shares of stock in the company from his personal portfolio. He did that

for several years in a row. "

The Christmas parties were extravagant affairs held at Music Hall. Entertainers included stars such as Sammy Davis Jr. and Andy Williams. And the annual gifts of five shares of stock from the personal holdings of Lindner and his brother Robert, were extended to everyone connected with the party. The year the Cincinnati Symphony Orchestra played for the party, each musician received five. Each member of Charles Kehrer's orchestra which entertained was given the five shares. Freddy, the wooden dummy of ventriloquist Aaron Williams, received five shares in 1972. And one year, in wishing all American Financial employees a Merry Christmas from the stage, Carl Lindner reminded an unseen assistant that the Music Hall janitors who had to clean up after the party should be given the same gift.

Early in his tenure, Lindner had department heads write reports about their visions of the future, what they wanted in staff, in space. Then he set about granting wishes.

"One outgrowth of that,"

recalls one of those involved in the project, "was an expanded business section, with much wider coverage of the markets. One of AFC's top executives worked with our business news staff. He told us not to worry about how much improvements would cost. Our job was to propose the improvements, and he said he would act as our advocate when it came time to getting the money to pay for them. The best business sections in the country were studied and adopted for Cincinnati readers. We got new space and staff and facilities. We also got an entirely separate department for the pictorial section . . . .

"Carl Lindner spent a good amount of money on the paper."

It was money well-spent. Four years after Lindner bought *The Enquirer,* the sale to CCC brought something like $34 million, net, to Lindner's bottom line. That deal was ann-

ounced in the paper on May 4, 1975, couched in the passive voice as if no actual human being had been involved.

"An agreement whereby *The Enquirer* would become part of Combined Communications Corp. (CCC) of Phoenix, Ariz., was announced Saturday.

"The present owner, the American Financial Corp.(AFC), would receive considerations from CCC consisting of cash, notes and ownership by AFC of 500,000 shares of common stock and 750,000 common stock warrants of CCC.

"CCC owns television, radio and outdoor advertising properties. CCC media interests are in 14 states and in Canada. CCC and AFC are both successful growth companies . . . .Lindner will become a member of the CCC board and will continue as publisher and board chairman of *The Enquirer.*"

Lindner remained as publisher until 1979, when CCC's merger with Gannett was consummated. Then Gannett appointed William J. Keating to the post. That merger resulted in Lindner's becoming one of Gannett's biggest stockholders. He later sold his shares.

FRANCIS L. DALE LEADS ENQUIRER, CIVIC PROJECTS

As publisher from 1965 to 1973, Francis L. Dale maintained certain traditions: He was every bit the civic booster and activist Moses Dawson and Washington McLean were more than a century before him, and he was as much in league with the economic power structure as John R. McLean was. He was also as intimately involved in politics. Dale's involvement, however, was in an era when that was not the fashion for publishers, and his publishing career ended with his political allies involved in the worst political scandal in American history — Watergate. The scandal, however, tainted Frank Dale only by association, if at all, which lets him be remembered for the immense amount of good he did for Cincinnati while he ran *The Enquirer*. Like his predecessor, Dale believed in community participation and served on boards of everything from the Council of Churches, Goodwill Industries, and the

local Red Cross chapter, to Bethesda and Catherine Booth Hospitals and Boy Scouts and Boys Clubs and the Salvation Army. He had been president of the Cincinnati and Ohio Bar Associations. After World War II duty as a destroyer commander in the North Atlantic, Dale — a graduate of Duke University and the University of Virginia law school — came to Cincinnati, joined the law firm of Frost & Jacobs, and was a partner there when he became publisher in 1965. Soon after arriving at *The Enquirer*, Frank Dale invented a slogan: "The paper with the power to get things done." Then he made sure it was what the slogan said it was. "His main man," remembers one contemporary, "was Charlie Carraher., our company secretary and community relations director. He'd say, 'Charlie, three weeks down the road I want a dinner for 800 people, with the governor and state senators involved and the

councilmen. When you get it arranged, let me know and I'll be there.'" A new stadium was a major issue when Dale became publisher. Crosley Field was half a century old, as well as in an area the city wanted for industrial development. There was talk of the Reds' moving out of town. Moreover, a new stadium was a prerequisite if the city ever hoped for a place in the exciting, world of profess-ional football. One reason for fears that the team would move was City Hall's dithering over building—mainly paying for — a new stadium. Dale took the initia-tive. He recog-nized the ne-

Francis L. Dale

cessity of hav-ing the urban core vibrant and alive, a fo-cal point of civic activity. The stadium be-longed down town. The Cham-ber of Com-merce, headed by Charles Staab, execu-tive vice president of *The Enquirer,* threw its resources into the project. To make sure that the Reds remained in town, Dale engineered a syndicate of 13 investors, incorporated as 617 Vine Inc., and bought the team for $7 million from William O. DeWitt. The deal in-cluded a 40-year lease to play at a new stadium on the river-front.

In 1967, with no little arm-twisting by Gov. James Rhodes, the deal was clinched and work began. The stadium opened just in time for baseball's All Star game in 1970. Dale was a tireless civic promoter. He pushed such ideas as Light Up Cincinnati and the photo contests that ensued, chess tournaments on Fountain Square, and unabashedly used the newspaper's power to support community projects and organizations, from United Appeal, the Red Cross and the arts, to the Chamber of Commerce and downtown development.

One annual exercise of journalistic muscle he decreed was a promotional special called "Perspective: Cincinnati," for which he ordered top-level ad executives to solicit major businesses for hefty cash in exchange for nothing more than getting their company logos printed in the section and an opportunity to

say they were involved.

It is widely acknowledged today that projects Dale threw *The Enquirer* behind so vigorously prevented Cincinnati's suffering the degenerative disorders that rotted the hearts out of other urban centers in the 1960s and '70s. He literally kept Cincinnati in the big leagues. As former *Enquirer* editor Luke Feck put it years after Dale retired: "A lot of people don't realize that Frank Dale saved downtown Cincinnati."

Dale remained as publisher for just over eight years, resigning in 1973, when Carl H. Lindner, chairman of American Financial Corp., took the title of publisher.

Dale then served briefly as ambassador to the United Nations' offices in Geneva, Switzerland, then was publisher of the *Los Angeles Herald-Examiner* from 1977 to 1985. He then became commissioner of the Major Indoor Soccer League and, after that, president of the Music Center of Los Angeles County. He makes his home in Pasadena.

TOO SMART OR TOO DUMB

At a time when the Vietnam War and Watergate scandal had politicians and media constantly at odds, Frank Dale was more than just politically involved. He was the founder of the very organization from whose loins the entire Watergate scandal had sprung — the infamous Committee to Re-elect the President, or 'CREEP.' He escaped personal taint by virtue of having stepped aside (leaving CREEP in the hands of such professional politicians as John Mitchell) by the time scandal engulfed the Nixon White House.

On Wednesday, April 7, 1971, there was no hint of the dark days ahead when *The Enquirer's* Washington Bureau reported:

"Francis L. Dale, president and publisher of *The Cincinnati Enquirer*, is heading a move for a national 'Citizens Committee for the Re-election of the President,' it was learned Tuesday . . . ."

He recalled that he was among those active in 1967 for Nixon's nomination and that *The Enquirer* was the first major newspaper to endorse him. "But what I am doing now, seeking out four or five people in various parts of the country to get this committee started, is on my own," Dale said.

Next day, Dale held a press conference at the old Gibson Hotel — a hangout of sorts for prominent Cincinnati Republicans before it was

razed — and named seven other committee members, including former astronaut Frank Borman and Olympic swim champ Don Schollander. "Just a beginning," Dale said.

On Oct. 5, 1973, two-and-a-half years after founding CREEP and 18 months after the Watergate break-in, Publisher Dale was chastising the media for misleading people into believing that President Nixon knew in advance about the break-in.

"The press has created a wrong impression," said Dale. "We have an obligation to correct that impression." The media, he said, had become "an active participant . . . a major factor in the course of events."

Before that October was out, Dale had resigned as publisher in favor of owner Carl Lindner, and within three months had been nominated by President Nixon to be U. S. representative to the European office of the United Nations in Geneva. At a Senate confirmation hearing to which hardly anyone but *The Enquirer* paid attention, Dale said his only contribution to Nixon's campaign was to attend two $1,000-a-plate fund-raisers. (His sons, he said, had contributed $30 to George McGovern's 1972 campaign.)

When the Senate confirmed his U.N. nomination, Dale said he had never worried about the CREEP connection: "I was either too dumb to know," he said, "or too smart to get involved."

BIRTH OF THE SUNDAY PAPER

In the beginning, in 1841, *The Enquirer* was an afternoon paper, appearing every day except Sunday, as was its predecessor, the *Advertiser.* The advantage of afternoon publication is that it provides readers with late-breaking news of the very day of publication. The problem afternoon papers face, however, is one of distribution: Its effective geographic range is limited by how far it can be delivered on the day it's published. The earlier in the day a paper is printed, the farther it can go before the news is stale.

In 1843, *The Enquirer* was growing in popularity in outlying Ohio, Kentucky and Indiana communities. Its circle of circulation widened so much, in fact, that the paper had to be ready for the early mail to reach them each day. That meant printing earlier. On March 25, 1843, the publishers, John and Charles Brough, took the logical step of making *The Enquirer* into the morning paper it has been ever since.

"Daily," however, still meant six days a week. Sunday posed a problem in an era when dying men refused ice to cool their brows unless assured it had been cut the day before. It simply wasn't acceptable to work on the Sabbath.

But a Monday morning paper doesn't get printed unless someone works on Sunday, a fact that led publishers James J. Faran and Hiram Robinson to begin producing a Sunday paper in 1848. It made business sense, too, because it gave *The Enquirer* a clear field for one day a week in a town with 14 other papers the other six days.

There was risk involved, however, and the decision was not made lightly. On Thursday, April 20, 1848, three days before the first *Sunday Enquirer* debuted, a long, thoughtful editorial appeared, explaining the decision. In all likelihood it was written by James J. Faran. Its reasoning was simple: To produce the Monday paper meant either working on Sunday or giving the readers old news by producing Monday's paper on Saturday. Except for the final distribution, *The Enquirer* assured its readers, the Sunday paper would be produced entirely on Saturday, and to avoid Sunday labor, there would be no *Enquirer* on Mondays.

At that time, only four other papers in the nation published on Sunday, and all four have long since folded or lost their identities through mergers. That leaves *The Enquirer* as America's oldest Sunday newspaper. Maybe.

As we say in the introduction to this book, we are not at all certain of this. The story that *The Enquirer* is America's oldest Sunday paper has been accepted as truth around the paper for a long time, so you can imagine our surprise to discover evidence in our files that at times between 1848 and about 1880, there were Sundays when there was no

Continued on next page

Enquirer. On the other hand, it is equally possible that the legend is entirely true and that the paper was produced but simply not filed.

The reasons for our uncertainty are legion. The old-time editors and printers were not always careful about changing the "folio" lines that indicate day, date, volume and number. (We've gotten better at it; since 1880, it has happened rarely. For example, on March 24, 1920, *The Enquirer's* front page was dated March 23.)

To add to the confusion about the old days, *The Enquirer's* own file of back issues was destroyed by the fire at Pike's Opera House in 1866. The modern record was built with what old papers the microfilming contractors could find at historical societies and libraries. Even after the paper moved into a new plant following the fire and began publishing seven days a week, there were Sundays and Mondays here and there for which no paper appears in the files.

A distinct possibility is that the libraries from whose collections the files were rebuilt didn't have Sunday papers for some weeks because they had no one working on Sundays to file them.

Anyway, as we were saying . . . The other early Sunday papers have all long since folded or merged, leaving *The Enquirer* the oldest Sunday paper in the United States.

Until the 1920s, there was but one *Enquirer* each day. The first paper off the press was identical to the last (unless some truly immense event required a rare, press-stopping makeover). During the 1920s — an era of intense competition — *The Enquirer* began producing two other daily editions. One was an evening edition, off the presses about 8 p.m., called the "bulldog" edition. The other was a Kentucky edition.

The name "bulldog" originated in New York, whose newspapers shipped early editions upstate by rail. To get to, say, Buffalo by early morning, they had to be on the train out of Manhattan the night before, and woe be unto any wagon driver who missed the train with his load. Indeed, fights sometimes broke out over who was ahead of whom among the teamsters queued up to unload at the depot. Perhaps inevitably, one promotion-minded paper boasted that its drivers "fought like bulldogs" to be first on the train, and ever since then, the word "bulldog" has applied to the evening edition of a morning paper. Later shortened to "the dog," the early edition of *The Enquirer* first appeared Oct. 2, 1922.

As a logical consequence, that was also the day the words "Final Edition" first appeared on page one.

The Enquirer bulldog was a familiar friend to Cincinnatians out and about in the evening on downtown streets. During night baseball games, newsboys would appear in the aisles during the middle innings, peddling the next day's *Enquirer.*

The bulldog had the scores of afternoon games around the league, and let horse-racing fans get a jump on other bettors by checking out the next day's entries at major tracks. *The Enquirer* dropped the "dog" on Aug. 31, 1973, because of a newsprint shortage and the cost of publishing it. The state edition, printed at 11 p.m., became the first edition.

The Enquirer has changed considerably in appearance and size in a century and a half. From its birth in 1841 until 1868, *The Enquirer* had four pages. New presses installed in 1868, following the move up Vine Street after the Opera House fire made eight pages possible, and from then until the late 1880s, *The Enquirer* was eight pages each day.

Readers grew very accustomed to what was on each page. National news — mainly from Washington and New York — appeared on page one. Page eight, the back page, was for local news. Pages three and seven were want-ads, personal ads and notices. Page two was where international news could be found. Page four was for hard-core political news and was where the masthead appeared, on top of a column or two of editorial comment from the proprietors.

Another new press in 1888 doubled the possible size again.

On many days, for a while, *The Enquirer* remained at eight pages, but by 1895 it was routinely larger and often ran 16. The big Goss presses in the new Enquirer Building in 1927 could churn out Sunday papers with hundreds of pages. The largest *Enquirer* ever, counting the comics pages, which are not printed at *The Enquirer*, was a behemoth of 326 pages on Dec. 6, 1953. Department store advertising was very strong.

The number of pages in each issue was shown atop page one from shortly before the turn of the century until the practice was discontinued on Nov. 22, 1956. In recent years, *The Enquirer* has been produced in sections, each with its own

Today's presses print five editions of **The Enquirer** *Monday through Saturday and three on Sunday. The pages from Aug. 19, 1991, show how page one changed from edition to edition as news broke. The presses print about 50,000 papers per hour.*

section-front page and its own page numbers.

After 1872, the use of headlines changed dramatically, too. Until then, headlines were modest in size, usually but a line or two, and often just a bold-faced word at the start of a story. McLean's aggressive editors evolved an attention-getting style in which key words and phrases were stacked up in "decks" calculated to entice the reader. The style was ideal for newsstand sales. Headlines that often ran more than halfway down the column forced the reader to pick the paper up to see what lay "below the fold." Once in the readers' hands, the reasoning went, the paper was as good as sold.

Editions of *The Enquirer* aimed at readers geographically came along in 1923. The first target was Kentucky, and the first Kentucky edition, on Nov. 12, was an ordinary *Enquirer* with a page of Kentucky news added. Called the "universal edition,' it got its own identity two weeks later with a Kentucky-oriented front page and the regular *Enquirer* front page inside. *The Enquirer* had maintained an office and reporting staff, at several different locations in Covington, beginning in 1872.

Later, "state" editions were born. Produced after the "bulldog" but before the "Final," they offered a page of local news for readers in outlying counties of Ohio or Indiana. The first, called the "Miami" edition, appeared on March 9, 1936. Through the years, since the advent of various editions, *The Enquirer's* page one has been made over for each edition when news warranted. This lets editors keep up with any breaking stories that are evolving even as the editions come and go, but that isn't always a blessing.

Continued on next page

Weekly Treated Its Readers Royally

*T*he Enquirer produced a weekly edition as well as a daily, from its very start in 1841 until 1921. The *Cincinnati Weekly Enquirer* was mainly a paper for farmers and other readers outside the city in rural Ohio, Kentucky and Indiana. It was a huge success, with circulation larger than the daily for many years; in an era when communications were less sophisticated, The *Weekly Enquirer* could reach its rural audience before the news it contained was stale.

The growth of farmers' weekly magazines and the Post Office's introduction of Rural Free Delivery after the turn of the century foretold its demise. But the *Weekly,* as it was known on Vine Street, was so popular that it hung on longer than it had any right to expect.

One reason for its popularity was that it cost but a dollar a year. Another was "The Enquirer Household Club," an organization of which every subscriber to The *Weekly* was automatically a member. The *Weekly* devoted a department to the club, and every year it underwrote membership outings in the big city, Cincinnati, at package prices which, even by the standards of that era, were trifling. At such events, Household Club members got an all-expense weekend in town, including railroad fare, hotel and meals. They assembled outside the Enquirer Building, were regaled with speeches and greetings from VIPs, and marched with brass band,

badges and banners to picnics, ball games, concerts and the Zoo.

Arrangements for these trips, like everything else connected with the *Weekly,* were worked out in one room on the fourth floor of 617 Vine St., where for more than half a century a man named Charles Bishop was the business manager. Everyone called him "Old Man Bishop," but it was not out of any disrespect. It was because hardly anyone knew his first name. ("The term 'Mister,'" as one old *Weekly Enquirer* hand explained in 1930, "was too formal for a business in which mere copy boys of a few weeks' service addressed the veterans as Tom, Dick and Harry, and reserved more respectful speech and manner for the one or two at the paper in whom reposed the power to hire and fire.")

At its zenith in the 1880s, under the editorship of a scholarly Kentuckian named Benjamin Franklin Sanford, the *Weekly* approximated the daily *Enquirer* in circulation and influence among its readers. Among its most popular features were columns offering personal advice and confidential counsel — especially about matters of romance and relationships. Sophisticated city folks found them amusing, but the faithful readers in the provinces swore by them.

The *Weekly Enquirer's* bailiwick was rural, Midwestern, Bible Belt. Editor Sanford maintained in his product a highly moral atmosphere, bordering on the downright religious and rooted in the assumption that all readers were good, upright, moral, Christian citizens. When Sanford retired, his son, James Sanford, succeeded him. At the turn of the century, the editor was Col. Robert E. Slater.

The *Weekly's* last editor was Samuel Fenton Cary Jr., son of a congressman and one-time vice-presidential candidate. Cary, a good reporter and graceful writer who sprinkled *The Weekly's* prose with his own verse, took his work with him everywhere. *The Enquirer's* tireless librarian-historian of the 1920s, Harry Pence, once wrote that Cary "edited the weekly at his home, on the streetcars, or anywhere he happened to find a table and chair."

The *Weekly* was finally laid to rest in 1921, the last issue appearing on Feb. 9 that year, and with it died the Household Club — both victims of modern transportation, rural free mail, and that hot, new medium of the Roaring '20s, radio.

Election nights are especially demanding. The 1974 race for governor between John Gilligan and James Rhodes was memorable for its nerve-racking progress: It had been a tight contest with no predictable outcome, and as returns came in on election night, the lead swung back and forth.

"Gilligan Beating Rhodes" read the four-column head atop page one in the state edition. When the final began rolling around 1 a.m., the head had been changed to reflect new certainty about the outcome: "Gilligan Defeats Rhodes," it said. His margin was razor thin, but even Rhodes himself had conceded publicly. Then came late returns from conservative Hamilton County — always the slowest in the state — and the lead swung back to Rhodes. The pressroom stopped the presses so the news desk could change the head again, and the last of the final editions could tell readers, "Rhodes beating Gilligan." It was just another election night on Vine Street.

'SNAKE SHEET' STARTED THE MAGAZINE

The first supplement even vaguely resembling a "magazine" began accompanying *The Enquirer* in the 1890s. Called *The Saturday Supplement,* it contained miscellaneous news features, mostly reprinted from other publications and from feature-distribution syndicates. Because of the often bizarre, exotic, sensational material used in it, it was laughingly referred to among insiders as "the snake sheet."

The snake sheet generally ran four pages at first, but often was as big as eight pages before the turn of the century. It was a victim of shortages in World War I. Reduced again to four pages in August, 1916, and to two pages a month later, it died altogether at the end of the year.

One editor of the snake sheet was Arnold Eisler, who, with artist Tom Collins, frequently slipped out to play cards on company time with colleagues who worked for the German-language papers. Then they would sneak back to work using the back stairs from Battle Alley — College Street — behind *The Enquirer's* buildings. Eisler also wrote poetry, which his fellows at *The Enquirer* groaned at having to hear him recite. He had such a weakness for stories about bears that he once received a curt and sarcastic note from publisher

John R. McLean informing him that no more than three bear stories should appear on any one page of the Saturday Supplement.

After World War I, a new magazine section appeared. It was born July 25, 1920, and accompanied *The Enquirer* on Sundays. It contained eight tabloid (half-size) pages, including the Sunday comics in color, and feature photographs. The comics were separated out later in the 1920s, and the *Pictorial* Sunday supplement was expanded to full-size until World War II, when it shrank again to tabloid size.

In those days, the *Pictorial* was printed in sepia-tone ink, and because it was mainly photos, was printed outside *The Enquirer's* plant by the "rotogravure" process," which used a harder metal printing plate and allowed finer screens for sharper reproduction of photos.

This was Cincinnati's version of "the rotogravure" that the song "Easter Parade" promised you'd get your picture in.

The *Pictorial Enquirer* lasted until the end of 1968, although by then it was less a tabloid section than a mini-magazine. That's why, in 1969, under an editor named Jack Cannon, the name was changed to the *Enquirer Magazine* and the concept was expanded to include serious, full-length features, analyses and occasional fiction.

The Enquirer Magazine lived another 16 years.

If any one person's name is connected in the readers' minds

with the *Enquirer Magazine* and its predecessor, *The Pictorial Enquirer,* it is Allan Kain, the veteran photographer whose brilliant color work— especially his outdoor and nature shots — graced the magazine's pages for two decades.

The Enquirer Magazine was printed by a Louisville company, Standard Gravure. It was such a popular local advertising medium in the mid-1970s, that at busy retailing seasons it often had more than the 96 pages the printer could accommodate on the press and had to run in two sections. *The Enquirer Magazine* for years was the nation's largest (in terms of ad lineage), locally edited Sunday newspaper magazine, and scored higher in readership surveys than anything in the Sunday *Enquirer* except the top news on page one.

Up until its last edition, the magazine remained profitable for the newspaper and very popular with readers. However, by 1980, changes in advertising incentives made it more attractive for department stores to print their own all-ad supplements and to pay *The Enquirer* to insert them into the Sunday paper. *The Enquirer Magazine* shrank year by year, its place largely taken by pre-printed ad stuffers and national magazines such as Gannett's *USA Weekend.*

Finally, in December, 1988, *The Enquirer Magazine* died. It hadn't run a bear story in years.

FROM FARNY TO 'F. STOP'

While neither man's obituary in *The Enquirer* so much as mentioned it, two of the most famous American artists — Frank Duveneck and Henry Farny — produced illustrations for *The Enquirer* as young, free-lance, commercial artists in Cincinnati in the early 1870s.

The technology for reproducing photographs was still two decades away, and newspapers illustrated ads and stories with drawings etched as woodcuts or copper engravings. One Sunday in November, 1874, both artists accompanied reporter Lafcadio Hearn in covering the grisly Tanyard murder. Their illustrations in the next day's paper are signed with monograms, "FD" and "HF." It may have been the greatest concentration of talent *The Enquirer* ever brought to bear on a breaking story.

The reporter had met Duveneck and Farny on one of his first assignments after joining the paper in 1872, a story about Cincinnati artists. Duveneck and Hearn were the same age, 24, and Farny but three years older; they all became personal acquaintances. In the summer of 1874, Hearn and Farny collaborated on the illustrated weekly humor magazine *Ye Giglampz*. It failed within three months.

The Enquirer began using occasional illustrations with the news in 1854 but had no artists of its own for years and hired artists such as Farny and Duveneck on a free-lance basis.

Illustrations became far more common after John R. McLean took over the paper from his father in 1872. Visual appearance was plainly part of his strategy to produce a popular paper with mass appeal. Drawings became even more common in the1890s. The paper set up its own photoengraving department in 1895 — with one eye on closer control of the increasing number of illustrations, and another on the new technology of "halftone" engraving that had just made it possible for newspapers to reproduce photographs.

The Enquirer spawned many artists and illustrators of renown. Chief artist Winsor McCay was one of the originators of the comics and later produced the first animated movie cartoon. McCay started at *The Enquirer* in 1900, when McLean offered him a better salary than he was making at the rival *Commercial Tribune* doing political cartoons about McLean and the Democrats. The former sign painter and dime-museum artist had just begun to be published in national humor magazines, which used his political cartoons critical of the war with Spain.

When McCay moved to *The Enquirer,* the paper was between technologies: The first photos had appeared in 1898, but illustrations were still the rule, and McCay often

Continued on next page

Winsor McCay and part of his illustration which appeared in The Enquirer on Feb. 15, 1903.

accompanied reporters on stories. One was a lynching of a gang of robbers in Osgood, Ind., which drew newsmen from as far as Chicago. In his 1987 biography of McCay, John Canemaker quotes McCay's recollection of getting a scoop because "the cameramen were out of luck. It was dark and flash lights were not so hot in those days."

Bribing a train engineer to make a special, late-night trip back to Cincinnati, McCay was able to reach town in time to get his drawings in the next day's *Enquirer,* ahead of all other papers.

The cocky, always-overdressed McCay became the paper's chief artist. In 1903 he drew his first famous comic characters, the "Jungle Imps." The weekly series illustrated poems by George Randolph Chester, a reporter who later became famous for short stories about a fast-talking promoter named "Get-Rich-Quick Wallingford."

In 1903, James Gordon Bennett, publisher of the *New York Herald,* saw McCay's work and offered him triple his *Enquirer* salary. McCay sought advice from *The Enquirer's* editor, who replied: "Tell them that if they send you a check for traveling expenses, you'll take the offer."

McCay did, and back came a check, much to the editor's surprise. In New York, McCay found fame. His comic strip, "Little Nemo," based on his son, Winsor Jr., was so popular that it became a Victor Herbert musical. In 1909, he produced the drawings for "Gertie the Dinosaur," the first animated movie cartoon, with which he toured vaudeville theaters nationwide. In 1912 McCay gave up his comic strips and became editorial cartoonist for the Hearst syndicate. In 1917, he produced the first feature-length animated cartoon, *The Sinking of the Lusitania.*

McCay's staff at *The Enquirer* had included a young man named Carll B. Williams, who stayed around a long time and not only became chief artist but established a family tie to *Enquirer* readers that lasted for decades.

When Williams started at the paper in the 1890s, few thought he'd amount to much. He was reserved, frail, quiet and deaf, according to his friend, Harry Pence, the paper's librarian in the 1920s. Pence wrote Williams' obit in 1928. In the beginning, he recalled, Williams had done the odd jobs in the art department and the luminaries such as McCay treated him with disdain. "From the very first day," wrote Pence, Williams didn't seem to realize that the veterans "viewed him rather critically and went to no great lengths to encourage, or instruct him." But, Pence went on, "assigned to tasks upon which he was expected to fail, he refused to recognize the possibility of defeat, and always his innate talent and perseverance enabled him to succeed."

Williams' frilly borders and fancy embellishments enhanced photographs in the paper until his death. More notably, his drawings gave life to the characters in Robert Schulkers' nationally syndicated features and books about "Seckatary Hawkins."

Four years after Williams died, his daughter Caroline followed him to *The Enquirer.* Her forte was buildings and cityscapes, and for decades one

Caroline Williams' cityscapes of Cincinnati and Franklin Folger's "Girls" were extremely popular.

of her drawings of "A Spot in Cincinnati" appeared each Sunday on the editorial pages. After 20 years of working at *The Enquirer*, she moved with her widowed mother to a log cabin in Burlington, Ky. She worked there, sent her drawings in and seldom came to town. "She loved the old buildings," said editorial page editor Thomas Gephardt shortly after she died in 1988. "She told me she hated to come downtown because the new buildings had no style."

Few of her thousands of fans realize that Caroline Williams, for all her renown as a pen-and-

ink artist, had studied at the Sorbonne, and that in the last two years of her life she produced fine watercolors as well.

Even more reclusive than Caroline Williams was Franklin Folger, creator of the syndicated

cartoon, "The Girls," which appeared in more than 100 newspapers. "The Girls" gently satirized the foibles of middle-aged American women. It first saw print in *The Enquirer*, in December, 1952. Folger was so uncommunicative that he had no telephone, accepted no visitors and hated transportation of any kind. He drew "The Girls" at his apartment on Fourth Street and sent them to Chicago's Sun-Times Syndicate via *The Enquirer*. The only person he

ever dealt with was *The Enquirer's* Mildred Miller, a former reporter and columnist

who became his secretary and dealt with his fan mail.

In 1977, when Folger refused a 25th-anniversary interview with the very paper where his success began, Miller submitted reporter Lonnie Wheeler's written questions and later gave him Folger's laconic, handwritten replies. Then, realizing how inadequate that must have seemed to Wheeler, she offered herself as a surrogate interviewee. "OK," she said, "I'm Franklin Folger. Ask me anything."

"In some ways," Wheeler wrote, "Miller must really feel like Franklin Folger. She has been playing his part for 25 years, paying his bills, writing his letters, speaking his words."

While Folger was hiding behind "The Girls" skirts, over on the editorial page, a cartoonist named L. D. Warren was making Cincinnati fall in love with his daily drawings. Warren, who didn't even start at *The*

Enquirer until he was 40, became one of the most prolific cartoonists in American newspaper history.

Other editorial artists marveled at the style, grace, clarity and detail of his work. "L.D.," says one contemporary *Enquirer* artist, "was an absolute master draftsman." He was also a tireless student, and until the day he retired in 1974, took and taught drawing courses at the Cincinnati Art Academy.

Warren's trademark character was John Q. Public, a cartoon Everyman modeled after his father, who appeared in L.D.'s first *Enquirer* cartoon, on July 29, 1947, regarding the city's flood-control program. John Q. tries to make the river "stay away from his door" with a broom. *The Enquirer* had had no cartoonist of its own since before the Depression, and Warren was a breath of fresh air after years of syndicated material.

The next year, he had a one-man exhibition at the Art Aca-

L.D. Warren, an acrobat as a young man, would entertain friends by standing on his hands and drawing with a pencil in his teeth.

demy and was honored by the Disabled American Veterans for his cartoons supporting their cause. In 1949 he won the first in an almost annual string of awards from the Freedoms Foundation at Valley Forge, Pa. He was a political conservative, and found his niche at the conservative *Enquirer* during the Cold War era. His wife, Julianne Baker, was a photographer at the afternoon *Post and Times-Star*, and they were as talented a couple as ever gave visual life to the pages of newspapers.

Warren's retirement in 1974 left a huge vacancy. But within two years a young cartoonist named Jim Borgman showed up at *The Enquirer*. He endeared himself to the paper and the city, as well as to the Pulitzer Prize selection committee. The day before *The Enquirer* celebrated its 150th birthday, he won the 1991 Pulitzer for editorial cartooning.

Sports has rated its own cartoons at *The Enquirer* since Harold E. Russell created his first "Danny Dumm" sports cartoon in 1926, 12 years after starting at the paper. Danny was such a familiar figure that thousands of readers thought it was the cartoonist's name, despite the distinctive "Russ" with which he signed his work. Russell produced a daily sports drawing until he retired in 1959, then continued doing a Sunday cartoon until he died in 1966. He was often compared with Willard Mullin, his contemporary on the *New York World Telegram*.

Russell was a knowledgeable racing handicapper, and for years included a list of "probable winners" in a box within his cartoons. When he retired, his cartoons in support of baseball earned him a lifetime pass to every National League game. His best-known character may be "Mr. Red," the baseball-faced symbol of the city's team which he first drew in 1969.

Jerry Dowling, Russell's successor as the paper's sports cartoonist, invented a symbol of

Harold Russell's character Danny Dumm was often mistaken as the artist.

his own, the humongous "Big Red Machine" that adorned the paper during the team's glorious years in the 1970s. Dowling was also the creator of a daily comic strip built around a newspaper character named "F. Stop Fitzgerald," which appeared in *The Enquirer* for a time in the 1970s. Caricatures of *Enquirer* colleagues frequented Dowling's work for years, until one editor — upset by a drawing perceived as unflattering — forbade the practice. Colleagues still occasionally think they detect them, however.

The present art director at *The Enquirer* is Ron Huff, who designed this book and who, before becoming art director, spent the better part of a year in Washington on assignment for Gannett as part of the team that designed *USA Today*.

His predecesssor as art director, Elmer Wetenkamp, is now near retirement from the staff. He started at *The Enquirer* in the 1940s and is a rich lode of anecdotes. One of his favorites was about something that happened one day in the 1950s, when the department was on the fourth floor with windows onto Vine Street. The entire art staff was intently watching a child at play in a room in a building across the street when, with no warning whatever, a man came hurtling down past the window and smashed into the second-floor balcony below — a suicide from the Enquirer Building's roof.

"Harold Russell was working on his Danny Dumm sports cartoon at the time," Wetenkamp remembers, "and he fainted. Just fainted dead away. He never did get his cartoon done. It was one of the few times he didn't make a deadline."

NEXT....

JIMBORGMAN

"I was so green," recalls Jim Borgman, the Cincinnati native who now wields *The Enquirer's* political cartooning pens, "that I remember hearing people out in that big open newsroom yelling 'COPY!' and then the sound of hurried footsteps in response. Only I thought they were yelling 'COFFEE!'"

That was 1976, when he was a raw kid, straight out of Kenyon College. "Hey," he says, explaining his naivete, "it sounded like a legitimate plea, like yelling 'MEDIC!' on a battlefield. I never tried it, but I came close, and I still wonder what the copy clerks would have done if I'd followed it up by yelling 'WITH CREAM AND SUGAR!'"

Jim Borgman is green no longer. In this, *The Enquirer's* sesquicentennial year, he became the paper's and Cincinnati's first-ever Pulitzer prize winner. He won for editorial cartooning. A celebrity now, Borgman had to pay the usual dues first. "It was three or four years, truth be told," he admits, "before I knew the Democrats from the Republicans. But Cincinnati seems to have forgiven me.

"By 1980," he adds, "I felt I had legitimate opinions to air."

The Enquirer found its Pulitzer-prize artist in a bar. Well, actually it was at the Cricket Tavern next door to the paper on Vine, which was where newspaper people hung out in those days.

The winter before he graduated from Kenyon, the young cartoonist had come to the attention of his father's employer, who just happened to know Graydon DeCamp, then editor of *The Enquirer Magazine*. DeCamp , as a favor to a friend,

Jim Borgman

agreed to meet the young man for lunch and to see whether the magazine would be able to use any of his work.

They met in the Cricket Tavern and after half an hour of small talk, DeCamp turned the conversation to Borgman's cartooning and asked for work samples. Borgman reached down by his feet and pulled out a large portfolio, spreading it open on the narrow table in the cramped restaurant booth.

Up to then, DeCamp had regarded the entire exercise as just another favor for a pal that probably wouldn't come to much. L. D. Warren's successor, Dwane Powell, was departing, and *The Enquirer* was looking for a new cartoonist, but DeCamp was not directly involved in the search for Powell's successor.

Five minutes into leafing through Borgman's portfolio of college-paper clippings, however, DeCamp knew he was on to something big. DeCamp immeditely took the portfolio to editor Luke Feck who said he also had received a Borgman portfolio from the *Philadelphia Inquirer*. Borgman had sent it there, seeking a job, but the paper didn't have an opening. The cartoonist at the *Inquirer* knew *The Enquirer* was looking for someone, so he sent it to L.D. Warren who turned it over to Feck.

Feck, editorial page editor Thom Gephardt and publisher William J. Keating reviewed the portfolio and the search was complete. *The Enquirer* hired Jim Borgman.

His first drawing for *The Enquirer* appeared a few weeks later, before he was graduated and became an

Enquirer employee. It was a color cover for an *Enquirer Magazine* story on the Ohio primaries.

"At Kenyon" says Borgman, looking back now through 15 years and a Pulitzer prize, "every cartoon I drew had been greeted with glee that, in fact, 'someone was paying attention to us.' I was virtually carried off the hill on everyone's shoulders at graduation and am still referred to as the only art major ever to repay his student loan.

"Suddenly, I walked into a major metropolitan newspaper, and angry, grown-up people were calling me on the phone to complain about my cartoons. The whole first year threw me for a loop. Thankfully, the work I did was so forgettable that everyone has forgotten it."

The fact is, Borgman's career as an artist began at Cincinnati's Carson Elementary School, in blue-collar Price Hill, when a crayon drawing he had done of Popeye appeared on a children's TV show. He remembers liking the attention a lot. He came by cartooning honestly: His father was a commercial illustrator who designed and painted truck-sized logos, lettering and designs. Jim swept the shop floor for his father and worked one summer applying decals to trucks. His father died in 1984. "He would have loved this," Borgman said in an interview after winning his Pulitzer. "He kept a scrapbook of every cartoon I ever published. He had something like nine volumes"

At St. William grade school, Jim amused classmates with scathingly satirical caricatures of teachers. One nun, anything but amused, told him he was wasting his talent drawing cartoons.

Borgman began "wasting his talent" on the pages of *The Enquirer* on June 10, 1976. Gerald Ford and Ronald Reagan were in the drawing. Among his most popular drawings are the Cincinnati Bengals' mascot waiting for its next Riverfront Stadium victim during the team's 1988 championship season and the domino theory catching up with Mikhail Gorbachev.

At first, Borgman recalls, he was cautious, very uncomfortable.

In an *Enquirer* story published after Borgman won the Pulitzer prize, he described his start at the newspaper as "just living hell. I wasn't used to the medium, so it was just pure labor."

An ulcer started, but Borgman stuck with the job. "I tend to be sort of responsible" he said in the story about him. "I didn't do outrageous work, and they came to trust me."

Eventually he did learn the difference between Democrats and Republicans and developed an outlook of his own, at variance on many issues with the conservative views ordinarily found on *The Enquirer's* editorial pages. He once offered to seek work elsewhere if his superiors didn't like what he was doing.

"No," he recalls being told, "Your name's on it. People will see it as your work."

Borgman has been named "best in the nation" three times — 1987, '88, and '89 — by his peers in the National Cartoonists' Society. He has won several "Best of Gannett" awards, the Ohio Governor's Award in Journalism, and the Thomas Nast prize for editorial cartooning.

The Pulitzer selections were announced April 9, 1991, which meant that news of Borgman's prize appeared on page one of *The Enquirer* on April 10, 1991, the newspaper's own 150th birthday.

'GIVE US MORE SECK!' WHICH WE DID

One of the most popular characters ever to spring from an *Enquirer* mind was a lad named Hawkins, who in 1918 began 30 years as secretary of an imaginary boys club that at one time had more than a million very real members. "Seckatary Hawkins" began as a short story in *The Enquirer* but went on to national syndication in more than 100 newspapers, became a daily cartoon strip, and then a serial on network radio.

In 1966, reporter Jim Golden wrote a biography of both the "the fat little fellow whose hair stood straight up" and his creator, Robert Franc Shulkers.

"My first Seckatary Hawkins story ran in *The Enquirer* 48 years ago this coming Feb. 3 (1966)," Shulkers reminisced. He related that he was born in Covington, Ky., in 1890, and grew up in a neighborhood just a block or two from the Licking River. "We had some exciting times around the river," he told Golden.

"In those days there were green woods upstream between Covington and Latonia, and we played there often." The river on whose banks many of the Hawkins episodes were set, said Shulkers, was a composite of the Licking and the Ohio.

Shulkers joined *The Enquirer* in 1911 as secretary to W. F. Wiley, then the managing editor. The next year he wrote a Christmas story for the children's page, and soon he was contributing regularly in addition to his secretarial work, as well as writing book reviews and occasionally a column of foreign news features called "Old World Chitchat." In 1918, Shulkers wrote a children's page story called "The Snow Fort" about a lad named Hawkins. It was "Seck" Hawkins' first appearance as a character, and ran in the paper on Feb. 3, 1918.

It was not intended as part of a series, but it was a hit, and H.N. Hildreth, the Sunday editor, suggested Shulkers write about Seck and his pals every Sunday. The first episode had been written in the third person. But on Feb. 17, Shulkers wrote a first-person episode — an extract from "Seckatary Hawkins' Club diary." Kids loved it, and Seck was in print to stay. The stories ran in *The Enquirer* for 17 years. Seckatary Hawkins was illustrated by Carll B. Williams, director of *The Enquirer* art department, and his drawings became an integral part of the series and gave Hawkins a visual identity.

The newspaper began to get so many requests for back issues that Wiley suggested a book. Stewart Kidd published *Hawkins in Cuba* in 1921 and *The Red Runners* in 1922. Both got excellent reviews.

But the syndicates just didn't seem interested. So Shulkers did what Hawkins probably would have done and took matters into his own hands. "In August of 1923," said Shulkers, "my wife, Julia, and I took off in our Oakland touring car. In 14 days we made 12 cities, several on the East Coast."

He was not without experience; as Wiley's secretary, he had handled syndication of the weekly "Luke McLuke" column by *The Enquirer's* James S. Hastings. "When we returned we had sold Seck to nine newspapers. Shortly afterward I signed with Metropolitan Newspaper Syndicate to handle the marketing."

Key to the series promotion was the "Seckatary Hawkins Fair and Square Clubs." The first was started by *The Enquirer* in response to letters from children who kept asking how to get to the riverbank clubhouse and join Hawkins' club. "Mr. Wiley suggested we oblige them," Shulkers said.

The oaths of membership consisted of about a dozen promises and rules aimed at courting parental approval. Later the pledge was drastically simplified: I shall always be fair and square, possessed with strength of character and honest with God and my friends and in later life a good citizen."

"Which we did." Those words, "which we did," were the trademark ending of Hawkins'stories.

Soon, via the syndicate papers, clubs were signing up members by the thousands all over the country: in Cincinnati, 170,000; in Pittsburgh , 300,000. There were parades, picnics, special theatrical entertainments. Some cities opened official clubhouses. Some clubs wrote their own songs.

Seck got his own radio programs in 1923, a Saturday evening half-hour on WLW and a Tuesday evening half-hour on WSAI. In 1930, Seckatary Hawkins became a daily children's feature on the NBC network.

His third book, *Stormy The Dog Stealer*, and a second edition of *Hawkins in Cuba* were published in 1925 by Appleton. In 1926, Shulkers bought back the copyrights and published a set of six on his own: *Stoner's Boy, The Gray Ghost, Knights of the Square Table, Ching Toy, The Chinese Coin* and *The Yellow Y*. In 1930 came *Herman the Fiddler*. Altogether, the books sold about 50,000 copies.

Carll Williams died in 1928 and artist Joe Ebertz took up the pen. That was the year that the newspaper started a daily Seckatary Hawkins comic strip and it continued until the mid-1930s.

The end came slowly. After the peak year of 1930, Shulkers said, "the Depression killed off a lot of juvenile stuff. It was called expendable." *The Enquirer* dropped the daily feature in 1935. Cleveland's *Plain Dealer* carried on until 1942, and a few smaller papers persisted until 1949.

Long after Hawkins had vanished, Shulkers returned in retirement to *The Enquirer* and worked as an assistant in the library. Many of his co-workers, new to the business since the war, didn't know who he (or Seckatary Hawkins) was.

In researching for this book, we kept finding old file cards, some bound together, some stuffed in with photos or clippings, but each containing a nugget of arcane historical trivia about *The Enquirer* — the date of the first color ad, or the name of the managing editors in the 1890s. It was amazing how often we would discover we needed some obscure fact, only to come across just that item of information on one of those file cards. We don't know who put them in the files. But we do know that in his later years, on slow nights, Shulkers spent hours poring over file cards, and we strongly suspect we had a lot of help on this book from Seckatary Hawkins, so we figured we'd better say thank you and tell you about it. Which we did.

Robert Shulkers

THE SHERIFF — DOC WATERS — JUDGE GRANBERY

ROBBY HOOD — BILL DARBY — JOHNNY McLAREN — JERRY MOORE — PERRY STOKES — SHADOW LOOMIS — SECKATARY HAWKINS — LINK LAMBERT — DICK FERRIS — ROY DOBLE — LEW HUNTER — HERB ACOMB

COMICS BECOME SERIOUS BUSINESS

One Sunday in 1894, New Yorkers found something startling on their newsstands. The *New York World* was wrapped in a section of amusing stories illustrated in full color. Readers who'd had nothing but black- and-white papers immediately dubbed it "the funny paper" and soon were buying three times as many as ever before. The name "funnies" has been a synonym for comic pages ever since.

The colored paper gave rise to another familiar term in 1896, when *World* artist Richard Outcalt produced what is now regarded as the first comic strip, "The Yellow Kid," for the *World's* funny pages. Readers called the *World* "the yellow paper."

It was in a furious circulation war at the time with the *Journal*, which William Randolph Hearst had just bought from *Enquirer* publisher John R. McLean. Hearst, stung badly, hired Outcalt away from the *World*, and Joseph Pulitzer paid another artist to produce the strip, and the Yellow Kid began appearing in both papers. Some straight-laced citizens considered the "Kid" vulgar, but that didn't bother Hearst or Pulitzer, whose sensationalism climbed to new heights daily. Soon, their circulation-building style came to be called "yellow journalism."

In Boston, the Christian Scientists established a paper, the *Monitor,* in an effort to offset the sensationalism of the yellow papers. The *Monitor* took a very high road indeed — no crime news, no scandal and, of course, no funnies.

It took six years for the comics to reach Cincinnati and *The Enquirer,* and when they arrived, they were only in black and white at first.

The Enquirer's first Sunday comics appeared on June 8, 1902. It is probably not a coincidence that this is just about the time of year when Hollywood releases movies aimed at young audiences nowadays — that is, about when school gets out for the summer. They consisted of two strips on page five, with some jokes as filler. The strips were "Happy Hooligan" by F. Opper and "Foxy

Grandpa" by Carl Emil Schultze, who drew under the *nom de plume* of "Bunny." On the same date, a third strip appeared on *The Enquirer's* children's page. It was Rudolph Dirks' "Katzenjammer Kids." By the time school resumed in the fall, the comics were a huge hit. More strips were added. Howarth's "Mr. and Mrs. Skinner" appeared on Oct. 12, and Opper's "Alphonse and Gaston" was added on Nov. 2. Howarth's "Lulu and Leander" debuted the Sunday after Christmas.

Then, a few weeks into the new year, on Jan. 18, 1903, the comics first appeared in color, as an entire supplement. The first page contained "Foxy Grandpa" by Carl Emil

BRINGING UP FATHER - - - By McManus

REGISTERED U. S. PATENT OFFICE. COPYRIGHT, 1921 INTERNATIONAL NEWS SERVICE

Comics in the daily **Enquirer** *debuted Oct. 26, 1918, with this strip featuring George McManus' battling couple, Jiggs and Maggie.*

Schultze and a strip by F. Swinnerton called "Mt. Ararat Animals." The second page of the section was entirely filled by "The Jungle Imps," a weekly fable illustrated by the *Enquirer's* own Winsor McCay, who later went on to far greater fame as the originator of the animated movie cartoon.

Page three in that first color comics section was a fashion feature — also in color. Page four contained "The Katzenjammer Kids" and "Happy Hooligan."

When McCay went to New York in 1903, his "Jungle Imps" was replaced by *Enquirer* artist Ap Adams' "Clowns."

The comics did not run in the daily *Enquirer* until 1918, when George McManus' "Bringing Up Father" began appearing on Oct. 26. It stayed for years; the domestic battles of Jiggs and Maggie remained popular well into the 1950s.

In the early days, comics were a mix of work by the paper's own artists and strips bought from syndicates, but after about 1920 were entirely syndicated until the 1970s. Then *The Enquirer* had one more fling with a locally produced comic strip. That was sports cartoonist Jerry Dowling's local strip built around a news-photographer character named "F. Stop Fitzgerald." It debuted in *The Enquirer* on Sept. 17, 1978, (the same day as "Garfield") and lasted 14 months.

Most Cincinnatians over 55 or so probably remember sitting by the radio as children and listening to the Sunday comics, following along as an announcer read them. The "radio comics" began April 15, 1934, and ran each Sunday at 8:15 a.m. on WFBE (which later became WCPO). The voice was Robert Bentley, an actor, singer and announcer at the station. In 1942, Bentley became *The Enquirer's* radio editor, writing a daily column called "Lend Me Your Ears." He later also announced a radio program called *The Voice of The Enquirer* on WSAI each evening.

Over the years, strips have come and gone, as times changed. Unabashedly funny — and often subtly satirical — at the start, the "comics" began acquiring dramatic qualities in the 1930s, and during World War II, children and adults alike awaited each day's action by such heroes as *Smilin' Jack* and *Buz*

F. Stop Fitzgerald

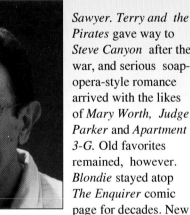

Jerry Dowling's F. Stop Fitzgerald began Sept. 17, 1978, the same day Garfield *first appeared.*

Sawyer. Terry and the Pirates gave way to *Steve Canyon* after the war, and serious soap-opera-style romance arrived with the likes of *Mary Worth, Judge Parker* and *Apartment 3-G.* Old favorites remained, however. *Blondie* stayed atop *The Enquirer* comic page for decades. New "funnies" caught on, too — *Dennis the Menace*, for instance. And in the serious political climate of the early '70s, we began seeing delightful social satire again.

The Enquirer has always understood how seriously its readers took their comic strips, because whenever anything changed on the comic page, the letters poured in. John Caldwell and Dennis Doherty came to understand better than anyone. As features editor — later reader editor

— Caldwell would conduct periodic reader polls on the comics, so he had a pretty good handle on what was popular, what wasn't. But on Palm Sunday, 1982, something misfired.

Polls had shown the "Judge Parker" strip to be waning in popularity. Doherty — newly promoted to assistant managing editor — pulled it and substituted a strip called *Duffy*. Next day, the calls came flooding in. Caldwell, now retired, calls it the largest unsolicited reader response to anything the editorial department ever did in his long career. (The only response greater had been the thousands of letters and calls objecting to glamorous photos in a women's underwear ad supplement placed by Shillito's department store about five years earlier.)

This makes the *Judge Parker* case even more intriguing, in deputy managing editor Doherty's mind, because on the same Palm Sunday the paper also ran a special section on homosexuals. It, too, engendered scores of calls from Cincinnatians who complained that it "glorified" the gay life. But up against Parker, homosexuals took a back seat among readers. "The calls about the piece on gays," recalls Doherty, "were outnumbered almost two to one by calls from people who wanted *Judge Parker* back. What's worse," he adds, "none of the people calling about the feature on gays canceled their subscriptions. Three canceled because of *Judge Parker*. Don't tell me how seriously people take their comics!"

THE CINCINNATI ENQUIRER

FRIDAY MORNING, APRIL 5, 1968 PRICE 10 CENTS

DR. KING IS SLAIN BY SNIPER BULLET

Nation Shocked, LBJ Pleads For Restraint

Dr. Martin Luther King Jr.

— AP Wirephoto

MEMPHIS, Tenn. (UPI)—Dr. Martin Luther King Jr., the Nobel peace prize winner who repeatedly walked in the shadow of death in his fight to bring integration to America, was slain by a white sniper Thursday night when he stepped onto the balcony of his hotel.

Police issued a bulletin for a young white man in dark clothes who dashed out of a building across the street after the shooting. The rifle, fitted with a scope, onto the sidewalk and fled his life.

"A prophet, a bridge" . . . page 31

President Johnson appeared on nationwide television two hours after the shot was fired. The President said:

As any American citizen," he said, "to reject the blind violence that has struck down Dr. King, who lived by nonviolence."

The President urged prayers for peace and understanding in the land and said:

"We can achieve nothing by lawlessness and divisiveness among the American people."

'I May Die'

NEW YORK (P) — Dr. Martin Luther King in 1962 after shots were fired in nearby houses, said . . . "I may get my crucified I may even die. But I want it said even if I die in the struggle that he died to make me free."

'Country's Shame'

WASHINGTON (AP)—Vice President Hubert H. Humphrey said Thursday night the assassination of Dr. Martin Luther King Jr. "brings shame to our country."

But he predicted that the slaying of the civil rights leader in Memphis will bring new strength to the cause for which King fought.

Humphrey's statement:

"Martin Luther King's death is a tragedy and sorrow to his family and our nation. The criminal act that took his life brings shame to our country.

"An apostle of nonviolence has been the victim of violence.

"The cause for which he marched and worked will find new strength. The blight of discrimination, poverty and neglect must be erased from America, an America of full freedom, full and equal opportunity shall be his living memorial."

Shock And Distress Felt In Nation

WASHINGTON (UPI)—Not since John F. Kennedy was assassinated on November 22, 1963, has the U.S. capital been so shaken by a murder, and feared repercussions of the slaying of Dr. Martin Luther King.

Leaders called for calm. Some in Congress said open housing legislation should now be passed as a memorial to the man who marched for it.

A $250-a-plate Democratic party fund raising dinner broke up early, its thousands of guests leaving the Washington ballroom in silence and disbelief.

Dr. King, said House Speaker John McCormack (D. Mass.), "was a man who strengthened the House as it concurs in the Senate civil rights bill."

The bill, adopted by the House earlier this year, would outlaw discrimination in the sale or rental of 68% of the nation's housing. It also preserves the major rights legislation—such as King's—a Federal crime.

Southerners too spoke in anguish.

"Violence," said Sen. James O. Eastland (D. Minn.) "is to be deplored. It does not have a place."

Sen. Edward W. Brooke (R. Mass.), the only Negro in the Senate, said this.

"In our anguish and bitterness over this event, let us not lose sight of the meaning of this great man's life . . ."

Richard Cardinal Cushing, Roman Catholic archbishop of Boston, said "An eloquent voice for the rights of all men was silenced, and with it everyone will mourn." In a statement, "had dedicated his life to the brotherhood of all men and now he has given his life for the ideals he so zealously preached. May his noble soul rest in peace and bless his loved ones."

Dr. Ralph J. Bunche, in a telegram to King's widow, called the shooting "a most grievous blow to all that is good and decent in our society and to achieve the goals for which Dr. King sacrificed his life."

Assassination Shock To City

Word of Dr. Martin Luther King's assassination fell like a bomb shell Thursday night on Mayor Eugene P. Ruehlmann's Conference on Commitment at the Exposition Convention Center.

"I have just been told that one of the 300 Cincinnati leaders who had gathered at the center to discuss root causes of the urban crisis.

Immediately upon learning of the assassination, Mayor Ruehlmann called for a moment of silence in Dr. King's memory.

Visibly shaken by the news, Councilman Myron Bush, nation's urban problems and he said later in a statement to The Enquirer.

"The most fitting tribute we can pay . . . is to work even harder and intensify our efforts and determination to eliminate the injustices of our society and to achieve the harmony throughout this country."

Visibly shaken by the news, Councilman Myron Bush noted that local leaders were working toward solving local and racial problems when the news hit.

Pray For U.S., RFK Urges After Slaying

INDIANAPOLIS, Ind. (UPI)—Sen. Robert F. Kennedy Thursday told a predominantly Negro audience that the slaying of Dr. Martin Luther King's family to pray for our country which all of us love."

Kennedy, whose brother, former President John F. Kennedy, was slain by an assassin's bullets 4½ years ago, was informed of King's murder in Memphis when he arrived here and was to make a campaign address at the Indianapolis airport on the last leg of a three-city campaign swing.

"The New York Democrat, who is entered in the May 7 Indiana presidential primary, made a brief statement. He recalled his brother's assassination in his reference to King's assassination.

"In this difficult day, in this difficult time for the United States, it is perhaps well to ask what kind of a nation we are and what direction we want to move in."

It is important to recognize the injustice but we have to make an effort to understand, to go beyond these rather difficult times.

"My favorite poet was Aeschylus. He wrote: In our sleep, pain which cannot forget falls drop by drop upon the heart until, in our own despair, against our will, comes wisdom through the awful grace of God.

Troops In Viet Fight Malaria Too

BOSTON (UPI) — An Army colonel said Thursday malaria causes more casualties than U.S. forces in Vietnam than enemy action every day.

Col. William D. Tigertt, director of the Walter Reed Army Institute of Research, indicated that malaria strikes "principally at the infantryman" but added a considerable number of other troops were affected by the disease.

The Army reported 9124 cases of malaria in Vietnam during 1967. Eleven of the men died, Tigertt said.

The colonel said malaria was nowhere near as crippling today as it was during the early day of World War II when it was encountered in the South Pacific islands.

That's Far Out

Maralo Sprague, who lives way the heck out in Batavia, advertised a house-for-rent-or-sale in The Enquirer Classified columns and rented the first day.

"It was a lovely house," said Mrs. Sprague. "So that the world's most beautiful people," Bush said.

Twenty-Mile Stand, Oneonta, Socialville and New Palestine some ideas Call 421-6500 to contact the far-out buyers and renters.

A Tragic Moment —And Time Stops

At the moment of a tragedy, in that second of time when we are face to face with inexplicable, senseless brutalism, a clock within us seems to stop.

Time stands still, while we try to grasp the meaning of what has happened.

Each of us in this nation must waste no time in assessing the meaning of the assassination of Dr. Martin Luther King Jr. That Dr. King, the vigorous exponent of nonviolence in pursuit of racial justice and equality, was felled by violence adds even more meaning to this national tragedy.

It came at a moment when passes were high that our growing awareness of our many problems was leading us to a better day.

If we are to save ourselves from the maelstrom of violence and murder based on insensate race hatred, we collectively must follow the course so well espoused by Dr. King—the course of rationality, justice, nonviolence.

The City of Cincinnati, every citizen in it, must now exercise reason.

At the moment of the killing, 200 citizens of Greater Cincinnati were assembled at the Convention-Exposition Center undertaking a study of the root causes behind the problems of prejudice, discrimination, social inequality—ills that beset every urban area of this country.

When Mayor Eugene Ruehlmann, at this Mayor's Conference on Commitment, announced the tragedy, he asked for a minute of silent prayer. Those in attendance observed that moment, then went back to their task.

They resumed their work in the same reasonable, calm, serious manner in which they had been working before the news struck.

In a way, there is a lesson there for each of us.

Unless we, as they did, resolve not to let the tragedy deter us from trying to correct these ills that so sorely beset us, there can be little hope.

God willing we will do so. We must.—An Editorial

"We must, never forget the courage and dedication which made a bright red hills of Georgia, sons of former slaves and the sons of former slave owners will set down together in a table of brotherhood.

"We in Cincinnati join the nation in the shock, dismay, at the death of Rev. King. Our sympathy goes out not only to Mrs. King and family but to all those who represent and followed his leadership."

Calvin H. Conliffe, the Negro member of the Cincinnati Board of Education who rendered the mayor's conference, said "this deep, personal grief over this tragic, violent death of a man who fought so hard for non-violence."

'I Have A Dream'

WASHINGTON (UPI)—"I have a dream . . . It is a dream deeply rooted in the American dream . . .

I have a dream that one day in the red hills of Georgia, sons of former slaves and the sons of former slave owners will set down together in a table of brotherhood.

These words were spoken in August 1963 by a 5-foot, eight-inch mahogany-colored Negro in the nation's capital before 200,000 persons participating in the much heralded "Washington march."

History has the man into this position, would both be immortal and a sign of ingratitude if I did not face by moral responsibility if I do what I can in this struggle."

The murder of Dr. Martin Luther King Jr. was so momentous that no other news appeared on page one. Rarely do newspapers have single-subject front pages.

EXTRA! EXTRA!

The Weather
Cloudy and colder today, with a low of 32 and a high of 48. Saturday, fair and warming.

Details: Map on Page 5

Local and Area News Pages 5'14

CAMERAS GET NEWS IN A FLASH

The first *Enquirer* was all type, and what few illustrations there were for the next half century were woodcuts or copper engravings. Usually too expensive for one-time illustration of news stories, they generally adorned advertisements whose repeated use justified the cost.

The Enquirer's first news illustration appeared Oct.1, 1854: a panoramic drawing on page one of the Little Miami Railroad's car shops and engine sheds at Pendleton, three miles upriver from the city. Another etching adorned the editorial page that day.

For years, the paper didn't do its own engraving but jobbed the work out to commercial engravers. (The paper must have been a good source of business, however, because after 1847, an engraver was always in business nearby.)

Photography was an infant technology in the 1850s. Although the "halftone" engraving process which allows printed reproduction of photographs was invented in 1852, the combination wasn't in widespread newspaper use for 50 years.

News continued to be illustrated by artists, not photographers.

By 1895, however, photography was common enough to be on the verge of replacing illustrations, and *The Enquirer* set up its own photoengraving department. It was mainly for advertising use at first. The first halftone news photos ran on Monday, Sept. 5, 1898 — a whole page of photos of dignitaries in town for an encampment of the Grand Army of the Republic. They appeared in a special supplement, prepared well in advance to give photoengravers a luxury rare in the newspaper business — time.

Two months passed before the paper ran more photos, on Nov. 20, 1898. These were photos of children and women in conjunction with Sunday society news — another use that allowed ample production time.

These early "news" photos were almost all head shots — studio portraits — by commercial photographers. *The Enquirer* didn't have its own cameramen then, although photographers were on staff at many other papers. Publisher John R. McLean preferred commercial photographers' work for his papers,

The Enquirer and the *Washington Post.*

One of the earliest photographers on *The Enquirer's* payroll was Paul Briol, later a well-known commercial photographer in Cincinnati. A 19-year-old from Spencer, Mass., he began as a photographer for a St. Louis paper in 1908, and went to work at *The Enquirer* in 1910. Photography was still so new that it wasn't a full-time job. Briol also was one of several staffers who produced the column, "Old World Chitchat." He made photographs for *The Enquirer* until 1920, then left to open a

Continued on next page

bookstore. When that failed during the Depression, he opened a commercial studio and started a remarkable collection of photos of the city and its people. More than 6,000 of his negatives and prints are in the collection of the Cincinnati Historical Society. Injured in an auto wreck in 1962, Briol died in 1969.

Because photography is relatively new to journalism, there are fewer photographers for the historian to keep track of, but there certainly have been some very memorable ones.

Robert Stigers, chief photographer of *The Enquirer* on its 100th birthday in 1941 and later a photographer across town at the *Post,* was among the most memorable. Colleagues knew he was soft and sentimental inside, but to outsiders, he seemed a gruff bear who respected no person.

Once he found himself assigned to photograph the goodwill visit of some minor nation's monarch. Did Stigers address him as "your majesty," as everyone else was doing? Absolutely not. "Hey, king!" he commanded. "Look over here." The mon-

arch did as he was told and Stigers got his shot — then asked the king for an autograph, and got that, too. He was secretly very proud at having photographed so many famous people. He was proud, too, of his frightening ability to reach news scenes first, and often spoke of the time he drove the 22 miles from downtown Cincinnati to an explosion site in suburban Loveland in 20 minutes — before expressways.

Three of his best known contemporaries were Herb Heise, Carl Wellinger and Ran Cochran. The latter — hand-

Paul Briol was one of The Enquirer's first photographers. This is his famous photo of the Tyler Davidson Fountain.

some, well-dressed, ruddy-faced and eternally youthful — was an *Enquirer* photographer for 10 years before World War II, won distinction for his combat photography during the war, then returned to become *The*

Enquirer's chief photographer for 20 years after it, until he died of a heart attack in 1969.

Heise was a whiz with a camera who was blessed with a good news sense and a sardonic wit. Late one day, nearing quitting time, a tired and harried Heise was returning to the office from an assignment in a car outfitted with a radio. The city desk was trying to reach him to cover a late-breaking story. He didn't reply, so the desk had to send someone else. When he finally appeared in the office, an irate editor demanded to know why he'd not responded by radio.

"Well, I was maintaining radio silence for security reasons," Heise explained with a perfectly straight face. "I didn't want the other paper to know about it."

Carl Wellinger's name brings

a smile to the face of Bob Firestone, retired now after a long, illustrious career as sports editor at the *Times-Star* and assistant city editor at *The Enquirer*. He still laughs as he recalls that Wellinger always referred to famous people as "dignaries." And he remembers that the Cricket Tavern next door to *The Enquirer* on Vine Street had a drink called "The Wellinger."

"No one seemed to know what was in it," Firestone says, "but I remember it was something awfully dark." The closest description of the drink is a double Manhattan cocktail.

Whether they know him or not, many older Cincinnatians remember Wellinger as the photographer who scuttled along in foul territory between third and home at Crosley Field. He crouched like a catcher to shoot action close-ups with his bulky Speed Graphic in the long-ago days when photographers were allowed on the field.

It has been so long since that was allowed that it is beyond

memory of the elder of today's staff, Fred Straub (although he and his col-

Herb Heise

leagues still roam freely on football sidelines, where they are much likelier to be overrun). The German-born Straub has never lost his old-world accent, and he takes part of his annual vacation at Oktoberfest time and returns to Munich for his beer and wurst. Like many photographers, he has technical

interests outside photography; his was flying. His late colleague, Bob Free, kept the paper's police radios working and was a serious wood-working artisan who made lovely flintlock muskets from scratch.

Ran Cochran

This was logical. Until word processing came along and demanded more, a reporter's tools were simple — pencil and note

pad. The photographer has always had to contend with technology, the physics of light, the mechanics of cameras, the chemistry of the darkroom. The earliest ones had to deal with huge wooden cameras, heavy tree-trunk tripods and hazardous flash powder. In the 1950s, the twin-lens Rolleiflex simplified matters, but not until the versatile, modern 35-millimeter camera came along did the photographer cease to be a beast of burden. These cameras are so small that most photographers carry at least two.

A few of today's photographers remember when photos were reproduced as halftones with 65 lines of dots to the inch. That's crude by modern standards (photos in this book are reproduced with 150-lines to the inch), and subtle shadings often got lost. Artists would retouch them, especially where people were shot against a dark background, and *The Enquirer's* files are heavy with old 8-by-10 glossies encrusted with retouching paint.

One artist, Stan Cohen, specialized in painting fake "windows" behind the heads, making them visible in print. Action photos of basketball, made in darkened gyms, often needed this doctoring.

Enquirer photographers, for years, have customarily driven their own cars on assignments and have been reimbursed for mileage. Once, in the '80s, unhappy over the paper's refusal to increase the mileage rate, most of the

Bob Free

photo staff's cars suddenly broke down one day and had to be garaged for repairs that lasted several days. Photographers took to calling cabs to cover assignments, and when the front office balked at that, a few began riding the bus, even to a breaking spot news scene Eventually, the job action ended, thanks to a spirit of compromise and the photographers' abhorrence of missing that good shot.

By the 1970s, *The Enquirer* not only had a "graphics editor," it was regularly using color as well as black and white. More than that, photographers were thinking up entire stories on their own and helping editors decide what to cover and how to cover it. The photo department's muscle was such that in the late '70s, when graphics editor Chuck Scott wanted to use a

Fred Straub

photo that was 16 inches wide and three inches high, he persuaded editor Luke Feck to turn it on its side and run it vertically on the page. Obviously, gone were those days when word editors could order photographers or artists to distort reality by retouching the photos.

A news editor named Bob Johnson once upset the photo desk by doing his own retouching when he couldn't find an artist. He wanted to use a photo of a group that included an extra person who wasn't named in the story. So he simply dipped into some white paint he kept in his desk and he changed the unwanted person into a tree.

Today wire photos arrive electronically. The temptation to alter them still exists, but strict rules prohibit that.

'WOMAN'S EYES' SETS TEMPO

It began in September, 1895, as a single column of news inside the paper, headlined "For Woman's Eyes," a weekly collection of items deemed of interest to ladies. It was without byline or other indication of who chose what to include, but a woman surely had at least some material input because part of the column was devoted regularly to descriptions of fashions under the headline reading, "Seen on Fourth Street." Few of the men on *The Enquirer's* staff in those days would have stood still for such an assignment.

The author may have been Olive Logan, who later worked in New York as a magazine writer and appeared in *The Enquirer* as a correspondent under the name "Clara Belle."

For some time before 1895, *The Enquirer* ran a column called "Random Notes" on Sundays, containing news primarily of interest to women. But no regular column was openly touted that way until "For Woman's Eyes" appeared on Sept. 25 that year.

This was less a column of society news than a precursor of modern feminism. The lead item in one of the earliest columns was about a "progressive Texas woman" who was visiting Cincinnati to drum up business. "Her husband met with reversals in the cattle business," the story said, "and she applied her talent to painting panels for hotels."

Other entries that day included a how-to piece on making "school bags of the old-fashioned purse pattern," and a paragraph on the accomplishments of "two illustrious English-women," Florence Nightingale and Jean Ingelow, who both celebrated their 75th birthdays that year.

A 15-year old black girl authored a column, "Mosaics," beginning in 1876. Delilah L. Beasley, a Hamilton, Ohio, native, went on to a successful career at the *Oakland Tribune* and is credited with leading the drive to remove derisive references to blacks from America's newspapers.

By 1897, "For Woman's Eyes" had expanded to more than a full column, and had acquired an illustrated logo consisting of a hand-lettered headline and a drawing of a handsome woman in Victorian dress staring formidably out at the reader.

The page on which it appeared one day in June that year contained abundant ads — ads for jewelry at Loring Andrews & Co., for the Peebles and Thompson Boarding and Day School, and for Cuticura soap (whose big, black type promised "SLEEP FOR SKIN- TORTURED BABIES").

By century's turn, women clearly had a solid toehold on the pages of *The Enquirer.* In 1902, graceful fashion sketches regularly topped what had become a full page of news and advertising under the "For Woman's Eyes" logo. Grooming was accorded a department of its own

Continued on next page

under the heading, "Milady's Mirror," and the ads included wigs from Japp's Hair Store, bureaus from Hartwell Furniture ($15.50 each) and preparations such as Mme. Yale's Hair Tonic.

Give a good woman's page an inch and it'll take a mile. By the time the *Titanic* sank in 1912, *The Enquirer* was giving "For Woman's Eyes" two entire pages every Sunday. One regular, datelined New York, was "Clara Belle's Chatter of Women and Their Ways." Typical of its fare was the fiction piece one October Sunday in 1911 about a bright, attractive, cultured girl who had a chance to marry well but didn't because she was choosy and took too long making up her mind. "Girls," it concluded, "when a rich man wishes to marry you, don't take too long to think about it."

During this period the page contained hundreds of brief items from outlying communities all over Ohio, Indiana and Kentucky — from Maysville to

The first women's story was about a Texas business woman. Soon, news for and about women became a magnet for advertising.

Richmond — about who had visited whom, who had had a dinner party, who had gone where for a holiday. These two- and three-line items, called "locals," were contributed by faithful stringers (part-time correspondents) in each town and were staples in the reading diet of small-town America. "Locals" still appear in many of the rural weeklies.

By 1920, "For Woman's Eyes" had vanished and had been replaced by a typographically similar one — "For Women and The Home" — that covered a wide range of topics. By then, too, "women's" news occupied a full page even on weekdays, and more on Sundays, and consisted not only of regular features on fashion, food and homemaking, but of hard news as well. One Saturday in 1918, for instance, there was a feature about new laws in Bolshevik Russia requiring girls to register at age 18 for state-arranged pairing with single men. "Girls Become State Chattels," read the headline.

A story the same day reported the travail of a young Cincinnati girl who had figured in a sensational divorce trial and been turned over to Juvenile Court.

Women not only got the vote, they also got the promotions, and by the Roaring '20s, *The Enquirer's* women's pages were being written, designed and edited mainly by women, as well as for them. The 1920s were a time of high fashion and sophisticated design, and *The Enquirer* went along, with full-page fashion-photo layouts each season that rival today's for stylish type faces and lavish white space. ("Waistline for Fall Frocks Higher Than Normal . . . Skirts of Street Frocks to be Comfortably Short," read one layout's headline in 1923.) The same Sunday's section included an entire page of "Intimate Ideas for the Woman and Her Home," and another of news about clubs and clubwomen.

The party ended in the 1930s, however. There was a Depression on. Lavish was out, austere in, and the women's page (singular) of 1931 combined all under a banner logo, "The Home, The Community and You." It was liberally sprinkled with features about such things as making and repairing clothes and getting the most out of leftovers. By then, too, along with the Ohio Truss Co.'s illustrated girdle ads, a new kind of advertising had appeared — ads for radio programs. One touted the *Dear Dr. Copeland* program on WKRC, featuring the same Dr. Copeland whose syndicated

Traditional women's news led the way to the paper's first lifestyle section, People Today, in 1976.

home-health column appeared in *The Enquirer* for years.

Through all these years, embedded somewhere near or among the fashion, cooking, homemaking, cosmetics, sewing, club and child-care stories, was the news labeled "Society." It was clearly understood that while the women's pages were for all women, only a select few would ever grace the columns labeled "Society," whose editor was one of the most powerful at *The Enquirer*.

Where many reporters were lucky to have a desk, Society Editor Marion Devereux rated an entire, spacious office next to the publisher's. She not only had a desk, but also a window on Vine Street, a sofa and chairs, a coffee table and tea set and a small table with a sherry decanter and crystal glasses to help lubricate her intimate little chats with nervous mothers of blushing debutantes and her tete-a-tetes with Cincinnati's grande dames.

By and large, even when American society began reshaping itself in the 1950s, the "Women's Pages" remained the home of all things of interest mainly to women, which often included, for some reason, comics and puzzles, pop psychology, health and hearth, cooking and sewing.

Then came the turbulent social consciousness of the 1960s and '70s. Poodle skirts, cashmere and crinolines gave way to the beehive, the shift and the chemise. By the time feminism became a force with which to reckon, men who didn't know whether to laugh or cry over leisure suits and turtlenecks were even more uncertain about the mysteries of the miniskirts, granny dresses, est and rolfing. Many had begun sharing homemaking and child-rearing as women pursued fast-track careers. Gender distinctions were blurring fast.

On Feb. 9, 1976, *The Enquirer* joined the many dailies which had dropped women's pages. "Women" became "People Today."

But don't worry, *The Enquirer* assured conservative read-ers, the new section would still contain all the elements of the old, but merely would lean more toward genderless features about cultural and social trends and issues. The new section was explained at birth by Luke Feck, then the executive editor:

"We have not created a neutered section . . . . People Today will have many of the favorite columns and features that were popular in the women's section. But the focus has shifted to helping, coping, enjoying.

"People Today is where you will find the 'how to' and those things that can have a direct, immediate and positive impact on your life. The section contains the news of how to work, travel, save, educate, play, invest, even sleep. . . .

"The amenities will not be gone. Eleanor Adams, our inexhaustible and charming society editor, remains on hand every day, writing the society news of the day on the third page of the People Today section. Page two will be the home of . . . Dear Abby, Action Line and Dr. Van Dellen. Other pages will be devoted to consumerism and money man-agement, a daily listing of upcoming meetings and events . . . .Men's groups will be as welcome as women's clubs."

Sheryl Bills, who had attended

Sheryl Bills

Indiana University before joining *The Enquirer* in 1968 as a general assignment reporter, was appointed the first editor of People Today. She had remarkable organizational skills as well as journalism talent. It was the first big career step for her. Later she would become *The Enquirer's* first female managing editor.

In 1969, *The Enquirer* accorded similarly collective treatment to all its cultural news — film, TV, music, theater, books, art — by dropping the old "entertain-ment" title and inaugurating a new section with the trendy name, "Now."

But trends inevitably involve both people and culture, and the distinctions are often unclear. Worse, the media age was making the cultural landscape into an ambiguous and amorphous swamp, which began yielding such mutant crops as advertorials, infomercials and docudramas. In 1982, *The Enquirer* again, instituted major change, blending together in one, new section what editor George Blake called "the best elements of our former People Today and entertainment pages."

"Tempo," the new section was named. It debuted on Aug. 22, 1982, and is still with us at our sesquicentennial.

The Tempo area of responsibility is vast. In addition to the lifestyle and entertainment news it publishes daily and in separate sections on Sunday, the Tempo staff is responsible for publishing a separate Food section each Wednesday, several special fashion sections each year, quarterly health sections and the travel news pages on Sunday.

BUSINESS BECOMES BIG NEWS

"On Oct. 30, the morning after 'Black Monday,' The Enquirer's front page headline blared: 'Stock Market Crashes Again; Sixteen Million Shares Sold.'"

Business has always been important business at *The Enquirer,* and with good reason: Newspapers often reflect their owners' interests, and four of *The Enquirer's* proprietors have also been successful businessmen in other fields. Moreover, in the early days when the paper was forthrightly political, even the politics were largely the politics of business interests.

The first of the publisher-businessmen was John Brough, who went on to success in the railroad business.

From the beginning, commerce was mainline news. Indeed, much news of general interest in the energetic, young river town was news of such things as shipments received and sent, and prices fetched for crops and manufactured goods. *The Enquirer* published daily fluctuations in commodities of local interest — flour, pork shoulders, cotton, whiskey — and kept close watch on the progress of the canals, highways and railroads that were weaving the West together in an age when "the West" meant Ohio.

Although Cincinnati was the West's leading city, the financial centers remained back East, and when the telegraph came in 1847, one of its first news roles was transmission of daily share prices from the eastern money centers.

Washington McLean was the next of the businessman-publishers. When he bought into the paper in 1857, he was already a thriving builder of steamboat engines and well connected in commerce between Cincinnati and the South.

Much news that went under other names in the mid-19th century was, in fact, business news. When *The Enquirer* printed daily AP dispatches on river conditions, it was not catering to mere curiosity but providing vital intelligence to merchants on the progress of cargoes in which their capital was at risk.

Washington McLean's son, John R., who built *The Enquirer* to national prominence, was even more of an entrepreneur-publisher than his father. Although his foremost business was newspapers, he invested heavily as well in utilities, urban transit, mining and banking. Not until the fourth of the businessman-proprietors — Carl Lindner in 1971 — did *The Enquirer* display such keen interest in business news.

When John R. McLean took the paper over in 1872, *The Enquirer* was already reserving space on one of its eight, daily pages — for years it was page six — for financial and commercial news.

We'll not call it "business" news, for that term is relatively new. In 1880, the "business department" was where the newspaper purchased its paper and ink, counted receipts and

Continued on next page

filled pay envelopes.

What we would call "business news" was the province of the "financial correspondent." He "did Third Street," which was Cincinnati's financial district then. Not until Dick Havlin took over the business desk in the '50s did the title change to "business editor."

One of the earliest correspondents was D.J. Edwards, who signed himself "Holland" and was regarded nationally as one who set standards for financial reporting.

By 1900, *The Enquirer* had a new press capable of 16 pages and was devoting parts of two pages daily to financial news. The columns leaned heavily to data in fine print, however, and the headlines hardly glittered. The top story was likely to be a stock-market summary. The rest of the data was usually grouped under such scintillating headings as "Cattle Market," "Butter, Eggs and Cheese," "New Suits Filed," and "Realty Transfers."

One of the things that made possible the daily publication of so much market data was new technology. In the old hand-type days, when every letter and digit was plucked from a type case by a printer's fingers and placed in a form, columns of sheer data were out of the question. There just wasn't time enough to do it. In 1895, however, the Linotype vastly enhanced typesetting speed and permitted *The Enquirer* to expand its financial news greatly.

The business news still shared space on its pages, however, and in 1900, alongside the bank clearings and news of oil explorations in Pennsylvania, were stories about a Lutheran convention in town and "Sensational Allegations made by Mrs. Myrtle I. Wells in Suit For Alimony."

A year later, following the arrival of young W. F. Wiley as managing editor, the financial pages seemed to brighten. The data, while still extensive, were less prominent, and aggressive reporting led to more colorful coverage. *The Enquirer* began keeping readers abreast of trends and personalities as well as transactions. One day in late 1901, for instance, one headline told of "New Ideas for the Street Car Line," and another disclosed a developer's plans to build a power plant to provide electric lights for a new apartment building in Avondale. The paper even wrote of a dispute that had surfaced within the Ohio Bill Posters Association during its convention in town.

A fixed feature of the financial pages from well before the turn of the century, however, was a table of daily weather data from around the country. Weather was of immense interest in an era when agriculture was a crucial economic engine (so much so that the U. S. Weather Bureau originated in the Commerce Department). Weather data remained a daily feature of *The Enquirer's* financial pages until the 1950s and ran there sporadically as recently as 1960.

By 1910, with the automobile here to stay, oil was headline news, and *The Enquirer* regularly covered exploration in Ohio, Indiana, Kentucky and West Virginia. The Midwest was hardly the Mideast, however, as demonstrated by a report in October, 1911, that "drills during the past week had little success at finding valuable new territory" and that six of 10 new wells in northwestern Ohio were dry.

Some things never change, however; the same day's report from Wall Street, under a headline as cautious as it was wordy, shows that even in that less complicated era, the stock market defied rational analysis:

"Stocks Are In Better Position, But Wall Street Is Uncerain Of The Outcome, Because It Recalls Other Periods of Activity When Movements Seemingly Set in One Direction Were Suddenly Swerved Into Another."

In 1920, with the "war to end all wars" finished, America was poised for one of the headiest financial roller-coaster rides ever. The 1920s were prosperous times, and business was big news. Before the end of the decade, even bootblacks and cabbies would be speculating in the stock market. By 1921, *The Enquirer* was not only carrying daily stock-market reports, but the financial pages also were laced with ads for steamship travel to Europe.

In this prosperous decade, *The Enquirer* expanded its financial staff, regularly covered local commodity markets and the Cincinnati Stock Exchange and produced regular columns on local business meetings and personnel changes — even reporting on the personal lives of local businessmen.

Then, in 1929, after some days of sharp selling, Wall Street plunged into the abyss. On Oct. 30, the morning after "Black Monday," *The Enquirer's* front page headline blared: "Stock Market Crashes Again; Sixteen Million Shares Sold."

The Enquirer devoted six entire pages to financial news that Tuesday, in addition to the full column of news on page one, and only one of those pages was stock-price data. It wasn't all bad news either: U. S. Steel declared increased earnings and an extra $1 dividend; a survey of top executives showed "confidence in fundamentals," and a Commerce Department official declared the economic structure "sound" despite "speculative uncertainties."

By 1931, however, the optimism was gone and not many folks were taking those European vacations any more. The typical financial page ad

Despite the severity of the selling on Wall Street, The Enquirer's *stock market head on Oct. 30, 1929, covered only three columns.*

was like Businessmen's Federal Savings and Loan's, urging readers to "start saving REGULARLY— TODAY!"

Hard times diminished the average reader's interest in business news and *The Enquirer* — no less affected by the Depression than many families — diminished its coverage, space and staff. On the first anniversary of the crash, financial news consisted of stock tables, wire-service reports on New York and Chicago markets, and exactly one local story — an account of prices at Cincinnati's weekly wholesale fruit auction.

Local business coverage slowly revived in the late '30s, partly because of city editor Lee Evans' stalwart campaigns for prominent play of local news. And once war came to Europe and American industry geared for defense, the "financial" pages became less about finance and more about industry. Two months before Pearl Harbor, an *Enquirer* business-page story reported that "Cincinnati and Richmond, Ind., plants of the Crosley Corporation will be affected by a priorities order issued yesterday in Washington requiring manufacturers of mechanical household refrigerators to cut production."

On Tuesday, Dec. 9 — after the first business day following the Japanese attack — *The Enquirer* had local stories regarding Procter & Gamble's stocks of ingredients from Asian sources (adequate, P&G said), and about orders for war materiel received by local manufacturers — one, a new company that got war orders the day after its founding. The paper also made a local story out of the Federal Reserve Bank's freezing of Japanese assets in the United States.

Following World War II, *The Enquirer's* business coverage seemed to fall into a comfortable routine and became as much an editing job as reporting. Cincinnati wasn't a financial center, and data on stocks, bonds, commodities dominated the business pages. It came by wire and required only routine headline writing and editing for publication. Local commercial news — absent a

FACT

The first telegraph report of New York stock prices in **The Enquirer** ran on Feb. 12, 1847.

major local story, of course —was relegated to a signed column by the financial editor. When Jack Dudley was financial editor in the early 1950s, it was titled "Along the Business Front," but by the time Dick Havlin was writing it a decade later, it had been simplified to "Business Front" the title it kept under his successor, Ralph Weiskittel, into the 1970s.

The last of our four businessman-publishers, financier Carl Lindner, bought *The Enquirer* on May 6, 1971, and within seven months, *The Enquirer* had drastically expanded the financial news.

The first change was announced on Nov. 24 that year, and *The Enquirer* soon was providing a bit more than the traditional New York and American

Jack Dudley

Ralph Weiskittel

Stock Exchange data. By 1973, the financial pages — in all editions — contained complete quotations on the American and New York Exchanges, over-the-counter stocks, bonds, government issues, mutual funds, bank and insurance stocks and a wider range of indexes.

Again, it was new technology that made it possible to publish so much financial data into print so fast. This time, the technology was a combination of computerized data transmission and phototypesetting. When this new "cold type" came along to replace the old hot-metal type-setting, the financial pages were among the first beneficiaries.

In 1976, *The Enquirer* gave business and finance an entire

daily section all its own. The first "Business and Finance" section was published on Tuesday, Aug. 17.

By 1980 — the start of a decade in which, as in the 1920s, business became almost an obsession in America — *The Enquirer* was routinely publishing as many pages of business news each day as it had devoted half a century earlier to the biggest business story of the century, the Crash of '29.

Expansion continued with the introduction on Oct. 6, 1986, of a special business report each Monday called "Business Monday."

It was readily identifiable because the cover was published in full color — the photos, the columnists' logos, even the nameplate for the page. Editor George Blake demanded that all of the stories in the section be local stories.

The section gained favorable reviews from readers. It contained about 24 columns of information, including the cover, and continues to improve in this sesquicentennial year. And its success has led to the publication of several special business sections each year.

FROM POLITICS TO PUBLISHING

When Carl Lindner bought *The Enquirer,* Frank Dale stayed on as publisher for more than two years until Lindner persuaded his friend and associate, William J. Keating, to resign from Congress to run the paper.

It was a stunning surprise. Bill Keating had become a fixture in southern Ohio politics. He had been in public life for 17 years, as assistant attorney general, Municipal and Common Pleas Court judge and Cincinnati councilman. He was a widely popular Republican whose support crossed party lines. Then in his second term in Congress, he was widely regarded as a prospect for the Republican nomination to succeed Sen. William Saxbe, who had already announced he'd not seek re-election.

Now, Bill Keating was chucking it all in favor of a new career in newspapering. When he moved into the fifth floor office suite on Vine Street in October, 1973, Bill Keating had no more newspaper experience than the newest copy clerk.

Looking back after 18 years in newspapering, Keating still seems at a loss to explain his hiring. "I don't know," he muses, "except that my philosophy might have matched theirs."

That philosophy — a consensus, seeking a blend of moderation and high moral tone — played well against a background of Watergate and polarized politics. "In my opinion," Keating said at the time, "politics is a proud and honorable profession. Through the years, I have developed a great respect and admiration for the men and women with whom I have served. Particularly in these times, I would like to have the ability to convey this impression to the American people."

And what qualities might he bring to journalism? "I expect my experience to be of great value in my being able, for example, to call on people whom I have come to know to see how they arrive at their beliefs on pending matters and issues."

Bill Keating was by no means the first politician in charge at *The Enquirer.* The paper's very founders, John and Charles Brough, had both served in the state legislature, and John had been governor. James J. Faran, co-proprietor from 1845 to 1872, had been a state legislator and mayor. And John R. McLean himself had run for both governor and vice president.

Still, politics and journalism had long since parted ways in the American scheme of things. In the charged, adversarial atmosphere of 1974, having a partisan politician in charge at *The Enquirer* induced a certain unease among the editorial staff. At times Keating found himself confronted by editors over real or imagined interference. Editors sometimes found themselves defending their professional skepticism to a

Continued on next page

man who was supposed to be a colleague.

Now, at *The Enquirer's* 150th birthday, Bill Keating has become an accomplished pro. On the verge of retirement, he has now spent more years in newspapering than he did in politics. He has run *The Enquirer* under three owners and seen it through drastic modernization of production and distribution facilities. After Gannett bought *The Enquirer* in 1979, Keating oversaw operation of numerous other dailies — including, at one time —Gannett's entire newspaper division. And when he retires in 1992, he will have spent 15 years on the board of the Associated Press — the last five as its chairman. He is an old hand with a new understanding of the peculiarly optimistic and good-humored skepticism with which journalists regard the world.

Bill Keating, in his 18 years of newspapering, has become an expert on something called "joint operating agreements," under which newspapers share production facilities and other, non-editorial operations. Soon after he arrived at *The Enquirer,* Scripps-Howard's

William Keating occupies the paneled office first occupied by W.F. Wiley.

financially troubled *Cincinnati Post* sought just such an arrangement, and by December, 1979, *The Enquirer* had taken over all its operations except the editorial department.

In 1984, Gannett moved Keating into its upper, corporate echelons in Washington, first as president of Gannett's Newspaper Divison and then as executive vice president and general counsel of Gannett Co., Inc.

Later, from 1986 to 1990, Keating organized the company that produces both of Detroit's

major dailies under another form of joint agreement.

He came back home after four years in Detroit.

Interestingly, through all of this, he has retained the title "chairman" of *The Enquirer,* even though it has been more than 10 years since *The Enquirer* had a board to be chairman of. There's a reason for this:

At first, under Gannett, *The Enquirer* was a corporation unto itself and Keating was chairman of its board. In 1982, Gannett did away with *The*

Enquirer as a separate corporation but permitted the officers of the old company to retain their titles. At that time, Keating was two years into a second five-year term on the board of the Associated Press, which has a rule that board members must be affiliated with AP newspapers. Thus, he was able to maintain his position because the Gannett reorganization had preserved the titles.

In 1990, when Keating returned to *The Enquirer* from Detroit, he returned as "publisher and chairman." For many Cincinnatians he is more than just that.

Among other things, he is a director of Fifth Third Bank, vice chairman of the board of trustees of the University of Cincinnati Foundation, a member of the corporate advisory board of UC's College of Business, a member of the board of visitors of the UC Law School, co-chairman of the fund drive for the Ohio Center for the Arts, a trustee of Xavier University, and a member of the Cincinnati Business Committee, the Downtown Progress Committee and the prestigious Commercial and Commonwealth Clubs.

'JOA' CONFIRMS ENQUIRER'S DOMINANCE

At the time in late 1973 when William J. Keating resigned from Congress to run *The Enquirer* for Carl Lindner, several circumstances were coming that would mean drastic change at *The Enquirer* by the end of the decade.

For one thing, the paper needed new presses. The sub-basement pressroom below 617 Vine St. was a dungeon, and the presses themselves — once a source of pride — were hopelessly obsolete. To make matters worse, in mid-1974, the U. S. Department of Labor inspected the plant and deemed it dangerous as well, because of noise that was literally deafening. The government ordered costly improvements.

At the same time, Scripps-Howard's *Cincinnati Post,* like many afternoon dailies, was not faring well because of competition from TV, diminution of its traditional blue-collar readership base, and increasing difficulty distributing the paper in afternoon traffic. There had been talk of something called a "joint operating agreement" between the *Post* and *The Enquirer,* under a federal law empowering the Justice Department to grant troubled newspapers exemption from antitrust laws.

A joint operating agreement — called a

Carl Lindner, left, and Karl Eller, favored a joint operation.
The Enquirer *and the* Cincinnati *and* Kentucky Posts *are printed in this plant at Liberty Street and Western Avenue.*

"JOA"— would reduce costly duplication of expense and solve *The Enquirer's* pressroom problem as well. The *Post* had relatively new presses in its building at 800 Broadway, and *The Enquirer* proposed to buy them for $2 million and produce both papers there.

Although there had been no public acknowledgement of a joint agreement, it became clear in February, 1975, that change was coming, when Lindner bought the *Post's* building.

The Enquirer's hierarchy was not

unanimous on the subject of a JOA. Keating opposed the idea, preferring simply to let nature and competition take its course. Lindner felt otherwise.

"I knew we would need a new plant," Keating recalls, "but I wanted no joint agreement . . . . Carl Lindner wanted two papers. It made business sense, and he felt the *Post's* plant was far better."

Within a few weeks, the third factor fell into place when Lindner announced he was selling *The Enquirer* to Phoenix-based Combined Communications Corp. The "sale" — closed in September, 1975 — extracted Lindner from direct ownership of *The Enquirer* but gave him a powerful minority position in Combined Communications.

Discussion of a JOA was postponed during negotiations between Lindner and Combined's owner, Karl Eller, but resumed when the sale went through. Keating still opposed the idea, and, he recalls, "I made one last try to talk Eller out of it."

But Eller bought Lindner's view, and in July, 1975, the other shoe dropped: the *Post* notified its unions it would ask the Justice Department to approve a joint agreement. It took two years to iron out the details, and in September, 1977, the *Post* and *The Enquirer* formally asked the Justice Department to approve a merger of all publishing operations with the exception of news.

Naturally, employees of both papers worried about the effect of a JOA on their jobs. Keating recognized this from the start, and both he and *The Enquirer* dealt with the issue forthrightly. On the Thursday before Christmas, 1977, *The Enquirer* produced a four-page special section on the proposed JOA. In it, labor reporter Marvin Beard quoted Keating as saying: "What is really happening is that the *Post* is going out of business, except for editorial. And we know that some will lose their jobs. At this point, we don't know how many." Beard wrote that it might be 550.

Long before the JOA was approved, Bill Keating had been casting about for alternative sites for a new production plant. At first, he had an eye on the possibility that the JOA might not come off. But it soon became clear, too, that even if it did, the *Post's* building at 800 Broadway might not be adequate. Presses aside, it didn't have adequate space for offices, newsprint storage, typesetting, photoengraving, composing, platemaking and distribution.

This time, Eller bought Keating's view and in March, 1977, agreed to the site Keating had chosen in Cincinnati's Liberty-Dalton urban renewal area. It was a good fit, with ready access to highways via nearby I-75. And the city would receive a $7 million federal

grant if *The Enquirer* built in the renewal area. Construction began in 1978 on Western Avenue at Liberty Street, near where the Reds had played until 1970.

As work went on, Combined announced it was merging with the Gannett Co., Inc., but it didn't slow the work. Construction rushed headlong toward a deadline: If the new plant could be "in production" by Dec. 31, Combined would qualify for an investment tax credit for the year. To speed work, parts of the new presses were installed on the concrete foundations before the steel building went up around them. Technically, *The Enquirer* made the deadline, using a partially finished press to print one section for a Sunday paper just before Christmas. It was well into the new year before they were used again.

On Jan. 28, 1979, *The Enquirer's* reader editor, John Caldwell, wrote about how another Cincinnati paper had installed new "lightning fast" presses a century before, capable of printing 10,000 eight-page newspapers an hour, and of how *The Enquirer's* original press in 1841 could produce but 250 four-page papers an hour.

The Enquirer's new, high-speed, offset presses in the plant that had been dubbed "Western" could crank out 72,000 112-page newspapers an hour. "Half a city block long and three floors high," wrote Caldwell, "they run with the precision of a wrist watch."

Over a weekend in late April, 1979, *The Enquire*r held its breath and cut the umbilical cord of history with 617 Vine St., moving delicate,

sophisticated, electronic typesetting gear across town to the new, $20 million "Western" plant. On Monday, April 23, *The Enquirer* was entirely produced there.

For the first time since 1857, a newspaper wasn't being produced on Vine Street.

The final piece fell into place in mid-1979 when, within a few days' time, the merger of *The Enquirer* into Gannett became final and the Justice Department approved the joint operating agreement. All that remained was to shut down the *Post* and merge its advertising, circulation, bookkeeping and production operations into *The Enquirer's*. The joint operating agreement went into effect on Dec. 7, 1979.

What pleased Keating, more than anything connected with establishing the JOA, is that *The Enquirer* accomplished it without serious labor problems. Unions sued the *Post* over its guarantee of "lifetime jobs" to many employees before the JOA. The *Post* had to pay out $11 million.

Not *The Enquirer*. "We didn't have one unfair-labor-practice charge filed against us," Keating said. "The biggest problem we had was in accounts receivable. The paperwork was humongous."

Keating, and his predecessors, have enjoyed good rapport with most of the unions representing *Enquirer* employees. Difficult negotiations with the printers (whose union was founded in Cincinnati), press operators and journalists do not stop him from acknowledging the contributions union labor has made over the years.

Members of the printers union were responsible for founding the credit union which has served all *Enquirer* employees for more than 50 years. Thomas J. Crowe, a printer, and 18 fellow workers used the profits from a nickel Coca-Cola machine in the composing room to capitalize the First Aid Credit Union, Inc. in 1939. The union had accepted responsibility for the machine in 1938 as a favor to publisher W.F. Wiley who had signed an advertising and promotion agreement with the soft drink company. The name of the institution was later changed to the Enquirer Credit Union and recently became affiliated with another institution.

Over the years the company has bargained with truck drivers, dock workers, machinists, electricians, mailers, photoengravers and plate makers, printers, press operators and journalists. There have been very few strikes and those have been short.

In more than once instance unions have joined in important cooperative programs that benefitted all employees. In the 1970s the company sought the cooperation of unions in establising a company-wide drug and alcohol abuse rcovery program. Differences that dominate bargaining sessions were put aside and a strong, successful program was instituted.

And at least once a year all employees, union and non-union, get together for a huge family picnic.

"Despite our differences, management and labor together have created the history we are celebrating this year," Keating says.

COMPUTERS COOL HOT TYPE

"... all the technology was in place for the classical era of American journalism, the hot-type age of The Front Page, ... and Citizen Kane. "

In 1841, the reporter, editor and printer were often one and the same person. A journalist would gather information, write the story out in longhand, then set it into type, one letter at a time, from a compartmented type case like the ones you see for sale today in antique shops. One by one, he'd pluck up characters with flying fingertips and place them in a "stick," building up lines of type at the rate of maybe three a minute, four if he was fast. Sometimes, especially near deadline, the editor would skip the longhand stage, composing the story straight into type.

Eventually, the tasks became the province of specialists. Reporters and editors kept track of events and gathered, wrote and edited the news. Printers set the type and pressmen ran the presses. As papers grew, especially following the Civil War, the number of printers required to set columns and columns of type by hand was prodigious.

In the late 19th century, automatic typesetting machinery began relegating the hand-type case to the antique shops. These machines mold-ed whole lines of type at one time from molten metal. The most important of these machines was Mergenthaler's Linotype, introduced in 1884. It allowed a skilled printer to set 12 to 15 lines of type a minute, casting each line as a single metal "slug."

New technologies didn't spread as rapidly then as they do now, and the Linotype wasn't universally adopted for some years. Hand type was used at *The Enquirer* until 1895.

On New Year's Day in 1878 (holidays being notoriously dull in the newspaper business), *The Enquirer* devoted its front page to just two articles.

One was an account of President and Mrs. Rutherford B. Hayes' 25th wedding anniversary party in Washington, D.C., on New Year's Eve. They'd married in Cincinnati, where Mrs. Hayes (Lucy Ware Webb) had attended college, so the story was a natural for page one.

The only other story, filling more than seven columns, was a detailed account of how the newspaper was produced.

Anyone in the business as recently as 1965 would have felt at home in *The Enquirer* composing room that New Year's Day in 1878. However, he or she probably would not have recognized the day's first order of business: At 1 p.m. the printers arriv-ed and spent four hours "distributing" the type from that day's paper — removing it, one letter at a time, from the printing forms (or "chases") and putting it back into the type cases, each letter in its proper compartment.

Capitals went in the upper case, of course, and small letters in the lower case.

Only after this preliminary chore

Continued on next page

was the composing room ready to set type for the next day's paper. The chronicler of that day in the life of a composing room in 1878 continued:

"By four o'clock the room is again deserted and the printers go to supper. At 7 p.m., the fore-man and his two assistants, the proofreaders, galley boys, regular and substitute printers are on hand . . . and the work of the night begins.

"An hour before, the first copy from the editorial and report-orial rooms, and the adver-tisements from the counting room, have been brought in and prepared by the foreman, and now this is given out to the printers, who call at the foreman's desk to get each take (so called because the printers would come and "take" them

Ernest Fredericks, above, works at his type case early in this century. Inset, a linotype operator setting hot type. The linotype enabled the newspaper to set more type in a shorter period of time and, consequently, to print more pages.

away to set the type; near deadline, news was set in "short takes" by many printers, in the interests of speed).

"By midnight, all the small advertisements have been disposed of . . . . Now it is found necessary to put on a fourth proofreader. Another galley boy is needed and the office is now at its best working capacity — all engaged in the final rush that takes place an hour previous to the closing of the forms."

Each printer worked at his own type case and was known by his case's number. Late in the evening, longer stories were broken down into short takes, each set by a different printer. The printers would place their finished "sticks" of type on the galleys in proper sequence, penciling their numbers on a slip of paper to identify who'd done the work. As an incentive for accuracy, any printer in

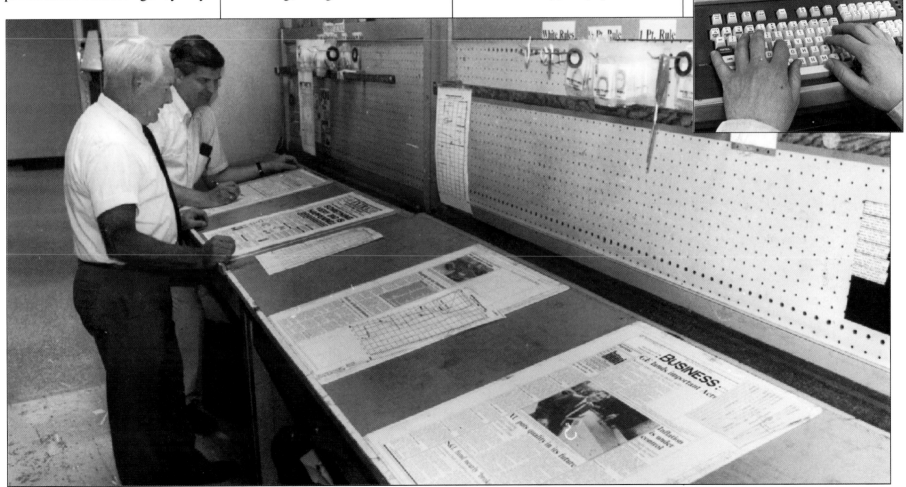

This video display terminal was part of **The Enquirer's** *first computerized typesetting system used by reporters and editors. Printer Don Burkey and make-up editor Frank Kappel check "cold-type" pages. Stories are photographed and pasted onto a grid sheet.*

whose take the proofreaders found more than three errors had to set the corrections for all the takes with fewer errors below his on the galley.

At 11 p.m., a hearty lunch was laid out for the composing room — roast beef or turkey, ham and eggs, oysters, potatoes, pie, coffee. It stoked the printers up for the final rush to deadline. That final rush, explained our man in 1878, was when the printers set into type "the sensations and current events of our own city, furnished by the ever-wakeful reporter, as well as the occurrences of the outside world transmitted by the electric wire."

The period from the Civil War until 1890 saw a great civic blossoming in Cincinnati, and the paper grew right along. At the height of the busy Christmas season in 1877, on Dec. 15, our man reported, "forty-nine compositors set up 717,000 ems of type."

That's about 60,000 lines, or,

NAG, NAG, NAG! PRINTERS LAMENT

For some reason, playing the horses has long been a way to pass time among printers (perhaps because they are among the first non-track people who are privy to the next day's entries). Whatever the reason, horse racing has long been a common topic among printers, and every big-city daily's composing room seems to have a resident bookmaker. Judge for yourself how pervasive the interest in horse racing is in this trade. The following appeared in *The Little Enquirer*, the in-house employee magazine, during the Roaring '20s, under the heading: "Composing Room Notes:"

"Many of the financiers of the composing room started out to make their fortunes when Latonia opened a month ago, and now that the races are over, here's the news: Harry Lavan is back at work. Chester Davis is back at work. Gary Nugent is back at work. Mike Barnes is back at work. Will Mooney is back at work. Spike Wolfenden is back at work. Charley Drummey is back at work. Will Shober is back at work. Will Hauer is back at work. Chester Wheelwright is back at work. George Boehler is back at work . . . "

On it went, naming dozens more before finally concluding " . . . and if your name is missing, just write it in."

per man, about three lines a minute for the entire shift. Plainly there were limits. A composing room could be only so large, and the speed with which a given number of men could pluck characters from the type cases helped limit the size of any day's paper.

The arrival of automatic typesetting machinery such as the Linotype in 1895 let *The Enquirer* leap beyond those limits by allowing a printer to multiply his output by five or six times, and the paper to add

more pages. Moreover — and this was the real gain — the Linotype eliminated the tiresome daily chore of redistributing the type from the previous day's paper. This magnificent machine redistributed its own letters as it went, removing them automatically from the mold after casting a line and conveying them back to the type case atop the machine for immediate reuse. The Linotype eliminated four hours of work for every printer every day.

When "halftone" engraving came along in the mid-1890s as well, allowing newspapers to reproduce photographs, all the technology was in place for the classical era of American journalism, the hot-type age of *The Front Page,* the *Daily Planet* and *Citizen Kane.* It was well-suited to the industrial age, with its metal type, its stereotype casting-boxes, foul black inks, marvelously complicated machinery and specialized tasks. The hot-type era lasted 80 years.

Ironically, the modern technology that supplanted it has taken us back to the point of beginning, away from specialization, breaking down the distinctions by putting printers' skills back in the hands of reporters and editors.

Cold type — type which is set photographically on paper — began replacing hot metal at many smaller papers in the 1960s and came to *The Enquirer* in the early 1970s. The change was gradual. For the first few years, Linotype operators continued to tap out news stories and ads in hot metal alongside a new device called an OCR or "optical character reader." The OCR scanned typewritten pages and transformed text into newspaper type electronically and photographically.

It was at this point, early in the 1970s, that *The Enquirer* replaced the reporters' beloved old manual Remington and Royal typewriters with IBM Selectrics, because the OCRs were designed to read the distinctive characters IBM put on its electric typewriter's bouncing ball.

The OCRs were but a way stop on the road to computers. Phototypesetting still required printers, but it required different tasks of them. Instead of dealing in the hot, metal type of the Linotype, they handled film and software and chemicals. Instead of using printers' rules and line gauges to compose galleys of heavy, metal type into frame-like, steel chases on a printer's stone, they used X-Acto knives and wax adhesive to paste strips of delicate, glossy photographic paper onto posterboard sheets.

Transition to cold type was not overnight. The paper was converted page-by-page over two years, until Tuesday, Sept. 17, 1974, the first day *The*

Enquirer was produced entirely of cold type.

Late on the evening of the previous Sunday — Sept. 15, 1974 — the last of the hot-type pages was closed for Monday's paper. The printers all paused in their work and watched. "No champagne or anything like that," Tuesday's paper reported. "But the printers knew, and remembered."

In late 1975, the Selectrics started disappearing and the first VDTs — video display terminals — arrived. Connected to a mainframe computer they began turning reporters and editors back into printers. The computer allowed editors to order type size, face, width and spacing as they wrote, then with a single key-stroke, transmit the text from the screen in front of them to a typesetting computer in the composing room. All the printer had to do was develop film, then cut and paste it on the page to be made photographically into a press plate. Dozens of printers found themselves faced with a tough choice: Learn the new, complex electronic technology or leave. Many left.

*For each daily **Enquirer** in 1991, an average of 2,540 miles of paper is needed. An average of 10,243 miles is needed for a Sunday edition. Each year the company increases its use of recycled newsprint.*

GUTENBERG STARTED IT ALL

Gutenberg did not invent the press. What he invented was "movable" type. Before him, presses made impressions from wood cuts which, once made, were immutable. Movable type consisted of individual letters, each a small "cut" unto itself. After they were composed in a form and locked tightly, ink was applied to the raised surfaces of the type and a page was pressed against the type. It's a system newspapers used until 1884 when Ottmar Mergenthaler invented the Linotype (which *The Enquirer* began using 11 years later).

The press Gutenberg printed his Bible on, like the one Ben Franklin used (and like the one on this book's cover) was a "flat-bed" press. The printer fed sheets of paper, one at a time by hand, and screwed the press down to make an impression. Much the same process was used in printing the first *Enquirer* in 1841.

With the advent of steam machinery in the early 19th century, power presses arrived, and soon after, automatic rotary presses did away with the printers' having to feed each sheet, one at a time. But even power presses had limits. *The Enquirer's* first was installed in 1847, two years after Robert Hoe invented it in 1845. A promotional story at the time proclaimed that it was "able to strike off 275 papers an hour, and to produce the entire day's run in five hours." (One wonders if the writer really intended to reveal the paper's meager circulation."

The offset presses at **The Enquirer's** *Queensgate printing plant use photoengraved, chemically treated plates. The lithographic principle that water and grease will not mix enables these presses to print fine color as well as black text.*

A newer Hoe press crashed through the burning floor to the bottom of the ruins when the offices and plant burned during the Opera House fire in 1866.

By coincidence, only a year earlier, a man named Bullock had introduced another advance in automatic printing, the "web" press. After *The Enquirer* moved to its present site following the fire, it was being produced on one of Bullock's machines, in which a continuous web of paper was drawn from big rolls and fed rapidly past curved printing cylinders.

One of the problems involved in developing fast, rotary, web presses was finding a way to convert rectilinear bits of type into curved printing surfaces. An early answer was to place the type into curved forms, called "turtles." It was not easy to compose thousands of tiny, individual type-metal characters in a curved form and then to transport it to the presses intact. Occasionally, someone did "pi"or spill everything.

A partial answer was the"mat" (slang for "matrix"), made by pressing wet papier-mache onto the page form, then drying the paper to leave a perfect mold for casting ("stereotyping") the printing surface of an entire page in one piece. The mat was flexible and could easily be curved to yield a metal plate that would fit a press cylinder. In one form or another, this technology lasted until the 1970s, when modern, computer-generated, cold type replaced hot metal. The metamorphosis was complete when offset presses replaced the web letterpress.

HUGE PRESSES HIT THE CEILING

Newspaper presses are massive machines, and when the old Goss behemoths cranked out final-edition *Enquirers* at night, the 617 Vine St building sometimes vibrated a little. Even passersby on the street outside could feel the earth shake a bit.

At first, in the 1920s, it wasn't a problem. But over the years all that vibration took its toll, and eventually bits of plaster took to cracking off every once in a while and falling from the ceilings. This was annoying but came to be accepted as nothing more than a familiar nuisance. So none of the editorial artists up on the fourth floor took notice when a few wisps of plaster dust began drifting down on them one evening in the 1960s as the presses started rolling.

"And then, all of a sudden," remembers one of them, "we heard this cracking, and we looked up, and the whole ceiling came down, all in one piece. All the plaster. We got up against the wall and, thank God, it didn't hurt anybody. We got a lot of plaster in our hair, and it was all over the room. It was like a bomb had hit. But we weren't hurt.

" Eventually, management put up drop ceilings, so that when the plaster fell, it wouldn't hit anything"

Trucks deliver what were then modern presses in 1949 to the back of the building at 617 Vine St.

The Cincinnati Enquirer/Michael E. Keating
The final out sent Barry Larkin into the air.

THE WORLD CHAMPS 1990

REDS

OCTOBER 21, 1990 SUNDAY

THE CINCINNATI ENQUIRER

FINAL/Single-copy price $1.25

A GANNETT NEWSPAPER

SWEEP!

Oakland can't touch Rijo, 2-1

BY JACK BRENNAN
The Cincinnati Enquirer

OAKLAND, Calif. — OK, so they weren't the Big Red Machine. But no Big Red Machine team ever won the World Series more convincingly than the 1990 Reds.

They completed a 4-0 Series sweep Saturday with a 2-1 victory over heavily favored Oakland, a team whose dreams of dynasty died with embarrassing ease.

"We were underdogs all year, but nobody can call us that now," said manager Lou Piniella. "We played our best baseball in the biggest games of the year. We deserve to be champions."

"As a kid," said pitcher Rob Dibble, "I never thought I'd make the big leagues, much less win the World Series. This is too much to soak in right now. It was almost over too fast."

In Cincinnati, more than 12,000 fans filled Fountain Square, celebrating.

Carrying brooms and chanting, "Sweep, sweep, sweep," fans danced and poured champagne and beer, eluding police who were confiscating beer and brooms in an attempt to maintain order.

Xavier University student Jeff Gonzalez watched the celebration and echoed the M.C. Hammer song that has become the Reds' anthem: "I'll tell you, you can't touch this!"

The only sad note involved Eric Davis, who was hospitalized in the intensive care unit of Oakland's Merritt Hospital. Davis was injured while diving for a line drive in the first inning. He might be hospitalized three to five days with what is said to be a bruised kidney, a Reds official said.

GANNETT AND THE FUTURE

On May 8, 1978, *The Enquirer's* Phoenix-based owner, Combined Communications Corp., agreed to merge with Gannett Corp., owner of one of the world's largest newspaper groups.

For Cincinnatian Carl Lindner's American Financial Corp., it was another sweet deal. Just four years earlier, an AFC subsidiary had transferred *The Enquirer* to Combined in exchange for a significant minority share of the Phoenix company. Now, each share of Combined would be exchanged for 1.2 shares of Gannett, and in selling *The Enquirer,* AFC had acquired 1.5 million shares of Combined plus warrants to buy another 750,000. At market prices on the day of the announcement, *The Enquirer* reported, AFC's profits from the sale could run as high as $72 million, even accounting for the $30 million AFC had invested in Combined.

It was a major deal for Gannett, too. In *The Enquirer*, the group was buying the biggest paper it had ever owned. CCC's *Oakland Tribune,* was its second largest.

Enquirer employees were naturally a bit concerned about the long-term implications of becoming part of a group of newspapers, especially about the possibility of coming to work one day to find they had a new boss or a new job in, say, Boise, Idaho.

But newspaper people are a mobile lot these days, and few journalists spend an entire career at a single paper. Working for Gannett, moreover, meant opportunities galore. Many an *Enquirer* staffer has moved on to greater responsibility at other papers in the huge and growing chain. This has been especially true for women, blacks and other minority-group journalists; Gannett is a determined believer and acknowledged leader in affirmative action.

Such opportunities work two ways, and many promising Gannett employees have moved up from smaller papers to *The Enquirer.*

In 1987, W. Curtis Riddle became *The Enquirer's* first black managing editor. He came to *The Enquirer* from *USA Today,* also served as assistant to the publisher and went on to become publisher of two other Gannett newspapers.

Gannett moved quickly and replaced Carl Lindner as publisher with William J. Keating, who had been *The Enquirer's* president. The sale took a year to consummate. Soon after it had been done, George Blake, then the 34-year-old editor of Gannett's Ft. Myers, Fla., *News-Press,* moved into the editor's office in 1980 when long-time *Enquirer* veteran Luke Feck became editor of the *Columbus.* (Ohio) *Dispatch.*

Blake has been editor of *The Enquirer* ever since. (He is literally married to Gannett because he and

Continued on next page

his wife, Mary Kay, both joined Gannett in 1973. She now is the company's director of recruiting and development.) Both his supporters and detractors — all editors have them — acknowledge that his tireless campaigning for news prerogatives has transformed *The Enquirer* from a paper driven by the business side of the company into a paper driven by news.

"Advertising now calls us and asks if late ads can be put into the paper," one senior editor says. "Circulation calls and volunteers to extend deadlines or change the sequence of the press run for editions when there is an important story."

Blake is responsible for the neighborhood news sections called "Extra." With strong support from the advertising division, the sections deliver an additional 48 columns of local news each week. Blake also conceived the Forum section which appears on Sunday. First he established a "Perspective" page for the Sunday paper, then expanded that into a section of opinion, commentary and analysis featuring a Jim Borgman drawing, in color, on the cover.

Keating remains as publisher,

...A JUG OF WINE AND, WHEW!

Gannett's CEO Allen Neuharth came to town just after Gannett merged with Combined Communications, for a Gannett board meeting and celebratory dinner at the Queen City Club.

Don Shepherd of the ad service department was one of the people helping set up the meeting. He was told that there was one, certain kind of wine that Neuharth drank and that it had to be in the hotel room when he came in, on ice, at 54 degrees, in a bucket, ready to drink.

One colleague of Shepherd's remembers the day, and Shepherd's consternation: "There was nowhere Don could find that wine. He went to Pogue's. Pogue's didn't have it. Shillito's didn't have it. He tried across the river and couldn't find it. He got a little desperate. So he went to the Maisonette, and they had quite a stock

EXTRA! EXTRA!

of it. But they said they didn't do brown-bag retail business and no matter what they weren't about to sell him a bottle. They said they got theirs from a wine supplier in Indianapolis.

"So Don calls his wife and says he's not coming home until late because he has to go to Indianapolis. He's only got four or four and a half hours. So he shags up there and buys two bottles, something like 62 bucks a bottle. He rushes back. He's worried about breaking the bottles. He's worried about being in a wreck. He's worried about getting a ticket. But it turned out all right. He got back in time and personally took the bottles up there and got them chilled right.

"He lost about 10 pounds on that trip."

---

too, although he spent nearly six years in other Gannett posts, and two other publishers ran *The Enquirer* before he returned in 1990.

The first was Gary L. Watson, who had been president and publisher of the Rockford, Ill., *Register Star* before coming to *The Enquirer* in 1984. He also followed Keating as president of Gannett's central region, as

Keating became president of the entire Gannett Newspaper Division. New publisher or not, Keating remained *The Enquirer's* chairman.

Watson, a hard-nosed journalist, ran *The Enquirer* and brought career journalism back to the publisher's office for the first time since W.F. Wiley died in 1944 and was replaced by ad-man Roger Ferger.

Watson had worked his way up in Rockford starting as a city hall reporter in 1969, and before becoming publisher there was editor of Gannett papers in Boise, Idaho, and in Springfield, Mo.

His philosophy of newspapering dovetailed beautifully with Blake's insistence that news come first. Veterans remember Watson's announcing that the production division — the composing room, engraving operation, pressroom and mailroom — was a service division. It meant that determining deadlines again was a joint decision between editors and production managers.

Watson was a publisher who felt most comfortable in the newsroom, and he spent a lot of his time there. That bade well and ill for the journalists who worked there. He could understand the problems they faced and discuss them empathetically; but woe to the editor who tried to fool him.

Gannett is not known as a group that stands still, and Watson stayed but 20 months before becoming president of the company's "community newspaper" group. Today he is president of Gannett's newspaper division. His successor on the fifth floor at 617 Vine was John P. Zanotti.

Zanotti was a Californian and a lawyer. He had been a group president of direct marketing for Harte-Hanks Communications Inc. before joining Gannett as assistant to the president of its newspaper division.

He ran *The Enquirer* for about four years and distinguished himself within Gannett as an astute business manager. In 1987 he was named Gannett's manager of the year and the next year he was named publisher of the year.

His business acuity did not preclude his involvement in the news end of the business. Special quarterly health and business sections began during his years at *The Enquirer*. He instituted an automotive section, the Business Monday section and launched a selected-market

Gary L. Watson

-coverage project in which a sample of the newspaper is mailed to non-subscribers.

Before he left in 1990 to become publisher of two dailies in Phoenix, Ariz., he oversaw the installation of new presses and the computerization of the mailroom. In 1991 he returned to Cincinnati as a broadcast executive.

Zanotti's departure left an

John P. Zanotti

opening in Cincinnati and Bill Keating returned from Detroit, where he had been overseeing the joint operating agreement between Gannett's *Detroit News* and Knight-Ridder's *Free-Press*.

In 12 years as part of Gannett, *The Enquirer* has become the city's dominant newspaper.

Like so many American dailies, it has followed the leads of television and such pioneering

papers as *USA Today* by adding color, aggressive page design and graphics, consistent anchoring of popular features and mega-coverage of special events. And the best is yet to come.

In this sesquicentennial year, Gannett has launched a project to transform all of its papers into papers of the future before the year 2000. The project requires journalists to listen to readers' needs and desires more carefully and to respond to them with a newspaper that is literate, useful and entertaining. It demands more careful protection of First Amendment rights and a true reflection of the diversity of the the paper's readership. When Gannett announced the News 2000 project, The Grand Old Lady of Vine Street was one of the first newspapers to begin building a new newspaper.

*I*n the envelope
on the inside of the back cover
is a reproduction of a daguerreotype made in 1848 by
Cincinnati photographers Charles Fontayne and W.S. Porter.
It shows the Cincinnati riverfront seven years after
The Enquirer published its first edition.
One of the few surviving daguerreotype panoramas, this is
the earliest known photograph of steamboats. The view is from
what is now John Taylor Park in Newport, Ky. The eight-plate
daguerreotype is in the collection of the Public Library
of Cincinnati and Hamilton County, which granted
reprint permission to The Enquirer.

This book was designed and edited on a Macintosh IIcx computer. The body type is Times and the headline type is
Century Old Style. Photo and illustration identifications are set in Helvetica and Times. Pages were generated using Aldus FreeHand
and Quark Xpress. Photos and illustrations were scanned on a flatbed scanner.
Negatives were generated through The Enquirer's color, electronic prepress system.
The book is printed on 80# Moistrite Matte Book paper.

Special resources and assistance were provided by Laura L. Chase and Linda J. Bailey
of The Cincinnati Historical Society; Alfred Kleine-Kreutzmann, curator of rare books and special collections of The Public Library
of Cincinnati and Hamilton County; Ruth Van Gorden of The Merten Co.; Paul Malott of QC Inc.; and these Enquirer employees:
Alan Vonderhaar, informational graphic specialist; John Bryan, systems editor;
Jack Cannon, copy desk chief; Martin Hogan Jr. and David Hunter, copy editors; James Schottelkotte
and Richard Macke, assistant sports editors; Owen Findsen, art critic; George Longfellow, artist; Ronald Cosby, copy clerk;
Larry Reynolds, prepress manager; Nick Ruter, John Orben, Herman Ashley and Dennis Williams, color systems operators;
Randy Burke, Jim Myers and John Lang, photoengravers; and Martha Flanagan, assistant to the president of The Enquirer.